Essential NLP

Teach Yourself®

Essential NLP

Steve Bavister and
Amanda Vickers

For UK order enquiries: please contact Bookpoint Ltd,
130 Milton Park, Abingdon, Oxon OX14 4SB.
Telephone: +44 (0) 1235 827720. Fax: +44 (0) 1235 400454.
Lines are open 09.00–17.00, Monday to Saturday, with a 24-hour
message answering service. Details about our titles and how to
order are available at www.teachyourself.com

Long renowned as the authoritative source for self-guided learning –
with more than 50 million copies sold worldwide – the **Teach Yourself**
series includes over 500 titles in the fields of languages, crafts, hobbies,
business, computing and education.

British Library Cataloguing in Publication Data: a catalogue
record for this title is available from the British Library.

This edition published 2010.

Previously published as *Teach Yourself NLP*

The **Teach Yourself** name is a registered trade mark of
Hodder Headline.

Copyright © 2010 Steve Bavister and Amanda Vickers

Typeset by MPS Limited, A Macmillan Company.

Printed in Great Britain for Hodder Education, an Hachette UK
Company, 338 Euston Road, London NW1 3BH, by CPI Cox &
Wyman, Reading, Berkshire RG1 8EX.

The publisher has used its best endeavours to ensure that the URLs
for external websites referred to in this book are correct and active
at the time of going to press. However, the publisher and the
author have no responsibility for the websites and can make no
guarantee that a site will remain live or that the content will remain
relevant, decent or appropriate.

Hachette UK's policy is to use papers that are natural, renewable
and recyclable products and made from wood grown in sustainable
forests. The logging and manufacturing processes are expected to
conform to the environmental regulations of the country of origin.

Impression number   10 9 8 7
Year   2014 2013

Front cover: Creativ Studio/Heinemann/Westend61/Photolibrary.com

Back cover: © Jakub Semeniuk/iStockphoto.com, © Royalty-Free/Corbis,
© agencyby/iStockphoto.com, © Andy Cook/iStockphoto.com,
© Christopher Ewing/iStockphoto.com, © zebicho – Fotolia.com,
© Geoffrey Holman/iStockphoto.com, © Photodisc/Getty Images,
© James C. Pruitt/iStockphoto.com, © Mohamed Saber – Fotolia.com

Contents

Welcome to *Essential NLP*

NLP changed our lives. Yes, we know it's a cliché, but it's true nonetheless. NLP changed our lives, and it can change yours too.

A decade ago we had a dream to write a book like the one you are holding. We've now had five such books published, with more in the pipeline. We wanted to set up a global business based around training and coaching, and we've achieved that as well. Our greatest aspiration, though, was to set up a charitable trust to help those unable to help themselves. This we have also done.

Was our success down to neuro-linguistic programming alone? Of course not. It required effort and action on our part. But using the methodology, tools, processes and techniques of NLP has enabled us to accelerate our progress. We have moved forward more quickly and more surely than we would have done without it.

Our aim in writing *Essential NLP* is to make the power of NLP available to as many people as possible. Everyone has the right to be able to live their dreams – and NLP makes that possible. We are living proof.

Essential NLP presents the central concepts of NLP in a practical, engaging way – but without dumbing them down. You will learn how to run your own brain, understand others better, make your goals compelling, build stronger relationships and a whole lot more.

Our expertise in NLP derives from each of us attending more than 100 days of NLP training, from running NLP courses ourselves and from using NLP in our work.

We are both Certified NLP Coaches, Steve is an Ericksonian Hypnotherapist, and we both have honours degrees in psychology.

Our expertise lies in business communication and relationships, including personal impact, networking, presentation skills and influencing. We use the principles of NLP daily, both to underpin our work and explicitly in training, coaching and therapy. We are directors of Speak First (www.speak-first.com), a company that offers our global clients consistent high quality training with local differences wherever their people are in the world.

Steve and Amanda

Only got a minute?

Some people initially struggle to understand what NLP is or grasp its essence. That's because it has both enormous breadth and depth, and can be used in so many different ways. It's been described as a science, a process, a study, a model, a set of procedures, a system and a technology – but the most useful way of thinking of it is perhaps as a form of applied psychology. Many NLPers – those who have studied NLP and make use of it – call it a 'User's Manual for the Brain'. For that reason it is widely considered to be one of the most powerful tools available for personal and professional development.

What does NLP stand for? The 'Neuro' part relates to neurology and the ways in which we process information we receive from our five senses – seeing, hearing, feelings, smelling and tasting. 'Linguistic' relates to the use of language systems – symbolism and metaphor as well as the spoken word – to code, organize and attribute meanings to our internal representations of the world. 'Programming' is about the way in which our experience is coded, stored and transformed to create habits and 'programmes' – similar to how software runs on a PC.

NLP was developed in California in the 1970s by a mathematician, Richard Bandler, and a linguistic, John Grinder, who drew upon a multitude of disciplines, including systems thinking, psychotherapy, cybernetics and general semantics. At the heart of NLP lie a number of principles known as 'presuppositions'. While these pithy, simple, proverb-like statements may not necessarily be true – the NLP approach is a pragmatic one – they are useful ways of engaging with the world.

One presupposition is, 'There's no such thing as failure, only feedback'. This leads us to think of mistakes as an opportunity to learn, and encourages us to try new things, without fear of failure. Three other presuppositions are: 'The map is not the territory', 'If one person can do something, anyone can learn to do it' and 'Experience has structure'. These presuppositions are at the core of NLP. Bandler and Grinder modelled excellence in others, such as therapists Fritz Perls and Virginia Satir, and demonstrated that once you understand the thinking patterns and behaviours used by talented people you can learn to do what they do.

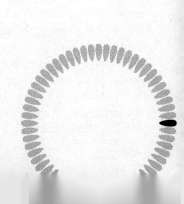

5 Only got five minutes?

The Meta Model is the result of the first modelling carried out by NLP's founders. They observed that certain types of questions asked by Satir and Perls helped people recover lost information and become clearer about their issues. This helped them function more effectively. There are 12 'Meta Model' questions that are categorized under:

▶ deletion (information from the external world that we delete to avoid being overwhelmed)
▶ distortion (simplifying an experience perhaps because we don't have all the information)
▶ generalization (using previous experiences to categorize information).

We will often, for example, leave important information out of a sentence, e.g. 'It's better not to rock the boat'. The question needed to recover this comparative deletion is, 'Better than what?' A common example of distortion is called complex equivalence. 'I was late for the team meeting – I'm absolutely hopeless.' You can challenge statements like this by asking, 'How does being late for the team meeting make you hopeless?' Generalizations happen all the time. In fact, there is one in the last sentence! 'All the time?'

Bandler and Grinder went on to model the world's foremost hypnotherapist, Milton Erickson. What they discovered was that he used language that was deliberately vague – as if he were deliberately setting out to delete, distort and generalize. The ambiguity of the language helped induce trance, which allowed him access to his patients' unconscious minds. These language patterns are useful when you're doing change work with people. Some of the categories of the Milton Model are the inverse of the Meta Model. Others have been added, such as embedded commands and ambiguity. Bandler and Grinder went on to discover a lot more about how we process and code information.

We take in the world through our five senses – or, as they're known in NLP, 'modalities'. Our neurological system uses the information gathered to create an internal representation of the world. Because we use our sensory modalities, working with our neurology, to create these internal representations, NLP calls them representational systems. They are also referred to as VAKOG: Visual – seeing; Auditory – hearing; Kinaesthetic – feelings; Olfactory – smelling; Gustatory – tasting. Although we use all the representational systems we tend to favour one of them more than the others – 'naturally' thinking in pictures, sounds and feelings. This is known as the primary system. The words people use provide a clue to the representational system they are using. When someone says, 'I like the sound of that', they are using an auditory word. Each of the sensory modalities has finer distinctions called submodalities. Sounds, for example, vary in volume, tonality and location. Images vary in brightness, colour, contrast, size and so on. They are extremely valuable in NLP because working with them allows you to choose and change the way you code your memories – making them more or less powerful, desirable or intense. Many well known NLP techniques, such as Swish, use submodalities to change the way you feel about something, such as removing the temptation of eating chocolate every time you fill up the tank at a petrol station.

Meta Programs are another way that we organize our thinking. Whereas submodalities are concerned with the sensory details of our internal representations, Meta Programs act like a filter of what we take in from the outside world and help us decide what comes out. Understanding Meta Programs gives you great insight into how you and others experience the world differently. If someone, for instance, wants to move house, their motivation may be to 'get away from' an area they don't like living in or it could be 'towards' the upmarket end of town. Most, but not all, Meta Programs come in bi-polar opposites like this. While they are context-specific we also tend to have dominant patterns. When you are able to recognize these patterns they help you to communicate more effectively with others.

The beliefs and values we hold shape our approach too. We often take our beliefs for granted because they operate in the background, guiding our behaviour. Many beliefs are about what should or should not be. These are called values. They are beliefs about what's most important to you. They form the basis of your identity and shape your personality. Beliefs and values can be incredibly powerful driving forces and they can be equally limiting. Children are often told they can't dance, sing, draw (the list goes on) and develop a belief that this is true even when it is not that stays with them throughout their adult life. When you believe something you act in a way that supports that belief. NLP offers many ways of challenging and changing beliefs that are no longer working – to create empowering beliefs that allow you to achieve what you want in life.

Understanding how people operate is an important aspect of NLP. Equally important, and tremendously valuable to many people, is the way it helps them achieve their goals. NLP focuses on outcomes rather than goals. An outcome is the result you get, whereas a goal is always something you want. In NLP, to achieve successful results you need to adhere to a set of 'well-formed' conditions, such as stating the outcome in positive terms, being as specific as possible and making sure the outcome is ecologically sound (if you had it would you want it?).

The emotional state you are in often affects how successful or otherwise you are in achieving an outcome. When you are unsure or negative you can end up feeling unresourceful – and you don't make as much progress as you hoped. Many people are not aware of how they're feeling most of the time and don't think it is possible to choose their state. With NLP it is possible. The first step is to know what state you're in, then you can either change or enhance it. Think for a moment about something you want to achieve. Imagine you've done it and everything turns out fantastically. The point here is to show how easily you can change your state by changing what is going on in your mind.

One of the ways NLP can help you change your state is by using anchors. These are naturally occurring associations we have – things we see, hear, feel, taste and smell that evoke memories and often feelings as well. They can be positive (we hear a piece of music and recall a wonderful time with a loved one) or negative (a time when we felt lonely or sad). Anchors can be set deliberately using a set of five well-formedness conditions. If you want to be in a particular state, or feel a certain way in a future situation, you can create an anchor that achieves that. Many NLP techniques, such as Change Personal History, use anchors. This pattern helps people change their perspective or feelings about a past experience that's still affecting them.

In order to work with someone effectively using one of the many NLP techniques, it's essential to build rapport with people and develop your sensory acuity. Many people find it easy to achieve rapport without thinking about it. When we share common interests with people we soon find we get along. In NLP this process is enhanced by behaving in similar ways to them. Someone with highly developed sensory acuity will have good observational skills. They will be able to pick up on changes in skin tone, voice tone and other small nuances in behaviour. They use this information to match the other person and deepen the rapport. The next step in developing sensory acuity is to notice patterns in behaviour – this is called calibration. When you are working with someone it is all too easy to focus on the process rather than the person and whether or not the technique is having the right effect.

One of the ways we can deepen rapport is by understanding other people's 'maps of the world'. This process can be aided by shifting from one perceptual position to another. There are three main perceptual positions: first position (perceiving people from our viewpoint), second position (mentally stepping into their shoes and seeing ourselves through their eyes), and third position (taking an external detached perspective where we can stand back and perceive the relationship between us and the other person). By moving from one position to another we gain insights that are useful in solving problems in relationships.

The work of Bandler and Grinder and many of their followers has left behind a trail of amazing techniques such as The Fast Phobia Cure, The New Behaviour Generator and The S.C.O.R.E. model. These can be used to greatly enhance the quality of people's lives. The benefits of NLP can be applied in almost any area of life including: personal development, presenting, sports, health, fitness, relationships, therapy, business, selling, negotiation, coaching, leadership, training, education and even spirituality. The only limit is your imagination, and NLP can help with that too!

1

What is NLP?

In this chapter you will learn:
- **different defintions of NLP**
- **what the N, L and P stand for**
- **about how NLP originated and where it can be applied**
- **what you'll get from learning NLP**
- **how to get the best from this book**

Defining NLP

'It makes a strange, loud sound, like a trumpet crossed with a factory siren.'

'It's enormous – about the size of a truck!'

'It can suck in water through its long, flexible nose – and even pick things up with it.'

'It can run at up to 15 miles an hour.'

'It's got thick white sticks coming out of its face.'

'It must weigh at least four tons.'

'It's grey and wrinkly.'

Describing an elephant so that someone who has never seen one can understand what it looks, sounds and acts like can be a challenge. All the descriptions above are true, but none on its own begins to give a sense of what a magnificent creature the elephant really is.

And it's the same with NLP. It has so many different facets that the best we can do at this stage is to give you a glimpse of it from some of the ways it has been defined or described over the years.

▶ *'The science of how the brain codes learning and experience.'*
▶ *'A process that analyses excellence in human behaviour in such a way that the results created by that behaviour can be duplicated by almost anyone.'*
▶ *'The study of the structure of subjective experience.'*
▶ *'A model of communication that focuses on identifying and using patterns of thought that influence a person's behaviour as a means of improving the quality and effectiveness of their lives.'*
▶ *'An attitude and a methodology that leaves behind a trail of techniques.'*
▶ *'A model of how we receive information, store information and retrieve it.'*
▶ *'A revolutionary approach to human communication and development.'*
▶ *'The difference that makes the difference.'*
▶ *'A modelling technology whose specific subject matter is the set of differences that make the difference between the performance of geniuses and that of average performers in the same field of activity.'*
▶ *'A system for describing, restructuring, and transforming a person's meaning and cognitive understanding of the world they live in.'*
▶ *'A set of procedures whose usefulness not truthfulness is the measure of its worth.'*
▶ *'An accelerated learning strategy for the detection and utilization of patterns in the world.'*
▶ *'A user's manual for the brain.'*

Understanding NLP

So, it's a science, a process, a study, a model, a set of procedures, a manual, a system, an attitude, a strategy, a technology … no wonder some people initially struggle to get a perspective on what NLP is or grasp its essence. The absence of any agreed definition or description means that everyone comes up with their own – and as you've seen, they're very different.

As you 'walked around the elephant' by reading the descriptions above you will have started to get a sense of what NLP is all about. And it's our intention that by the time you've finished reading this book you will have a clear understanding of the key principles, models and patterns, along with the ability to put them into practice.

Unpacking the N, the L and the P

Perhaps the easiest way of explaining NLP is to say it is a form of applied psychology. That's not the whole story, but it's how many people use it – as a means of achieving more for themselves and being more fulfilled in their personal and professional lives.

Another problem for NLP is the technical nature of the name. Happily, these days it is better known, but the reaction when you mention Neuro-Linguistic Programming from those who have never heard of it is still to ask, 'What on earth is that?' Although many of us wish the founders had come up with a name that was snappier, clearer and – for those of us who earn a living from NLP – sexier, in fact 'Neuro-Linguistic Programming' is simply an accurate description of what it is. Let's take a look at why each of the terms came to be used.

NEURO

The 'neuro' part relates to neurology, to the ways in which we process information from our five senses through our brain and nervous system.

LINGUISTIC

'Linguistic' relates to the use of language systems – not just words but all symbol systems including gestures and postures – to code, organize and attribute meanings to our internal representations of the world, and to communicate internally and externally.

PROGRAMMING

And 'programming' comes from information processing and computing science, on the premise that the way in which experience is stored, coded and transformed is similar to how software runs on a PC. By deleting, upgrading or installing our mental software, we can change how we think and, as a result, how we act.

When you link all the words up you have Neuro-Linguistic Programming, which is essentially concerned with the processes by which we create an internal representation – our experience – of the external world of 'reality' through language and our neurology.

The NLP model

We experience the world through our five senses: sight, hearing, touch, smell and taste. Because there is so much continuous information coming in our direction we consciously and unconsciously delete what we don't want to pay attention to. We filter the remaining data based on our past experiences, values and beliefs. What we end up with is incomplete and inaccurate because some of the original input has been deleted altogether and the rest has been generalized or distorted. The filtered information forms our internal map, which influences our physiology and 'state of being'. This in turn affects our behaviour.

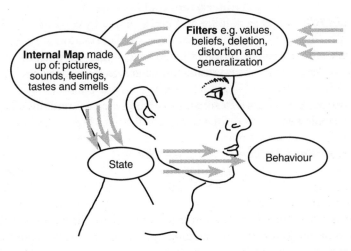

The NLP model.

The story of NLP

At the heart of NLP, though, is the 'modelling' of human excellence – and that is where the story of NLP begins in the early 1970s, with the collaboration of Richard Bandler and John Grinder at the University of California.

Bandler, a student of mathematics with a particular interest in computer science, got involved in transcribing some audio and video seminar tapes of Fritz Perls, the father of Gestalt Therapy, and Virginia Satir, the founder of Family Therapy. He found that by copying certain aspects of their behaviour and language he could achieve similar results, and began running a Gestalt Therapy group on the campus.

John Grinder, an associate professor of linguistics at the university, was intrigued by Bandler's abilities, and reputedly said to him: 'If you teach me how to do what you do, I'll tell you what you do.'

It wasn't long before Grinder, too, could get the same kind of therapeutic results as Bandler and Perls, simply by copying what Bandler did and said. Then, by a process of subtraction – by systematically leaving various elements out – Grinder was able to determine what was essential and what was irrelevant.

Realizing they were on to something, Bandler and Grinder joined forces and went on to write the first NLP book, *The Structure of Magic*, which was published in 1975. Subtitled *A Book about Language and Therapy*, it introduced the first NLP model, the Meta Model – 12 language patterns distilled from modelling Perls and Satir.

Already the essence of NLP had been defined. By studying carefully and analysing thoroughly – modelling – those who are geniuses in their field, it's possible for anyone to copy the crucial elements and achieve the same results. If you want to be an expert golfer you need to model someone who is excellent at the game – observing what they do and say, and then asking questions about what's going on mentally. In doing so you create a template for success that anyone can use.

The crucial discovery, though, was that our subjective experience of the world has a structure, and that how we think about something affects how we experience it. Drawing on the work of Alfred Korzybski, NLP makes a clear distinction between the 'territory' – the world itself – and the internal 'map' we create of it. This is often expressed succinctly as 'The map is not the territory'.

The linguist Noam Chomsky who developed transformational grammar, in which Grinder was an expert, had shown that our map will always be an incomplete and inaccurate version of what's out in the world because of the processes of distortion, deletion and generalization that occur as information is funnelled through our neurological and linguistic channels. When people have problems it's often because they mistake their improverished map for reality. As their map is made richer by asking Meta Model questions or using other techniques available in NLP, so the person develops more choice and finds it easier to achieve what they want.

'An attitude and a methodology'

One of the quotes we used earlier – 'NLP is an attitude and a methodology that leaves behind a trail of techniques' – comes from co-founder John Grinder, and is crucial to understanding NLP. So far we have talked mainly about the methodology, but in many ways it's the attitude that's more important. This can be summed up in a single word: curiosity. Moreover, in the words of L. Michael Hall, it's a *'passionate* and *ferocious* curiosity'. We would also add *relentless* to that list. Having an NLP attitude involves wanting to 'see inside other people' and wondering how they come to behave the way they do. It involves questioning, challenging, searching, and not taking anything at face value. The question that most epitomizes an NLP attitude is, 'How do you know?'

When it comes to techniques, NLP has produced some of the most powerful patterns ever devised for facilitating change in people. Some, like the Fast Phobia Cure, are well known, and often when discussion turns to NLP it's the techniques that are mentioned first. But, as John Grinder makes plain, they are the product of NLP's attitude and methodology – the result of modelling and inquiry.

Following their modelling of Perls and Satir, Bandler and Grinder went on to model Milton H. Erickson, the world's foremost medical hypnotist. The result was a different set of language patterns, the Milton Model, and the publication of the second NLP book, *Patterns of the Hypnotic Techniques of Milton H. Erickson MD.*

There followed a feverish period of inquiry and research, both by Bandler and Grinder and others, including Robert Dilts, Judith DeLozier, Leslie Cameron-Bandler and Steve and Connirae Andreas, during which many NLP patterns, techniques and models were discovered and developed, including representational systems, submodalities and anchoring.

NLP now

The Bandler and Grinder partnership came to an end in the late 1970s, and they went their separate ways. Both, though, continue to be active in the NLP world.

Bandler has gone on to create a number of trade-marked models, including Design Human Engineering and Persuasion Engineering. He has written several books, and regularly leads training in NLP and hypnosis, both in the UK and overseas.

John Grinder, with Judith DeLozier and others, developed 'New Code' NLP. Whereas 'Classic' or 'Old Coding' NLP drew its inspiration primarily from linguistics, Gestalt and systems theory, 'New Code' has its roots in information theory and the books of Carlos Casteneda. The result has been many new models, patterns and techniques, including Perceptual Positions. These days, one of Grinder's principle collaborators is Carmen Bostic St Clair.

Also a student at the university, Robert Dilts was one of the first people to get involved with Bandler and Grinder, and has been one of its most vigorous innovators, generating an enormous number of change patterns and models, and adding considerably to the published information on the subject.

As we move forward in the twenty-first century, NLP continues to evolve, with new models and techniques being added every year by a growing number of practitioners and developers.

NLP in action

NLP originated as a better way of carrying out therapy, and has been enthusiastically taken up by those in the helping professions as a fast, effective and safe way of curing phobias, removing unwanted habits, and helping with trauma. It can be used to relieve stress, improve confidence, and tackle many of the problems that people have.

But as NLP has become better known – thanks in part to best-selling books such as *Unlimited Power* and *Awaken the Giant Within* by Anthony Robbins – the areas in which it is applied have spread far beyond therapy.

Business, after some initial reservations, has embraced it strongly, and NLP concepts and processes now form the backbone of many company training programmes. Because of its practical focus on finding what's useful and putting it into action, it can enable individuals and teams to achieve their peak performance in areas as diverse as management, sales, communication, new product development and coaching.

Because the principles of NLP can benefit virtually any area of enterprise, it's now used in many areas including education, health and sport.

What you'll get from learning about NLP

But it's the personal benefits of learning about NLP that hold the key to its increasing success. Many thousands of people around the world are reading NLP books, going on NLP training courses and as a result living their dreams. What will it do for you? Here are just a few of the benefits you can expect. It will:

▶ *help you know what you want and how to get it*
▶ *help you to build stronger, deeper relationships*

- *enhance your self-confidence and self-esteem*
- *strengthen your ability to connect with others*
- *put you in the driving seat of your life*
- *enable you to communicate more effectively and persuasively*
- *help you to perform at your best for more of the time*
- *change limiting beliefs about yourself and the world*
- *enable you to be even more creative*
- *help you to control the way you think, feel and act*
- *enable you to accomplish your personal and professional goals.*

And that's just for starters. Yes, really. No kidding. NLP works. This is one time when you can believe the hype. By taking control of your own thoughts you can banish negative thinking and achieve more than you ever thought possible.

Insight

NLP has changed our lives. While this may sound like a cliché, it is demonstrably true. It has changed the way we think, the way we work – the way we are in the world. It's been instrumental in helping us make enormous changes, such as leaving a secure well-paid job (in Amanda's case) and switching direction (in Steve's case) from the world of media to the world of learning. Without it we would probably not have been able to set up a successful worldwide training business and write several best-selling books including this one.

Now have an experience ...

But only if you put it into practice. Although reading about NLP can be valuable in its own right, it's only when you put the principles and patterns into use that you gain the full benefit. Right now, you can have an experience that will demonstrate how powerful simple techniques can be.

Start by bringing to mind a memory that's slightly uncomfortable. Things didn't work out how you wanted for some reason, and you ended up feeling disappointed, unhappy or embarrassed. Mentally replay what happened, allowing yourself to see, hear and feel again what you did at the time.

Now take on the role of movie director in the cinema of your mind. You have full authority to change anything you want. Perhaps you'd rather have a cartoon. Play the memory again, only this time make the action more like *Tom and Jerry* or *The Simpsons* or some of your favourite characters. You might like to give the people in your movie cartoon voices as well.

How about adding background music? Make it something you find amusing, perhaps like the soundtrack from an old silent movie. Now play the memory again with the music turned up to just the right volume.

What you've done, without knowing it, is to 'recode' the way you represent that memory to yourself. So when you recall it, you won't feel the same. It may not bother you at all, and at the very least the feeling of discomfort will have diminished.

Now think of another situation, one where you had an argument or disagreement with someone, and you still feel bad about it. This time you're going to be a sports commentator, who's standing back and describing what's happening between you and this other person. Since your role is to entertain as well as inform, you may want to point out anything that seems interesting or amusing.

As you play the movie in your mind – say it's a disagreement with a colleague at work – your commentary might go something like this:

'Well, here we are again in Jill's office for another bruising battle with Jack from accounts. And Jill's straight in there with her complaint. No messing about here. But Jack was ready for that – he's pulling some papers out of his file. Jill's got her argument ready though ...'

Have some fun doing this. Really get into the character of the commentator. It will probably take you less than a minute to review the crucial part of what happened. Now step into the memory and play it again, this time through your own eyes. Almost certainly you won't feel as bad and you may also have gained some valuable insights about how you could act differently in a similar situation in the future.

The elephant we talked about at the beginning of this chapter may never forget, but human beings can. And as we change our memories, our perceptions, our beliefs and our thoughts, so we are able to choose new ways of acting and behaving that allow us to live the life we want. And that's the power of NLP.

How to use this book

While you may, if you wish, dip into the various chapters in *Teach Yourself Essential NLP*, you may find it useful, if you are new to NLP, to read it in sequence. That's because some later chapters assume knowledge of things that were explained earlier in the book.

To get the most from your reading, you will find it beneficial to pause and carry out the various exercises we've included to bring the concepts to life. Understanding NLP is one thing – experiencing it and being able to put it into use is quite another. You could never learn to play a saxophone by reading a manual. And it's the same with NLP. The only way to know it is to do it.

NLP in action

▶ *Apply the exercise at the end of this chapter to various memories.*
▶ *Think about the areas of life where you would like things to change. How specifically would you like them to be different?*

TEN KEY POINTS TO REMEMBER

1 *NLP is a form of applied psychology that can be defined in many different ways.*

2 *'Neuro' relates to the ways in which we process information from our five senses.*

3 *'Linguistic' relates to the use of language systems to code, organize and attribute meanings to our internal representations of the world.*

4 *We experience the world through our five senses: sight, hearing, touch, smell and taste.*

5 *To cope with the multitude of information coming in our direction we delete, distort and generalize.*

6 *We filter the data that remains based on our past experiences, values and beliefs.*

7 *NLP originated from 'modelling' excellence – and that principle is still at its heart today.*

8 *Richard Bandler and John Grinder co-created NLP in the 1970s.*

9 *The attitude of NLP can be summed up in one word – curiosity.*

10 *Learning about NLP will enable you to transform your life.*

2

The foundations of NLP

In this chapter you will learn:
- *about the four pillars of NLP*
- *about the NLP Presuppositions*

Like any form of applied psychology, NLP is underpinned by a framework of beliefs and attitudes which together form a coherent model. Much NLP thinking is embodied in a series of presuppositions, which will be discussed in detail later in this chapter. A useful starting point, though, are four core aspects of NLP which are often referred to as the 'Four Pillars'.

The Four Pillars

PILLAR ONE: OUTCOMES

What do you want? It's a simple question, but one that many people never really ask themselves. Instead they go through life with no clear sense of direction, drifting from one thing to another. Yet knowing what you want is an essential part of getting it. In everyday life we talk about having an aim, goal or target, but in NLP the term used is outcome, and the enormous value of knowing your outcome in any particular situation is the reason for it being one of the pillars on which NLP is built. Focusing on what you want helps to orientate all your resources towards achieving it.

Outcomes can be small, such as learning to play a song on the mandolin by Christmas or changing the carpet in the bathroom, or much bigger, such as finding the partner of your dreams or retiring at the age of 50 as a multi-millionaire. At any one time most people will have many different outcomes relating to various aspects of their life, some of them with a short time scale, others covering much longer periods.

Moreover, NLP offers a comprehensive process for refining outcomes to make them 'well-formed' – describing them in detail and imagining what it's like to have them already. The more clearly you know what you want the more likely you are to get it. We will be exploring well-formed outcomes later in the book.

PILLAR TWO: SENSORY ACUITY

Acuity is 'the capacity to observe or detect fine details', and NLP's second pillar, sensory acuity, concerns using your senses to be aware of what is going on around you. People vary enormously in what and how much they notice by looking, listening and feeling. Some are extremely observant, while others' focus of attention seems to be more on their own thoughts. Close your eyes for a moment, and then describe as accurately as you can your surroundings. What colour are the walls? The floor? What's the shape and design of the furniture? If there are other people around, what are they wearing? How do they move when they walk? What colour are their eyes? This simple visual exercise may highlight the fact that we are often unaware of much of what's going on around us.

Sensory acuity is considered important in NLP because it gives you information about whether what you are doing is giving you what you want, i.e. moving you closer to your outcomes. If you are trying to sell a product, for instance, or putting forward a proposal for approval, paying careful attention to the reactions of your prospects or audience – their expressions, body language, voice tone, etc. – can be the difference between success and failure. Throughout this book your attention will be drawn to the ways you can develop your sensory acuity, and know much more accurately what other people are thinking and feeling.

PILLAR THREE: BEHAVIOURAL FLEXIBILITY

Pillars one and two are the first stages of a simple but crucial feedback loop. When you start by knowing what your outcome is, and use your sensory acuity to observe what's happening, the feedback you get allows you to make adjustments in your behaviour if necessary. If the actions you are taking are not leading you in the direction you want to go it's obvious that you should try something different, but many people lack behavioural flexibility and simply keep on doing the same thing.

If your outcome is to clinch a sale and your long-winded, laid-back presentation with lots of examples doesn't seem to be winning over your audience, maybe you need to swap to a shorter, sharper style of getting your message across. And if your prospect is sitting with their arms folded across their chest it's clear you need to take another tack if you're to have a chance of achieving success.

PILLAR FOUR: RAPPORT

The first three pillars – outcome, sensory acuity and behavioural flexibility – will allow you to achieve pretty much whatever you want, unless other people are involved. Then you may need their co-operation, and for that you need a relationship based on mutual trust and understanding. The secret of establishing and maintaining such relationships is rapport, the fourth pillar of NLP.

Rapport can be thought of as the glue that holds people together. Most of the time it seems to happen naturally, automatically, instinctively. Some of the people we meet seem to be 'on our wavelength' or 'feel right' to us and there are others we just simply don't 'hit it off with'.

But NLP considers rapport to be a skill that can be enhanced and developed and we'll be looking at many ways of doing so, such as adapting our communication to suit the other person or altering our body language to match theirs. Just listening to someone and respecting their view can be a powerful act of acknowledgement.

But there's another dimension to rapport that is not so obvious, and that is the rapport we have with ourselves, in particular the rapport between our conscious and unconscious minds. Sometimes we feel torn, with part of us wanting to do one thing and another wanting something entirely different. The greater the rapport you have with the various aspects of yourself, the more inner peace you will experience.

The presuppositions of NLP

We will be returning to the four pillars in one way or another many times throughout this book. The four pillars are the basic building blocks of NLP, complementing and reinforcing a comprehensive set of beliefs that underpin the whole approach.

As we discussed in Chapter 1, in formulating NLP Richard Bandler and John Grinder drew upon a diverse range of disciplines, including systems theory, cybernetics, transformational grammar, general semantics and logical positivism, not to mention the many fields of therapy they studied. In doing so they embraced many of the underlying concepts of these various approaches, which they synthesized into what came to be known as the 'presuppositions' of NLP.

Because of the organic way in which they arose there is no definitive inventory, no 'Ten Commandments' of NLP. Most trainers and developers list somewhere between 10 and 20 presuppositions, often with additions of their own. The 15 chosen here are widely accepted as embodying the founding principles and fundamental beliefs of NLP, and its essence today. And the great thing about them is that they're sharp, pithy, statements that are easy to remember and use.

What does it mean for something to be a 'presupposition'? When we presuppose something we take it as given, accepted without proof, and this is the situation here. In fact, it's not even claimed that NLP presuppositions are true – although there is plenty of evidence to back many of them up. What's considered more important is that they're 'useful', that operating from them leads you to achieving your outcomes.

Some of the presuppositions will strike a chord and feel right immediately – perhaps reflecting things that you understood already. With others the thinking will be more unfamiliar, and it may take a short while for you to picture how they fit with your experience. Some may even sound plain wrong initially but if you are willing to suspend your disbelief and act 'as if' they were true you will almost certainly find you feel more comfortable with them in time.

While each of the presuppositions stands on its own, together they form an interconnected, interdependent matrix of thinking. But they should not be thought of as abstract philosophy that is merely a 'starter' for the NLP 'meal' to come. They are a practical, vibrant set of 'principles to live by' (Dilts) that can, in themselves, provide a platform for significant personal and professional growth. Beyond that, they are the theoretical framework underpinning many NLP patterns, models, change techniques and perspectives.

THE MAP IS NOT THE TERRITORY

This metaphor is at the heart of NLP. In the same way that a menu is not a meal, and an orchestral score is not a piece of music, so the experience we have of the world is not the world itself. The 'map' is your mind, or own perception, and the 'territory' is reality, the physical world that exists independently of your experience of it. Many people believe their internal map to be a true representation of reality, when in fact it's merely one interpretation.

EVERYONE LIVES IN THEIR OWN UNIQUE MODEL OF THE WORLD

We tend to think other people are like us, but given that 'the map is not the territory', it follows that each of us must have our own unique internal model of the world, which is why there is so much variation in the ways individuals behave and think. If you reflect for a moment on some of the people you know or who work with you, you'll be able to recognize how their approach may differ from yours. One person may think his boss has 'high standards' while another thinks of him as 'fussy about detail'. How we react in any given situation is based on our subjective perceptions. Three people may watch the same event, read the same book, or eat the same meal, yet each have a very different experience. We only ever know our own version of reality. We naturally think our version is right, and often when people argue it's because their maps are different, when everyone's map is equally valid.

EXPERIENCE HAS A STRUCTURE

NLP is based on the premise that experience has a structure – that the distinctions we make through our five senses, the ways in which we filter and pattern reality, and how we 'code' things such as time, emotions and memories in our brains and bodies are not random, but coherently and systematically organized. Once you understand the way someone is structuring their experience you can help them make changes.

LIFE, MIND AND BODY ARE ONE SYSTEM

While we tend to think of ourselves as separate, autonomous individuals, in reality 'no man is an island'. Leading NLP developer Robert Dilts expresses this elegantly when he says, 'Our bodies, our societies and universe form an ecology of complex systems and sub-systems all of which interact with and mutually influence each other'.

The Universe is a system made up of galaxies and planets. Society is a system consisting of cultures and sub-cultures made up of people. People interact with society and yet contain systems themselves.

The human body itself is a great example of a system in action, with the many different organs functioning separately yet interacting to form a whole unit. In NLP, mind and body are thought of as one system, each directly influencing the other. You can, for instance, change the way you feel by what you think, and what is happening within your body affects the thoughts you have. For example, when you think about making an important presentation your muscles are likely to tense, your breathing could be affected, and certain emotions come into play.

Life, mind and body are one system is one of the central NLP presuppositions because it's important to understand that it's not possible to isolate just one part of a system. Equally, when you change one aspect of a system, you will have in some way changed the rest. People inevitably affect each other by their actions and will be affected by what others do. When working on your own issues, or with other people, you need to be aware of the wider systems that will be involved.

THE MEANING OF A COMMUNICATION IS THE RESPONSE YOU GET

Have you ever had the experience of saying or doing something you thought was innocuous or harmless, yet the response you got was unexpected, surprising, and perhaps seemed to you out of all proportion? That's because the message we intend to communicate is not always the one that others receive. What seems acceptable from our 'map' may not be to others. There are two main reasons.

The first is that your communications are channelled through the unique perceptual filters others have, which means their own 'stuff' comes into play. So if someone is sensitive to people who shout, it won't matter what you say if you speak in a loud voice, the response will be the same.

The second is that your communication may not be as 'clean' as you think it is. If, for instance, you were giving praise to a member of staff but were offhand in your manner, they might think you were being false and respond accordingly.

The great value of this presupposition is that whatever is going on we are obliged to take responsibility for our communications, which means we can no longer blame others for not listening or for responding in the 'wrong' way. That's one of the reasons why sensory acuity is so important. You need to be aware of the response to know if your communication has been successful, or whether you need to adapt your approach.

YOU CANNOT NOT COMMUNICATE

It's obvious that when you speak you are communicating, but in fact everything you do affects the people around you. Research has shown that more than 70 per cent of communication is non-verbal, that we unconsciously pick up subtle nuances of position, gesture and expression in our interactions with others. And when we do speak, others are as aware of rhythm, tone and inflection as they are the words said. Even silence can be interpreted as having meaning. If you were to look at someone sitting quietly by themself, in just a few seconds you would have distinct impressions about them. Our mind and body are part of the same system, so the thoughts we have affect our physiology, and 'leak' non-verbally. Because *you cannot not communicate* it's essential that you communicate as clearly and as accurately as you can, rather than leaving it to chance. One way of illustrating this is to imagine finding yourself in a team meeting where an argument develops between two people. Whatever you say or do may be taken as a signal that you have taken sides with one party or that you are neutral. If you want to remain neutral you need to make sure the verbal and non-verbal ways you communicate are as aligned as possible, so that you come over as congruent.

UNDERLYING EVERY BEHAVIOUR IS A POSITIVE INTENTION

It can sometimes be hard to understand why people behave in the often bizarre, destructive ways they do. What would cause someone to drink excessively, sabotage their relationships, or act aggressively towards others? Yet human behaviour, according to NLP, is not random. There is always a purpose, a reason, a 'positive intention' behind it, which arises when the behaviour is first established. Many people, for instance, start to smoke at the age of 14, in order to feel grown up and impress their friends. Many years later, though, they find it hard to stop, because although the situation has changed, the 'part' responsible is still active. Sometimes the positive intention is far from obvious, and that's because it's operating, as is often the case, out of conscious awareness.

A number of NLP 'change techniques' involve discovering the positive intention of a behaviour and finding alternative ways of satisfying it.

Insight

In my (Amanda's) experience many people push back against this presupposition. The important thing to remember is that when you acknowledge someone's positive intention you're not condoning their unacceptable behaviour. Once you set aside your concerns, it's easier to focus on discovering the positive motivation that triggers someone's behaviour and respond to that. This can help you achieve the outcome you want.

PEOPLE MAKE THE BEST CHOICES AVAILABLE TO THEM

According to this presupposition, any behaviour, no matter how strange it may seem, was the best choice available to the person at that moment in time, given their life history, knowledge, beliefs and resources, and viewed from their frame of reference. You might regard them as mistaken, misguided or misinformed, and would have done something different in the same situation, perhaps with more effective results. Then again, there are surely times in your life when someone else would have handled things better than you did. The simple fact is that people, yourself included, do the best they can at the time and could probably do better if only they were aware of other options available to them. Examining the way we operate, our beliefs and thinking processes allows us to access new ways of doing things in the future.

THERE'S NO SUCH THING AS FAILURE – ONLY FEEDBACK

When babies are learning to do new things, such as crawl, stand or walk, they have no sense of failure. They simply have a go, and if that doesn't work they have another go, repeating the process until they get what they want. If, when they tried to stand up for the first time and fell down with a bump they decided they had failed, nobody would be able to walk. Instead, they get feedback about what does and doesn't work, and do more of what does work. Yet by the time they get to be adults most people have become less willing to make 'mistakes', less willing to risk 'failure', perhaps because that might lead to them thinking of *themself* as a failure. They seem to expect to do things well immediately, coming to the conclusion they can't do it at all, instead of using each set-back as feedback and as a learning opportunity.

Eliminating what doesn't work can be an effective way of finding out what does. Thomas Edison used this approach when searching for the right material to use in a light bulb. Rather than regarding each attempt that didn't work out as failure, he considered it a success in that it narrowed the number of ways that were left to try.

This presupposition is one of the most liberating because once you embrace it you can try all of the things you were once afraid of doing. The more 'failures' you have, the more you learn. So one strategy for learning might be to 'fail' more often!

IF WHAT YOU ARE DOING ISN'T WORKING, DO SOMETHING ELSE

If you tried a key in a lock and found it wouldn't open, what would you do? Keep trying the same key in the same lock, over and over again? Amazingly, that's what many of us do in certain areas of our lives, like a fly continually hitting itself against a pane of glass in an effort to get outside when there's a gap just inches away.

Instead you'd try another key or another lock until you found a combination that works. 'If you always do what you've always done', as the saying goes, 'you'll always get what you've always got'. Flexibility is an essential component of getting the result you want. If you try one way of tackling a problem and don't get the required results, have a go at something different, and keep varying your behaviour until you get the response you're after.

WE HAVE THE RESOURCES WITHIN US TO ACHIEVE WHAT WE WANT

Have you ever heard the expression, 'I didn't know he had it in him'? Many of us are limited by what we believe it's possible for us to achieve and are then surprised when we pull it off. This presupposition asserts that people can bring about change or achieve their outcomes by using the rich pool of inner resources they already have available inside, built up from a lifetime's experience. All that's needed is to access these resources at appropriate times and places. If there is a problem to be solved it could be that an approach you took when tackling something else provides you with the perfect solution.

Insight

It's easy to put forward reasons why it's not possible to do something. Thoughts like this limit you. If you catch yourself saying, 'Well he or she can do it because...' or, 'I'll never be as good as David Beckham', you may be right. You may also be creating a self-fulfilling prophecy. In my view (Amanda's) most people are pleasantly surprised when they discover they are capable of achieving far more than they thought. When you hear yourself saying 'can't', ask yourself if it's really true.

IF ONE PERSON CAN DO SOMETHING, ANYONE CAN LEARN TO DO IT

This presupposition encourages us to extend our performance and break through the barriers of what we believe might be possible for us. It's not only a fear of failure that holds us back, it's also our sense of our own limits. But our perceived limits are not our actual limits, and in reality we have virtually infinite potential. While it's not absolutely true to say that if one person can do something, anyone can do it – there are sometimes physical, practical or psychological reasons why that may not be possible – the spirit of the presupposition remains powerful. Sometimes it's just a matter of removing limiting beliefs or adding resources. There's also a connection with the NLP process of modelling excellence. If you want to get an article published, for instance, you could find someone who is brilliant at writing and 'model' how they do it.

PEOPLE WORK PERFECTLY

People who have issues such as phobias, social problems or simply don't do something the way they would like to are often thought of as being 'faulty' or 'defective' in some way. But that's not the way in which NLP views things: no one is 'wrong' or 'broken', people work perfectly. So if someone is hopeless at following directions, for instance, the NLP perspective would be that they're good at getting lost or finding a different path to take. Of course, this may not be the outcome they have in mind, in which case it may be necessary to examine things like their strategies and beliefs so they can be more effective. In NLP, the positive self-worth of an individual is held as a constant? with a clear distinction being made between the person and their behaviour.

IN ANY SYSTEM THE PERSON WITH THE MOST FLEXIBILITY WILL CONTROL THE SYSTEM

This presupposition derives from systems thinking, where it is known as the Law of Requisite Variety. The word 'control' perhaps overstates the situation; there are sometimes other factors at play, and a better way of expressing the sentiment is 'the person with the greatest flexibility has the best chance of achieving what they want'. Flexibility gives you more options. The solution you had to one problem may have worked well in that specific culture, environment or context but won't necessarily be effective in another. Situations change, you can't just repeat what you did before. The more complex the system, the more flexibility is required.

CHOICE IS BETTER THAN NO CHOICE

Richard Bandler, one of the originators of NLP, once said, 'The whole point of NLP is having more choice' and many of the presuppositions, along with most of the techniques, relate to increasing the number of choices available in any given situation. Having just one choice is no choice at all. That's what happens with a phobia: every time you see a spider you panic, you don't feel you have any other choice. The more choices you have, the more freedom you have to be in the driving seat of your life.

NLP in action

▶ Start to consider how you can apply the principles behind the four pillars – outcomes, sensory acuity, behavioural flexibility and rapport – in your everyday life.
▶ Look out for examples of the presuppositions in the rest of this book. You will find they come up in various guises in almost every chapter.

TEN KEY POINTS TO REMEMBER

1 *NLP is underpinned by a number of 'presuppositions' which can be thought of as principles for living.*

2 *Central to NLP is the presupposition, 'The Map is not the Territory' – meaning that the internal representation we create of the world is not the world.*

3 *There are four core aspects of NLP that are sometimes known as the 'Four Pillars' – outcome, sensory acuity, behavioural flexibility and rapport.*

4 *Knowing the outcome you want in any situation greatly increases your ability to achieve it.*

5 *Outcomes can be small and short-term or large and long-term.*

6 *Sensory acuity is important because it gives you information about whether what you are doing is giving you what you want – it forms a feedback loop.*

7 *If what you're doing isn't giving you what you want you need to do something different – in NLP this is called having behavioural flexibility.*

8 *When others are involved in you achieving your outcome you need to build and maintain rapport.*

9 *Rapport happens naturally and can be enhanced by using the principles of NLP.*

10 *NLP draws upon many disciplines including cybernetics, gestalt therapy, systems theory, hypnotherapy and general semantics.*

3

3

Representational systems

In this chapter you will learn:
- *about the five representational systems – visual, auditory, kinaesthetic, olfactory and gustatory*
- *about lead, primary and reference systems*
- *how to read eye accessing cues*
- *about overlapping and synaesthesia*
- *how to strengthen your least favoured system*

When you're sitting in a restaurant enjoying a meal, your senses are being bombarded with stimulation. You smell the food, the perfume of the people you're with, the flowers on the table. You hear the sound of people chattering, of plates and glasses being rattled, of cars passing by outside. You see the room, the customers and staff, and everything on the table. You taste the food, the wine, and if you smoke, perhaps a cigarette. You feel your weight on the seat, the knife and fork in your hand and, towards the end of the meal, a 'full' sensation.

We take in the world through our five senses or, as they are often called in NLP, modalities. That's how we know what's happening around us, there's no other way. Our neurological system then uses the information gathered from our eyes, nose, ears, mouth and the nerve endings in our skin to create an internal representation of the world. It's not a true, complete representation of reality and never could be, because our senses are relatively poor instruments, and can only take in data across a limited range.

We can only pick up sounds, for instance, from 20 Hz to 20,000 Hz, yet many animals can hear well outside that range, and with far greater sensitivity in respect of volume. What we can take in with our eyes is only a narrow part of the spectrum – unlike bats and other creatures, we can't 'see' in the dark. And it's a similar story when it comes to smell, taste and feeling.

But our internal representation is all we have, and we use it as the basis for all aspects of our mental processing as if it were the world itself. Because we use our sensory modalities, working with our neurology, to create this internal representation, they are called *representational systems* in NLP.

The representational systems are often referred to collectively as VAKOG, which is shorthand for: visual (seeing); auditory (hearing); kinaesthetic (feeling and touching); olfactory (smelling); gustatory (tasting). In NLP, most emphasis is placed on visual, auditory and kinaesthetic since they're the ones that are most essential to us in everyday life.

As we think about the world around us, we do so using pictures, sounds, feelings, tastes and smells.

When asked to recall a meeting you attended last week you bring to mind an image of the room or the people who participated. Maybe you remember what someone said – you hear the sound of their voice. Perhaps the weather was cold or the heating too warm. And there might have been a musty smell or tasty food.

Imagine taking the holiday of your dreams. Where will you be going? What will you see when you first arrive? What sounds will you hear? How will it feel to finally visit this place? When we think about the future we use our senses to create mental pictures, sounds and sensations. The world we create inside our heads can be as vivid as the world around us.

Primary system

Although people use all the representational systems available to them, they tend to favour one in particular, 'naturally' thinking in pictures, sounds or feelings. Some individuals find it easy to 'visualize', to see what happened in a memory or construct an image of what could transpire in the future. Others are great at recalling the tune of a piece of music or making up conversations in their mind. And some people are very aware of their feelings. We, of course, use all of the senses to some extent on a daily basis.

The representational system someone uses most of the time is known as their primary, or preferred system. It's normally highly developed, and capable of more discrimination than the other systems. As we grow up we develop an unconscious preference for a particular system and normally by our teens we have a visual, auditory or kinaesthetic disposition. Socialization can play an important role. If as children we spend several years learning to play a musical instrument, the auditory modality may come to the fore. Ballet or martial arts will help strengthen the kinaesthetic sense. And painting will do the same for the visual modality. Playing computer games is likely to develop both visual sophistication and kinaesthetic dexterity.

People often have occupations or hobbies that relate to their primary systems: photographers need strong visual awareness, recording engineers need auditory subtlety, and aerobics teachers need excellent co-ordination. For every system that's developed there are inevitably others that are not. If your visual modality is well developed at the expense of the other two, you may not take to the guitar or gymnastics with ease. But most of us are reasonably balanced, and have access to all five systems when we need them – looking at scenery, listening to the radio and receiving a massage using the appropriate representational system.

Predicates

Although we're not aware of it, the words and phrases we use indicate the representational system we're using at any one time. When someone declares they 'can see the light at the end of the tunnel', you know they're processing visually. When your boss 'likes the sound' of your idea, it's an auditory modality in operation. And when your friend wants you to 'grasp the nettle', you know they're thinking kinaesthetically.

If you listen carefully to someone speaking for even a short while you'll notice a pattern in the kinds of words and phrases they choose that reflects either their primary system or the particular context they're involved with.

Exercise

Stop for a moment and, before reading on, brainstorm a few words or phrases that you think might relate to the visual, auditory and kinaesthetic modalities.

How did you get on? If you struggled with certain representational systems, that may indicate you don't use them as much. Here's a list of common words and expressions relating to the three main modalities.

VISUAL

Appear, bird's-eye view, catch a glimpse of, clarify, clear-cut, dark, dress up, enlighten, examine, expose, focus, glance, glimpse, graphic, hazy idea, hindsight, illusion, illustrate, in light of, in view of, look, look into it, make a scene, mind's eye, notice, obvious, outlook, perspective, picture, pinpoint, reveal, see, short-sighted, spectacle, take a dim view, tunnel vision, under your nose, vague.

AUDITORY

Audible, call, clear as a bell, clearly expressed, compose, discuss, earful, earshot, harmonize, hear, hidden message, listen, loud and clear, manner of speaking, mention, note, outspoken, remark, report, say, scream, shout, silence, sing, sound, speechless, tell the truth, tongue-tied, tune-in, voice, well informed, word for word.

KINAESTHETIC

Affected, bear, boils down to, carry, cold, cool, crash, crawl, emotional, foundation, get a load of this, get in touch with, grab, grip, handle, hang in there, hassle, heated, hold, hot-headed, impact, irritate, lay cards on the table, lukewarm, motion, muddled, nail, pressure, rub, shallow, sharpen, shift, shock, slipped my mind, solid, sore, stir, stress, strike, tap, throw, tickle, tied up, touch, wring.

All the above include words that are known as predicates, sensory-based process words in the form of nouns, verbs, adjectives and adverbs. During the next few days pay attention to what people say. Notice how many predicates relating to a particular representational system they use. You may find it easier to listen to people on the radio, that way you won't be distracted by any visual input.

You'll often be able to spot in books and magazines the primary system of the writer. Take a few moments to read the following pieces of text and attempt to uncover the preferred system.

1   *The task weighed heavily on Helen. She usually grasped new ideas quickly but this time it felt too much to handle.*

2 *He heard what his manager had to say and then said what he thought about the subject. To him they were simply not on the same wavelength.*

3 *Caroline was delighted with the clear illustrations in the article. She could see how it would add to the overall picture for the readers.*

Answers:

1 *Kinaesthetic – 'weighed heavily', 'grasped', 'felt' and 'handle'.*

2 *Auditory – 'heard', 'say', 'said' and 'wavelength'.*

3 *Visual – 'clear illustrations', 'see' and 'picture'.*

Matching predicates

The great value of knowing someone's primary representational system is that you can use it when communicating with them. It enhances communication enormously because you are literally 'speaking their language', the language they use to think.

What do you observe about this exchange?

> A   Can you give me a hand? I'm having trouble grasping these concepts, they're very hard.
>
> B   I'll see what I can do to clarify things. Hopefully I'll have a bright idea.

You probably noticed that A is using kinaesthetic language and B is responding with visual language, which may hinder communication. A better response might have been:

> B   Just hang in there, I'll get to grips with it and try to get things moving.

Using the same modality of sensory-based predicates, the other person favours, irrespective of your primary system, is extremely effective in rapport terms. If you're unsure about what predicates to use, either because you've only just met the person, or there's a group of people, mix in visual, auditory and kinaesthetic expressions. That way you'll appeal to everyone.

Reference system

Our reference system is what we use to verify the decisions we make. When someone has a kinaesthetic reference system they have to feel right inside to know they've made the right choice. Those with a visual reference system would experience an internal picture that gave them an insight into the situation. People with an auditory reference system would hear some kind of internal dialogue that tells them things are okay. Over the coming weeks start to become familiar with your own system for checking decisions. It won't take long for you to work out how you know you are taking the right course of action.

Lead system

Since our primary representational system is our preferred system, you might have expected we'd all use it for every aspect of conscious processing. In fact, though, some of us have a separate 'lead' system for bringing things into awareness, whether they're from the external environment or generated internally.

Bringing to mind a memory is a good way to check what your 'lead' system is. Do you get a picture, sound or feeling first? Try it with a few memories, some recent, some when you were younger. If it's always the same modality, that's your lead system. What's important to understand is that it's not the full representation, just the key that unlocks the door. For every memory, or visualization, you normally have a full VAKOG representation stored internally. And the way you gain access to it is by first seeing a picture, hearing a sound, having a feeling, or experiencing a smell or taste.

Eye accessing cues

The quickest and easiest way of discovering someone's lead system is by watching their eyes carefully when you ask them a question. You may have thought eye movements are random or, more likely, never thought about them at all – but in fact they clearly indicate the representational system someone is using at any one time. And as the modality changes, so does the direction in which the eye looks.

These eye accessing cues, as they are known – 'cue' in this context meaning a signal that something is happening – are virtually universal. While many people have the pattern below, there are individual differences – in left-handed people, for instance, the pattern may be reversed.

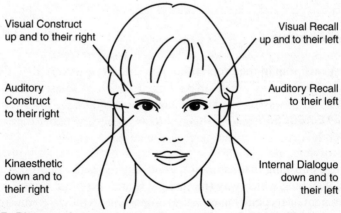

Visual Construct
up and to their right

Visual Recall
up and to their left

Auditory
Construct
to their right

Auditory Recall
to their left

Kinaesthetic
down and to
their right

Internal Dialogue
down and to
their left

NB. Diagram shows eye accessing cues for a right-handed person as you see them

Eye accessing cues.

People look up when they're processing visually. When they look up to their left they're recalling a picture they've seen before, such as their front door. When they look up and to their right they're constructing an image they haven't seen before, such as a pink tiger with yellow stripes.

When people's eyes move directly to their left they're recalling a sound they've heard before, such as their boss's voice, and when they look to their right they're hearing an unfamiliar or constructed sound, perhaps a melody they're making up.

When someone looks down to their left they're listening to their own internal dialogue. Most of us experience an internal voice – it can be like having your own running commentary on life. When people look down to their right they're in touch with their feelings.

Insight

When I (Steve) first learnt about eye accessing cues I spent many hours observing other people's eye movements as part of my practitioner programme. There really is no substitute for practice if you want to be able to do this in the moment. Several years on, it's something I do naturally, often asking them what they're looking at in their mind's eye, or what they're saying to themselves. When you start to work with other people using some of the techniques described in this book it helps you to tell how they are processing information at each step in the process.

EYE ACCESSING CUE QUESTIONS

Identifying a person's lead system in a given situation is simply a matter of asking them a question that requires internal processing and watching which way they look. The best way to become proficient at recognizing eye accessing cues is to practise. One of the most effective ways to do this is to enlist the help of a friend who has some time to spare. With them sitting in front of you ask the following questions and notice which way their eyes move.

Be on the lookout to identify their lead system and where their eyes move to next.

VISUAL RECALL (VR)
What colour is your front door?
Is there a fireplace in your house?
What can you see from your bedroom window?

VISUAL CONSTRUCT (VC)
What would you look like with pink eyes?
Picture a doctor with two heads.
What would your hair look like if it were dyed purple and green?

AUDITORY RECALL (AR)
Think of your favourite piece of music.
Hear the sound of a cat.
Listen to the sound of chalk on a blackboard.

AUDITORY CONSTRUCT (AC)
What's the sound of a barking budgie?
Make up a brief melody.
Listen to a crying motorbike.

KINAESTHETIC (K)
Feel what it's like to be tickled on the feet.
Which is cooler, your right or left hand?
Feel the wind on your face.

INTERNAL AUDITORY DIALOGUE (AD)
Think about the rights and wrongs of capital punishment.
Make up the opening lines of a speech you'd give at your old school.
Ask yourself what happiness means.

If you get any unusual results ask your partner what they were thinking about. It's just possible that they may, for example, not have a fireplace in their house and were picturing what it would be like if they had one. If this happens they are likely to look up to their right instead of their left as you expected. Or they could be repeating the instruction to themselves first before acting upon it, in which case they'll start each time by looking down to their left.

Matching representational systems

Knowing how someone is processing at any one time makes it possible to be more sophisticated in your communications, rather than simply relying on the primary system. You may know that someone's preferred modality is visual, and be about to use visual language yourself, but observe that they're looking across to their right, indicating that they're listening to an auditory memory, so auditory language would make it easier to connect. Having a better understanding of their map of the world in this way helps you develop stronger rapport.

Another advantage with observing eye accessing cues is that you can use the information to bring about a change in the state of another person. If someone you know is 'down in the dumps' and feeling sorry for themselves, they're likely to be looking down to their right. If you then use words and gestures to allow them to see the bright future ahead of them they'll often follow your gesture and start to look up to their right where they can't help but start to construct a visual image of a happier scene.

Recognizing strategies

Eye accessing cues don't exist in isolation. As you watch people, you'll notice there's a pattern to where their eyes go. They might first talk to themself (auditory lead/down to their left) then make a picture (visual construct/up right) and finally check the result (kinaesthetic/bottom right). This sequence is called a 'strategy', and NLP has a notation system that's used to record it. Using the letters VAKOG to indicate the representational system, an 'i' or 'e' is added after the letter to denote whether the sense is internal or external. For instance, Ae means auditory external and Vi stands for an internal Visual image. Vc is Visual construct and Ar is auditory recall. We'll explore strategies in more depth in Chapter 18.

Other kinds of cue

In addition to language patterns and eye movements, there are other cues which indicate the representational system someone is using at a particular moment in time. The following is a 'rule of thumb' checklist:

VISUAL
Breathing – shallow and high in the chest
Voice – high pitched
Speech – fast
Muscle tension – in the shoulders
Gestures – finger pointing
Head position – tilted up

AUDITORY
Breathing – evenly distributed across the chest
Voice tone – clear and precise
Speech – medium paced
Gestures – arms folded and telephone position – auditory internal dialogue
Head position – slight angle to one side

KINAESTHETIC
Breathing – deep and low in the stomach
Voice tone – low and deep
Speech – slow, with pauses
Gestures – arms bent and relaxed
Head position – tipped slightly forward

Overlap and synaesthesia

Sometimes in NLP one representational system is used to gain access to another. For instance, we might create a mental image of something and then add sound. Any two sensory modalities may be linked together in this way. NLP practitioners sometimes use overlapping as a therapeutic intervention by guiding the person's attention from one representational system to another. The following exercise gives you an opportunity to practise overlapping.

Steps

1   Pick a subject, such as riding a bike or going for a swim.
2   Start with the representational system that comes most naturally to you. If feelings are familiar territory, begin there. Get in touch with the sensation of water next to your skin or how your muscles move as you kick your legs behind you to propel yourself forward.
3   Then add another modality, the one that's almost second nature to you and yet not quite. If this is visual, you could find yourself picturing the water around you, seeing your arms as they take turns appearing in front of you. Perhaps there are other people around and you see their faces or partially submerged bodies.
4   Then add your weakest submodality. In our example this would be sounds. Perhaps the faces act as a trigger for you to add their voices, or the sight of your arms crashing into the water leads you to recall the sound splashing makes.

Sometimes two representational systems become so connected that one can't operate without the other, one allows access to the other.

This is often visual or auditory to kinaesthetic, sometimes referred to as a 'see-feel' or 'hear-feel' circuit. In the latter case the person gets the feeling from what they hear. Hearing a violin playing, for example, could automatically create a feeling of intense pleasure. Without the music the feeling would not be experienced. This is called synaesthesia.

Strengthening your least developed representational system

To be effective at NLP you need to be able to 'speak' three languages: visual, auditory and kinaesthetic. Most people have a well-developed representational system and others that are weaker. To establish rapport well you need to be able to use all three effortlessly. Becoming aware of your own preferences and those of people around you is a great start. Another effective way of achieving this is by using overlap exercises.

When you use overlapping you can add tastes and smells as well if you want to. By doing this you'll end up with a full sensory experience. It's important to open with your strongest system and then gradually add the rest. The more you practise accessing your weaker system the stronger it will become.

NLP in action

▶ Reflect on your own language patterns or better still create a tape-recording of yourself talking and identify your own primary system.
▶ Practise observing people's eye accessing cues and identify their lead representational system.
▶ Develop your least favoured representational system using the overlapping exercise.

TEN KEY POINTS TO REMEMBER

1 *We take in the world through our five senses or, as they are known in NLP, modalities.*

2 *We use the information from our senses to create an internal representation of the world.*

3 *The acronym VAKOG is often used as short-hand for our representational systems: Visual (seeing); Auditory (hearing); Kinaesthetic (feeling); Olfactory (smelling); Gustatory (tasting). It's also sometimes reduced to 'rep systems'.*

4 *Although we use all of the representational systems we tend to favour one in particular – this is known as the primary or preferred system.*

5 *The words and phrases we use when we think and speak often indicate which representational system we are using.*

6 *We use our reference system to verify the decisions we make and our lead system brings things into awareness.*

7 *Eye accessing cues – where we look when accessing information can reveal to observers the representational system we're using.*

8 *Matching another person's representational system can help us build rapport with them.*

9 *In addition to language patterns and eye movements there are other cues that indicate the representational system someone is using such as the way they breathe or their voice speed.*

10 *Sometimes one representational system is used to gain access to another – this is called overlapping.*

4

Submodalities

In this chapter you will learn:
- **how submodalities work**
- **how to recognize your internal representations**
- **new ways of thinking about and reacting to your internal world**
- **the difference between analogue and digital submodalities**
- **how to create change using submodalities**
- **about the Swish and the Compulsive Blowout techniques**

By now you're familiar with the five representational systems – visual, auditory, kinaesthetic, olfactory and gustatory – but this is only part of the story. For each of the sensory modalities there are finer details and distinctions, which are known as submodalities.

When we're thinking visually, for instance, the pictures in our mind's eye have colour, brightness, contrast, depth, size and so on. Sounds have volume, location, tonality, etc. The feelings within our body have temperature, intensity, duration and more. The same is true of our olfactory and gustatory senses.

Submodalities are the way we code and make up the structure of our internal experience. As with so many other things, most of the time this happens outside of our conscious awareness. Every thought we have, whether a memory or vision of the future, is formed out of these nuances of pictures, sounds, feelings, tastes and smells.

How submodalities function

The best way – arguably the *only* way – to understand how submodalities function is to experience them. And to do that you need to engage with your own experience.

So, allow yourself to think back to a time when you were relaxed and happy, perhaps on holiday. Tune into the visual element of your memory and, looking through your own eyes, recall what you saw at the time. Is your image in colour or black and white? Is it moving or still? Is it panoramic or is there a frame around it like a picture? How far away or near to you is it? Does it have a specific location? You may find you can make more distinctions than this.

Now play around with it. As you look at your image turn up the brightness. Does it alter how you feel about it? Then gradually make the image dimmer until you can barely make it out. Many people find there's an optimum brightness at which their feelings intensify, and when it's too light or dark they don't have any feelings for it at all.

If the image is moving, make it frozen, like a postcard. If it's already still, give it movement. How does that change things? If it's colour turn it to black and white, and if it's already monochromatic, fill it with colour. What's the effect? Move your mental image further away, then closer, to the side, and up and down. How do you feel when it's in those different locations?

Now tune into the auditory element of your memory and recall what you heard at the time. What sounds are you aware of – voices, music or a noise of some kind? How many sound sources are there? Are the sounds close by or some distance away? Which direction do the sounds come from? Do they sound as clear as a bell or are any of them muffled? If there are voices are they pitched high or low? Are they speaking quickly or slowly?

Try turning up the volume and get a sense of the difference it makes to your experience. Now turn it down to a whisper. If there are a number of voices or sounds adjust the tone of each one, much like you would if you were using a graphic equalizer. Move the sounds around into different locations. Try changing the speed. What effect do each of these changes have on the way you feel about it?

Finally, get in touch with any feelings you experienced at the time. Where in your body were they? How would you describe the sensations? Were they strong or weak? Diffused or focused? What happens if you move them around or change their intensity?

What you've just done is to briefly experience the 'fabric' of your submodalities – how they're made up. You may have been surprised when you started changing the way your memory was coded, that it could have such a significant effect. Most people have never thought of altering the brightness of an internal image or the volume of an internal sound to feel differently about things.

What you were doing was changing your internal representation, and you can do it with any memory, 'good' or 'bad', strengthening those which you value and weakening those which cause you problems. You can also use the same process when planning what you want to do in the future. By optimizing the submodalities, you can make your 'outcomes' compelling.

Recognizing submodalities

To recognize submodalities all you need to know is what to look for. You can practise by describing an everyday experience in detail and check the list below to find out how you've coded your experience.

TYPICAL SUBMODALITIES

Visual representations
Associated – dissociated
Moving – still
Framed – panoramic
Foreground or background contrast
Horizontal or vertical perspective
Location of image
Dull – bright
Black and white – colour
Colour balance
Fast – slow – still
Distance: near – far
Clear – blurred
Three-dimensional – flat or two-dimensional
Shape
Size

Auditory representations
Stereo – mono
Location of sounds
Volume: loud – soft
Tone: bass – treble
Pitch: high – low
Tempo: fast – slow

Close – far
Rhythm
Melody
Quality: clear – muffled
Continuous – discontinuous
Soft – harsh
Number of sound sources
Kind of sound: music, voice – whose voice?

Kinaesthetic representations
Constant – intermittent
Location of sensations – internal or external
Strong – weak
Large area – small area
Texture: rough – smooth
Dry – wet
Temperature: hot – cold
Pressure and weight: heavy – light
Still – moving
Rhythm – regular or irregular
Intensity

Auditory digital representations (internal voice)
Sensory based or evaluative
About self or others
Current – past – future
Location of words
Volume
Pitch
Simple or complex

Analogue and digital submodalities

There are two main types of submodalities, digital and analogue. Digital submodalities are either on or off. A mental picture, for instance, is either moving or still. There are no intermediate positions. Analogue submodalities, on the other hand, are infinitely variable between the extremes. Sounds vary along a continuum between quiet and loud. The majority of submodalities are analogue, with just a handful that are digital.

Submodalities and language

In Chapter 3 we discussed how the words people use reveal the way they're representing things internally. This is also true of submodalities. Some typical examples are: 'I hear you loud and clear', 'We've barely scratched the surface' or, 'He'll take a dim view of this'. The things we say often reflect not only the sensory specific predicates but also the associated submodalities. They give more precise insight into what people are thinking about and how they're coding their experience internally.

This relationship is sometimes apparent in non-verbal communication too. People often, for instance, indicate the exact location of the image they have in their mind's eye by pointing to it. Or they may use their hands to define the shape of something. Once you're aware that such movements are not random, you'll become more accurate at recognizing how people spatially structure their experience using gestures.

The value of submodalities

You may be wondering how knowing about submodalities might be of use to you. In fact it's extremely valuable, because it allows you to choose the way you code your memories and dreams for the future. And in doing so you can alter their meaning and make them more or less memorable, desirable, credible or intense.

Creating change with submodalities

The impact and meaning of a memory is affected more by the
submodalities used to code it than the actual content. Once
something's taken place it's impossible to change what actually
happened, but what can be altered is the way the experience is
coded. This alters the meaning of our internal representation of the
original event, and how we feel about it. The desired outcome of
many NLP patterns is either to diminish or amplify the intensity of
a remembered experience.

Many people have memories that are unpleasant and
uncomfortable, and which cause them problems in the here and
now. There might have been a traumatic incident or some other
kind of significant emotional experience. The result is a phobia, a
panic attack, or an irrational fear that is debilitating and makes life
difficult.

What happens is that when we recall the event or something
happens to trigger a memory of it, the emotion comes flooding
back. Since the event itself is in the past, what's causing the
problem has to be the way it's been coded into memory. And that's
largely down to the submodality distinctions. By changing crucial
details of the coding, it's possible for the intense emotion to be
drained from a memory, and for the person never to be troubled by
it again. We'll be looking at specific techniques to achieve this later
in the book.

Another thing that can be changed is how believable something is. Some people, for example, have an internal voice that gives them a really hard time, pointing out all their 'mistakes', reminding them of their stupidity and utter worthlessness. If this happens to you why not change the quality of your internal voice? Make it sound like Mickey Mouse or slow it down until each word is drawn out. The voice will soon lose its credibility. According to Richard Bandler, when people say they're depressed they often have an internal voice that's so quiet it can barely be heard. This means the voice has a hypnotic effect. One solution is to turn up the volume and change the tonality so the voice sounds cheerful.

It's also possible to change the meaning and impact of your internal coding for future outcomes, hopes and dreams. The right submodalities will make your goals appear attractive to you, undesirable or somewhere in-between. Simply adjusting your submodalities can make an outcome totally compelling.

You may or may not be surprised at the ease with which you can make these changes. The only way to discover the power of submodalities is to play around with them. The more you experiment the more you discover. As Richard Bandler says in *Using Your Brain for a Change* – one of the definitive books on using submodalities – 'All the things that go on in your mind affect you, and they're all potentially within your control'.

CONTRASTIVE ANALYSIS

One of the most useful techniques in working with submodalities is contrastive analysis, which can be used to find 'the difference that makes the difference' between two states or internal representations. Contrastive analysis is used in many NLP processes and is especially useful where one experience gives a desirable outcome and the other produces undesirable results.

If we experience one memory as emotional and one as neutral, there must be a difference in the way they are coded. By identifying

the submodalities that are different – the *critical* submodalities –
it's possible to effect a change, quickly and easily.

MAPPING ACROSS

Because the way in which we experience a memory depends
primarily on the way it's coded, changing the submodalities of an
unpleasant memory to those of a pleasant memory will mean it
becomes, as far as our neurological system is concerned, a pleasant
experience.

The process by which this is achieved in NLP is called Mapping
Across. It simply involves 'copying and pasting' the submodalities
that are different from the pleasant to the unpleasant memory. This
is normally done one at a time, until what had been the unpleasant

memory has exactly the same submodalities as the pleasant memory. Although it may sound complicated, or difficult, it's actually straightforward.

THE DRIVER SUBMODALITY

Sometimes, as you transfer the submodalities, you'll change one and many others will change at the same time. This is called the driver submodality, and it is the most 'critical' of the critical submodalities. It's like a master switch that controls all the others. This is sometimes referred to as 'the domino effect'. There's not always a driver, but if you encounter one you don't need to complete the mapping across process – in a sense the job has been done for you.

Ecology in change

It's important to mention at this point that sometimes submodalities are as they are for a good reason, and there can be unforeseen consequences in making the change. NLP places great importance on 'ecology' in assessing the impact a change will have on someone and other people in their lives. There's detailed information on this vital process in Chapter 7.

Swish

Swish is a pattern devised by Richard Bandler that uses critical submodality changes to programme the brain to work in a different way. It's a generative pattern, which means that it generalizes to other appropriate areas of a person's life, making it particularly valuable. Swish is often used to break habits such as a compulsion to eat chocolate, smoke cigarettes or stop nail-biting. After using Swish the person will still have the option of doing the behaviour, they just won't feel compelled to.

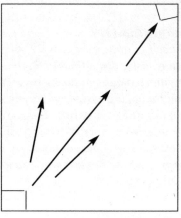

Unwanted behaviour

Image of
replacement
behaviour

Swish pattern.

Steps

1 *Think of a behaviour or response you'd rather not have. It may be a habit you could do without. Make it something you'd like to change or a situation where you want to respond differently. Identify a 'cue image' that triggers the response. There will always be one. This is your 'point of choice'. If you want to stop eating chocolate, it may be the moment you unwrap the bar or bring it up to your mouth. Sometimes the cue image is generated internally. You think, 'I must go and buy some chocolate'. Either way, take a mental 'snapshot' of the cue image.*

2 *By experimentation, identify two submodalities in the visual system that change the way you feel about it. Try size and brightness first.*

3 *Now think how you would look if you didn't have this problem, if you were the kind of person for whom this wasn't an issue. As you observe that other 'you', it's possible to tell it's someone who is resourceful, confident, etc. You don't have to know how they got that way. Spend as much time*

as it takes to make that person someone you'd really like
to be.

4 *In your mind's eye create a 'frame' in front of you, and
fill it with the cue image, optimized according to the two
submodalities you identified earlier. Then place the resourceful
image of yourself in one of the corners, small and dark.*

5 *Now, simultaneously, make them swap places, so the large
cue image becomes small and dark and the small 'resourceful'
image fills the frame, big and bright. Some people find saying
'Swish' helps; others find it a distraction.*

6 *When you've done this make the frame go blank and then
repeat the Swish process ten times, getting faster each time.
Make sure you create a blank screen after each one or if your
eyes are closed simply open them instead. This will change
your internal state. What this does is to broaden and deepen
the 'pathway' for the new experience. You're re-programming
yourself to respond to a different cue.*

7 *Test to see if you can restore the cue picture. If you find it
either won't come back or is shaky or dim you're done. If not,
go back and repeat the process.*

Designer swish

Swish works well with around 70 per cent of us. There are people,
for instance, who respond more to a dull image than a bright
one. This means if you use brightness in the usual way it has the
opposite effect to what you intended. In some cases people have
either an auditory or kinaesthetic cue related to their undesired
behaviour rather than a visual one. The Designer Swish overcomes
these issues because it's tailor-made to match a person's individual
submodalities. This advanced technique involves identifying the cue
submodalities by asking the person a series of questions, creating
a cue for the replacement behaviour and testing it to make sure
it has the desired effect. A plan is then created to determine how
best to create a shift between the two submodalities. For a detailed
explanation of this we recommend you read *Change Your Mind
and Keep the Change* by Steve and Connirae Andreas.

The compulsion blowout

Many people experience a compulsion to do something in a particular context. They may feel they have to check for dust when they walk into a room, or make sure pictures are hanging straight on the wall. The Compulsion Blowout, which was devised by Steve and Connirae Andreas, can often be the solution where a response is so deeply ingrained that techniques like Swish don't shift it. As with Swish when you complete the Compulsion Blowout you'll still be able to carry out the behaviour, you just won't feel compelled to. The Compulsion Blowout includes both contrastive analysis and identifying a driver submodality. The best way to understand it is to try it out for yourself.

Steps

1 *Think of a compulsion. To start off with it's useful to make it something fairly minor such as feeling compelled to check emails every few minutes for new messages or resisting eating a packet of crisps.*

2 *Think of something similar to the compulsion where you get a neutral response. Compulsions can operate in two directions, towards and away from. If you choose something you find repulsive it would just be another form of compulsion. An example of this would be choosing a food you found disgusting, say tripe, when you felt compelled to eat crisps. Instead you might choose peanuts, assuming they're a neutral experience for you.*

3 *Use contrastive analysis to find out what the differences in submodalities are between the compulsive behaviour and the neutral one. Make sure you cover all the representational systems. Discover the difference that makes the difference.*

4 *Uncover the driver submodality. Test each submodality difference by changing the compulsion experience. Test it both ways, so this might mean with the volume up and down. You're looking for an analogue submodality that puts the power behind it, the one that drives it. If the compulsion is to*

eat crisps, for instance, the driver may be that the closer the image is the more compelled you are to eat them.

5 Next, experience the feeling of compulsion really intensely. In our example it would mean moving the image of crisps really close so they seem irresistible to the point you can barely stand it. You're seeking to shift the analogue submodality of closeness along the continuum to a place where it loses its intensity.

6 You then repeat the process of getting closer over and over and faster and faster until you feel something shift. The aim is to cross a kind of threshold.

7 Allow a few moments before checking if you still feel compelled.

NLP in action

▶ Each evening for the next ten days pick an event from the day and replay the scene in your mind's eye. See how many submodalities you can detect.

▶ Pay attention to your internal voice. Change the submodalities, such as volume and pitch, relating to this voice. End up with your inner dialogue working in the way that sounds best for you.

▶ Pick a neutral everyday memory and turn your mental picture into a Disney cartoon. Now add some sparkle. When you're done return your mental image to whatever looks good to you.

▶ Select something you'd like to change and identify the driver submodality using contrastive analysis.

▶ Think of something you'd like to SWISH and follow the steps in the exercise.

TEN KEY POINTS TO REMEMBER

1 *For each of the five sensory modalities (senses) there are finer distinctions known as submodalities.*

2 *Submodalities are the way we code and make up the structure of our internal experience.*

3 *You can change the way a memory is coded by altering the submodalities.*

4 *Digital submodalities are either on or off – e.g. a mental picture is either moving or still.*

5 *Analogue submodalities are infinitely variable – e.g. sounds vary along a continuum between quiet and loud.*

6 *We reveal our submodalities through language and non-verbal communication.*

7 *Once something has happened it's impossible to change it, but what can be altered is the way the experience has been coded.*

8 *We can also change the meaning and impact of our internal coding for future outcomes – by making them more compelling we're more likely to attain them.*

9 *Contrastive analysis is used to identify the difference in the way two memories are coded – it is then possible to effect a change in the submodalities.*

10 *Swish is a generative pattern that uses submodality changes to break habits such as eating chocolate or smoking cigarettes.*

5

Meta Programs

In this chapter you will learn:
- *about Meta Programs and how people access information*
- *how some of the most common thinking patterns work*
- *how it's possible to enhance everyday relationships by paying attention to thinking styles in language*

Understanding Meta Programs

Have you ever wondered why some people like to think about the big picture and others prefer to get down to the detail? Perhaps you've come across people who seem to find the flaw in every idea that's put forward, and others who focus on all the reasons why something will work. NLP explains these differences in terms of 'Meta Programs' or unconscious filters which help us deal with the huge amount of sensory-based information in the external environment. Because we're only able to handle seven (plus or minus two) pieces of information at any time, and in order to avoid sensory overwhelm, we delete, distort and generalize. This process is described in detail in Chapter 13.

Leslie Cameron-Bandler identified around 60 different Meta Programs that help us organize our thinking and decide where to focus our attention; there are potentially many more. Whereas submodalities are concerned with the sensory detail of our internal representations, Meta Programs define the approach we take to issues we come across; they filter the types of things we let into our internal world and what we allow out.

RECOGNIZING META PROGRAMS

Once we're aware of what Meta Programs there are, it's possible to detect them by paying attention to what people say. If you drop a pile of books some people will rush to help and others leave you to pick them up yourself. Two people will react differently to the same message, story or joke depending on the Meta Programs they're 'running' in that context.

Most Meta Programs come in pairs of bi-polar opposites. In the dropped books example this would be 'self' and 'other'. This does not mean that we are either at one end or the other of a scale, we can also be somewhere in the middle of the continuum. Not all Meta Programs come in pairs. They can be in sets of three or four. Some are also separate and distinct patterns.

Meta Programs are 'context specific'. The patterns we use vary in different circumstances – at work, at home with the family, out with friends or with different relationships such as a boss, colleague, spouse, child, close friend or a situation such as buying a car. At work someone might find change stimulating and at home prefer things to remain the same. Having said that we also tend to have dominant patterns, a bit like a default setting on a computer program. While it's important not to put people's behaviour in pigeon-holes it's possible to identify patterns that people regularly use across a wide range of contexts. These patterns can also be defined for groups of people and organizations.

THE VALUE OF UNDERSTANDING META PROGRAMS

There are many advantages to be gained from understanding our own and other people's Meta Programs. Not least of these is developing self-awareness which, if acted upon can be applied in many different ways. Understanding Meta Programs:

▶ *improves our ability to establish rapport – being able to recognize other people's thinking patterns allows you to match their language and communicate more effectively*

- *enhances our influencing skills – when you recognize how other people think, you can present ideas to them in a way they're likely to buy into*
- *helps us make good recruitment decisions – some companies use Meta Programs when interviewing candidates for jobs so they don't end up with round pegs in square holes.*

NLP perspectives
Meta Programs – Shelle Rose Charvet

'Meta Programs are important in NLP because they add a depth of understanding of how people take in information from the outside, how each person processes that information differently. This affects their emotions, changes their behaviour, and impacts what they will like or dislike. These "filters" operate at a below-conscious level, outside of normal awareness. Leslie Cameron-Bandler (now Lebeau) identified them based on Noam Chomsky's seminal work on how people create their own individual Model of the World; through making below-conscious Deletions, Distortions and Generalizations. Understanding these filters can give incredible insight into how different people experience their lives, and why it can sometimes be so challenging for individuals, groups, cultures and countries to get along.

When individuals practise NLP with their clients, the knowledge, understanding and use of Meta Programs enables practitioners to adapt each of the protocols to fit how their client gets motivated and thinks. For example if a client were motivated to move "Away From" losing another job, the practitioner would be able to use Away From language so the client would stay motivated. "Because you want to avoid this happening again, I suggest we..."

(Contd)

Similarly, if you knew that your coaching client had a high need for change (a Difference pattern), you could help keep them focused by using Difference language: new, changed, switch, shift, etc.

It is difficult to believe how powerful changing the words you use to fit the motivation and internal processing patterns of other people can be. In fact most people don't believe it until they see the evidence for themselves. In my work with people and organizations around the world, I now know that whether we are talking about one-on-one communication, small group or mass communication, the skilled and ethical use of Meta Programs can help solve even the most intractable conflicts and improve understanding between people. It is my hope that the world will do exactly that; learn these tools (along with the rest of NLP) and make the planet a better place for everyone.'

Shelle Rose Charvet is the author of *Words That Change Minds: Mastering the Language of Influence*, *The LAB Profile Consultant/Training Certification Program*, *Conversational Coaching with the LAB Profile*, *Solving Communication Problems with the LAB Profile*, *Building Long Term Relationships; Decode What Your Customer Really Wants*.

www.WordsThatChangeMinds.com

www.LABProfileCertification.com

Some of the most important Meta Programs

We've selected a few Meta Programs for discussion, the ones we believe it's most useful to understand. As you read them you'll find you can identify your own or those of other people you know well. None of the patterns listed is better than its polar opposite but some are more useful in certain situations. When you're brainstorming, for instance, it's useful to spend time coming up with lots of ideas (the options pattern). But when you need to make progress, this filter may mean you're not as focused as you could be on getting the job done.

'Towards' or 'Away From'

Chris is a Sales Manager who's full of energy. People often describe him as 'achievement-oriented', because he's always trying to beat his targets and get a bonus. He's got his eyes set on a holiday cottage in France. Chris joined his present company because he knew it would give him the opportunity to move forward in his career. If he hasn't got a clear goal, he can easily become demotivated.

Bill's in his present job because he didn't like his last company. He gets stuck into each task he's set, whether it's writing a project report or preparing implementation plans, with the intention of getting it done. He aims to complete it by the deadline so that Linda, his boss, doesn't give him a hard time. Having said that there are times when he can be easily distracted. All it takes is a nice juicy issue to arise and he's there ready to play detective.

Insight

'Towards' and 'Away From' is just one of the patterns we incorporate into our 'Speak First Influencing with Impact' courses because there are so many ways you can apply the technique. Advertisements often use the power of this pattern to influence you to take action. There are so many advantages in using this when preparing a presentation, in meetings or any situation where you want to influence or persuade others.

...s on future goals characterizes the Towards ... People with this pattern put lots of energy into ... they want. They sometimes do this to such an extent t... ...on't pay sufficient attention to potential pitfalls. They usuall... ...ave lots of energy but can easily become demotivated if they don't have anything to aim for.

People using an Away From pattern avoid or move away from potential problems – they notice what could go wrong. Sometimes they have difficulty prioritizing because they're attracted to dealing with problems and this means they often get side-tracked. They're great to have around when there are issues to resolve and tend to be cautious in their approach.

COMMUNICATING WITH PEOPLE WHO HAVE A TOWARDS OR AWAY FROM PATTERN

To influence or build rapport with someone with a towards pattern, use words like 'get', 'have', 'obtain' or 'achieve'. Place emphasis on what can be accomplished rather than what might go wrong.

If you want to influence someone demonstrating an Away From pattern, use words like 'avoid', 'overcome', 'solve' or 'prevent'. They're more likely to think you understand them if you talk about potential obstacles or issues. If you're making a request of them, pose it as a problem for them to solve.

'Internal' and 'External'

Have you ever noticed that some people have a need for feedback to guide them on the best course of action to take while others rely on their own judgement? Take the following two individuals. When Jodie sings she knows she's performed well by the way she feels inside, and when people start to clap it merely confirms for her what she instinctively knows already. She appears self-assured but can be difficult to handle sometimes because she tends to act as if she has all the right answers. Caitlyn needs to hear the applause from the audience before she's convinced about the success of her performance. She's really open to feedback from her coach and tends to rely on him to advise her of the best songs to choose.

UNDERSTANDING INTERNAL AND EXTERNAL PATTERNS

This difference in approaches is all about where the locus of control lies. This can either be within the individual (internal) or it can arise from an external source.

People with an Internal pattern use their inner feelings as their main way of evaluating success. They know inside when they've done well and don't need other people to tell them. When taken to extreme this means they don't care what other people think. They seek out information from external sources and then come to their own conclusions. If feedback doesn't fit with their sense of the situation they'll reject it. They don't like being told what to do.

Those with an External pattern seek evidence to confirm their achievements from an outside source, such as feedback from another person or research data. They need external information to be able to assess properly how they've performed and want others to let them know how they've done. They often think of external information as providing direction and may even appear lost without it.

COMMUNICATING WITH PEOPLE WHO HAVE AN INTERNAL OR EXTERNAL PATTERN

To communicate effectively with someone who has an Internal pattern, start by asking for their opinion and make it clear they have a choice in how to respond. Use phrases like 'it's up to you' or ask them for their opinion. To influence someone with an External pattern let them know what you recommend as the best course of action. Ideally find research from experts to back up your argument.

'Self' or 'Other'

Dan and Harry couldn't be more different. When you walk in
the office where they both work Dan immediately looks up and
makes eye contact, smiles and gives his full attention to whoever
is speaking. Harry appears self-absorbed and only seems to be
interested in things that affect him. He speaks when he's spoken
to and doesn't join in with the office banter. Harry rarely offers to
give other people a hand when they're busy whereas Dan will drop
all of his own work to help out.

UNDERSTANDING SELF AND OTHER

The 'Self' and 'Other' patterns reflect how much we instinctively
notice and respond to other people. When it comes to recruiting
people for a job this is valuable information to have especially
if the role involves dealing with customers. People with a Self
pattern respond to others on the basis of what they have to say
and don't appear to be aware of non-verbal communication. This
makes it difficult for them to build and maintain rapport. They can
appear self-absorbed and sometimes find it difficult to maintain
eye contact. If you drop something they're unlikely to bend down
and pick it up for you. Rodger Bailey's research suggests that in a
work context only 7 per cent of people have a Self pattern with the
remaining 93 per cent being Other. Someone with an Other pattern
will be aware of the behaviours and reactions of those around
them. They quickly recognize changes in other people's facial
expressions or body language. They seem naturally to relate well to
other people.

COMMUNICATING WITH PEOPLE WHO HAVE A SELF OR
OTHER PATTERN

When you come across someone with a Self pattern the best way
to communicate with them is to concentrate on the content of what
you want to say. And with those having an Other pattern, all you

really need is to be able to build and maintain rapport well. You'll find communication comes easily with people who operate an Other pattern.

'Options' and 'Procedures'

It can be hard to pin Helen down. She seems to relish having an almost endless list of things on the go at the same time. When you press her to choose she has real difficulty plumping for just one thing. She enjoys working freelance because it allows her to get involved with a whole variety of different projects. Her brother Jack prefers to follow a set path and likes to see things through to a conclusion before starting something else. He's great at following instructions and explains things clearly in a logical order. He finds it hard to keep up with his sister's approach which he describes as 'scatty' and 'all over the place'.

UNDERSTANDING OPTIONS AND PROCEDURES PATTERNS

The Options pattern is easy to spot because these people love variety and bending the rules, even though they quite like creating them for others to follow. They thrive on choice, opportunities and new ideas. They don't relish making a decision because it limits the number of possibilities they have. Freedom is important to them and they enjoy being able to control their own future. If you know someone who is great at starting something but rarely finishes it they're likely to have an Options pattern.

The key to identifying a Procedures way of thinking is when someone wants to take things step by step. People with this pattern like to finish what they've started and can feel overwhelmed when there's too much choice. Following rules feels right to them and they can find it uncomfortable if they're asked to deviate from the norm. The other thing to listen out for is the way they like to explain things a stage at a time.

This difference in people's behaviour can be evident in organizations as well as individuals. Many people associate banking with a fairly Procedural approach where the employees follow the rules. When someone's looking after our money this is likely to be a good thing! Media companies on the other hand are often creative and come up with an almost endless stream of new ideas.

COMMUNICATING WITH PEOPLE WHO HAVE AN OPTIONS OR PROCEDURES PATTERN

When you're communicating with someone who has an Options pattern the key to success lies in choice, options, possibilities, alternatives, variety… Put the ball in their court and ask them if they can think of another way of doing something. Key words to use when someone has a Procedures pattern are 'reliable', 'proven' or 'tried and tested'. When you're explaining something, match their behaviour by covering each thing in a logical order one after the other.

'General' and 'Specific'

Some people feel at home when dealing with details and others prefer the big picture. Jackie's well known among her friends for not reading instructions and avoiding detail like the plague. When she is asked to proof-read a document she sometimes misses small errors. She loves abstract conversations about concepts and likes to think holistically. Caroline gets great satisfaction from obtaining every tiny piece of information she can lay her hands on. She enjoys 'number-crunching' and checking that written work is entirely accurate. She loves telling stories but when she loses the flow she has to start from the beginning again.

UNDERSTANDING GENERAL AND SPECIFIC PATTERNS

The General–Specific Meta Program is sometimes known as Big Chunk–Small Chunk in NLP. It concerns the level of either specificity or generality in thinking style. Most people start from one and move to the other. So if they start with the big picture they 'chunk down' to the detail. As Tad James and Wyatt Woodsmall describe in their book *Time Line Therapy and the Basis of Personality*, if you take any concept or idea you can either 'chunk down' from general to specific or 'chunk up' from specific to general.

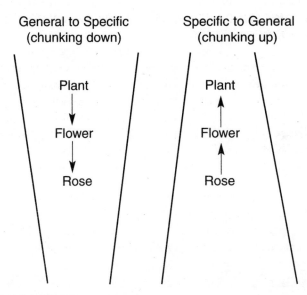

General to Specific
(chunking down)

Plant
↓
Flower
↓
Rose

Specific to General
(chunking up)

Plant
↑
Flower
↑
Rose

Chunking up and chunking down.

In NLP the idea of chunking up or down is used extensively. Questions are asked to elicit the next level of information and bring about a new way of perceiving a situation. For instance to 'chunk up' a useful question to ask might be 'What is that an example of?' To 'chunk down' ask 'What would be an example of this?'

One of the best ways to identify someone with a general pattern is to bombard them with lots of detail. They'll soon let you know because it usually drives them crazy. They love abstract concepts and have difficulty following a sequence step by step because they tend to process things all in one go. They don't tend to offer much small chunk information and can sometimes miss out important details.

People with a specific pattern love detail. They feel satisfied when they have successfully dotted all the 'i's and crossed the 't's. As the saying goes, they sometimes don't see the wood for the trees. Like the Procedures pattern, they deal with things step by step. The difference is that with a Procedure there are points where another route can be taken. If you interrupt someone with a specific pattern when they're telling you something they usually need to start from the beginning again. This is because they follow a sequence, which unlike the procedures pattern they don't deviate from.

COMMUNICATING WITH PEOPLE WHO HAVE A GENERAL OR SPECIFIC PATTERN

People with a General pattern prefer it when you keep the detail to a minimum. They like an overview of what you want to convey and enjoy abstract discussions. When you're communicating with someone with a Specific pattern, it helps if you use words such as 'precisely' or 'exactly'. Present information in a linear step-by-step way.

'Matching' and 'Mismatching'

Picture the scene. Wendy, Simon and Holly are at a meeting to discuss next year's budget proposals. Wendy has just presented her case for extra funds to the other two. Holly acknowledges the points Wendy has made and goes on to reinforce her case by giving further reasons why it would be a good idea. Holly has a reputation for seeing the best in people and has lots of friends in the office. Simon steps in and points out two or three disadvantages. He rarely agrees with anyone on the team, which doesn't make him as popular. One view of this might be that Simon rained on Wendy's parade and another that he could have saved the company from making an expensive mistake.

UNDERSTANDING MATCHING AND MISMATCHING PATTERNS

People have two ways of understanding external information. We either notice how things are different or how they are the same. Sorting for similarities between things is called Matching; sorting for differences is known as Mismatching.

When people Match they listen for things they have experience of and make a connection between what they hear someone saying and what they know. They focus on what works and what has been achieved. They tend to be good at building rapport with others. They can be good mediators who are able to bring about consensus between people. When taken to the extreme, Matching behaviour can appear insincere.

When people Mismatch they look for what seems to be missing or the flaw in what other people have to say. Mismatching can give the impression of criticism, which means it can be more difficult for them to build rapport with others, unless of course the other person is a Mismatcher too. Because Mismatching concentrates on things that may not work they're often good at encouraging new ways of thinking. They challenge the *status quo*.

COMMUNICATING WITH PEOPLE WHO HAVE A MATCHING OR MISMATCHING PATTERN

When you come across people with a matching pattern, emphasize commonality and sameness for effective communication. To communicate well with someone who mismatches, emphasize what is different or doesn't fit. If you present an idea to a Mismatcher be prepared for them to find at least one flaw in it.

Convincer patterns

There's another filter people use, the Convincer pattern, which has two parts to it. The first is how people know when they're convinced about something or are confident that it's true, for instance knowing when someone is capable of doing a job well. The second is how often they have to experience it before they're convinced.

1 *What convinces people that someone can, for instance, carry out a task efficiently? There are different ways people know:*
   ▷ **See** – *they have to see someone perform a task before they're convinced about the person's ability to do it.*
   ▷ **Hear** – *they're convinced if they hear someone else say the person can do it.*
   ▷ **Read** – *they're convinced if they read about the person's capability.*
   ▷ **Do** – *the person has to do something before they're convinced about it.*
2 *The convincer mode – how often does someone have to demonstrate something before another person is convinced? There are a number of patterns people unconsciously use:*
   ▷ **Automatic** – *they're immediately convinced. For instance, some customers will buy a product straightaway from a salesperson with only a small amount of information.*
   ▷ **Number of times** – *they need two, three or more occasions before they're sure.*
   ▷ **Over a period of time** – *this person needs much longer to assess the situation. This can be weeks or even months.*
   ▷ **Consistently** – *this person is never convinced. It would have to be proved every time. They work on the principle that people are only as good as the last job they've done.*

Meta Programs and change

Meta Programs don't of course operate in isolation from one another. We're unconsciously running these filters all of the time and together they create a complex mix with one pattern working alongside and affecting another.

Our Meta Programs, though, are not fixed. You can't say someone is a Towards, Options, Specific, Mismatcher – though it may sometimes seem like that. We are not our filters. The Meta Program patterns we have can be changed if we're not happy with the outcomes they're producing.

The starting point for change is being aware of your own patterns and the alternatives that are available. For instance, if you know one of your patterns in a work context is General and you have some detailed jobs to do it would be useful to be able to switch to Specific for a while.

You may simply be able to decide to work that way. Some people can, others find it difficult. If so, one way of bringing about change is to work with submodalities because Meta Programs are made up of sensory-based representations. Carry out a contrastive analysis between how you code General and Specific. This may mean finding an example of Specific in another context. Once you're aware of the difference between them you'll be able to choose a different way to experience completing the task. As mentioned in Chapter 4, when carrying out change work it's important to consider the consequences of making a change. See Chapter 7 for more on ecology issues of this nature.

There are also a number of other NLP techniques that can be very useful. A good source of additional information on this can be found in Tad James and Wyatt Woodsmall's book *Time Line Therapy and the Basis of Personality*.

The LAB Profile

In the late 1970s Rodger Bailey, a student of Leslie Cameron-Bandler-Lebeau's, created the Language and Behaviour (LAB)

Profile from the Meta Programs. The LAB Profile has only 14 practical categories of patterns divided into two sections: The Motivation Traits (what people need to become and stay motivated) and The Working Traits (how people process information, what they need to be productive, how they respond to stress and the steps they go through to become convinced). He also added other new developments: Questions to elicit the patterns in conversation and Influencing Language that would motivate individuals and groups, once you knew their patterns. Rodger also figured out that LAB Profile patterns are contextual; people behave differently at different times and places. As their behaviour shifts, so do their patterns and this has been verified many times in market research studies.

As a result of these developments Shelle Rose Charvet began to experiment with different applications of the LAB Profile. It is now being used extensively around the world for recruitment and selection, career development, coaching, managing, team building, market research, mass communication, sales, complex problem-solving, negotiations, conflict resolution, training design and delivery, as well as NLP modelling of skills. This is what is important about the development of the Meta Programs and the LAB Profile; they are powerful tools for understanding, and for improving communication.

► Become aware of your own Meta Programs in various contexts. Notice if some of them start to feel like familiar friends. Catch yourself saying things and work out which patterns you're using.

► Practise noticing other people's Meta Programs in their language and behaviour. Pay attention to the words they use and their body language.

► Ask someone why they chose their current job and listen to the response. What pattern can you detect in their response? Is it full of possibilities and options or do they tell you a story in a procedural fashion?

► What is your Convincer pattern? Do you have to see, hear, read or do to be convinced?

TEN KEY POINTS TO REMEMBER

1 *Meta Programs are unconscious filters that help us organize our thinking and decide where to focus our attention.*

2 *Meta Programs come in pairs, sets of three or four or separate and distinct patterns and are 'context specific'.*

3 *People with a 'Towards' pattern put energy into getting what they want and those with an 'Away From' pattern are motivated to avoid or move away from problems.*

4 *Those with an 'Internal' pattern rely on their own judgement to gauge their success whereas people with an 'External' pattern seek evidence from an outside source.*

5 *People with an 'Other' pattern notice and respond to others while those with a 'Self' pattern – a relatively small percentage of the population – are more self-absorbed.*

6 *People with an 'Options' pattern love variety and those with a 'Procedures' pattern prefer to stick to the rules.*

7 *Some of us prefer the big picture – a 'General' pattern – and others the detail – a 'Specific' pattern.*

8 *People have two ways of understanding external information: they 'match' for similarities or 'mismatch' by noticing how things are different.*

9 *The 'Convincer' pattern has two parts – the first relates to how people know when they are convinced by something and the second is how often they have to experience it before they are convinced.*

10 *Meta Programs are not fixed and, once you are aware of them, can be changed – though it can take conscious effort to do so.*

6

Values and beliefs

In this chapter you will learn:
- *about the nature and power of beliefs and values*
- *where beliefs come from*
- *how to challenge and change limiting beliefs*

Believe you can, believe you can't – either way you're right.

Henry Ford

May 6 1954 marked a turning point in world athletics. Up to that date it was believed to be impossible for anyone to run a mile in under four minutes. No one had ever achieved it. The last time the record had been broken was in 1945, and it stood resolutely at 4:01:4. But one man, Roger Bannister, a 25-year-old medical student from Harrow, believed it was possible – and on that date he proved it, crossing the finishing line in a time of 3:59:4. Yet within 46 days, his great rival John Landy, whose best time thus far had been 1.5 seconds outside the four-minute barrier, ran even faster than Bannister, recording a time of 3:57:9. And over the next three years, 16 runners were to log sub-four-minute miles.

We may not be planning to beat a world record, but beliefs play a crucial role in all our lives. If we believe something is possible we may seek to achieve it. If we believe it's impossible we probably won't even try. Once Roger Bannister had made the four-minute mile a reality, others were able to believe they could do it. They broke through their psychological barriers and, literally, followed in his footsteps.

Beliefs are not trivial, unimportant things. People are willing to die, and kill, for them. When, on 11 September 2001, two American aeroplanes were hijacked and flown into the Twin Towers that dominated the New York skyline, razing them to the ground, it was a belief in something more important than life that motivated those responsible. And when President George Bush responded by attacking Afghanistan and then Iraq, his actions were underpinned by an unswerving and absolute belief that terrorism must be defeated whatever the cost.

Understanding beliefs and values

In his article *Beliefs 1*, L. Michael Hall describes the ubiquitous nature of beliefs and how they operate:

> **As you woke up this morning and moved out into the day, you did so by gathering up a host of beliefs to take with you. You then put them on as spectacles through which to view the world. You have beliefs about yourself, your skills, your value and dignity, etc. You have beliefs about other people – what makes them tick, what they want, how to relate to them, etc. You have beliefs about work, play, recreation, hobbies, volunteer activities, etc. You have beliefs about the world: politics, education, crime, police, the justice system, other countries, wars, journalism, environment, etc. You have beliefs about a thousand different concepts: time, history, the past, the future, causation, personality, emotions, destiny, etc. Further, because you 'have' these beliefs, you operate from them as one uses a map to navigate territory. Beliefs as mental maps govern our life, emotions, health, skills, and everyday experiences. Pervasive 'things' these belief maps.**

More succinctly, in *Unlimited Power*, Anthony Robbins defines a belief as 'Any guiding principle, dictum, faith, or passion that can provide meaning and direction in life'. Beliefs are, then, assumptions and presuppositions we have about ourselves, other people, and the world in general.

Our beliefs arise within a specific cultural setting, and are often shared by others in our family and social circle. As a result they are invisible much of the time. We take them for granted and, more importantly, accept them as true. It's typically only when we encounter someone who has a different set of beliefs that we become aware of our own.

'Pure' beliefs are largely emotionless. You believe them but they evoke no feelings. You believe the sun will set at the end of the day. You believe your house will continue standing. It's no big deal, it's just the way things are. Some beliefs, though, are also judgements about the way things should be. These are called values, because they imply an evaluation.

'Values,' says Anthony Robbins, 'are private, personal, individual beliefs about what is most important to you. Your values are belief systems about right, wrong, good, and bad.' Values, then, are a guiding principle, an internal compass, by which we live our lives, shaping the kinds of experiences we seek out and those we avoid.

Core beliefs and values, those which we hold most dear, and which permeate across many areas of our lives, form the basis of our identity and the backbone of our personality.

The importance of beliefs and values in NLP

If your mind can conceive it, and your heart can believe it, you can achieve it.

Jesse Jackson

Beliefs and values are considered important in NLP for a number of reasons:

▶ **They're perceptual filters.** *Like Meta Programs, they determine to a large degree the way we experience the external world.*

In fact, our beliefs and values act both to create our internal representation of reality and to confirm it.

▶ **They're distortions.** *Every belief and value is essentially a generalization we've made about the world, and every generalization is essentially a distortion. When someone has a problem there's often a distorted belief or value at the root of it. Becoming consciously aware of what's being assumed or presupposed opens the door to their accuracy and usefulness being challenged.*

▶ **They have motivational importance.** *Beliefs in general, and values in particular, are motivational. They're not just static maps; we use them to choose routes and plan journeys. Because we tend to move towards what we value and away from what we don't value, we put energy behind what's important to us. If we value the family, we'll prioritize it, and schedule time and activities. If we value success or money, we might be prepared to work long hours at the office.*

The power of beliefs

There's considerable evidence for the power of beliefs across a range of fields, but the Placebo Effect is probably the most compelling. Placebos are pills containing sugar or starch, or liquids containing no active agents. Yet research has shown time and again that a significant proportion of patients who are given placebos believe them to be therapeutic and actually get well. The success rate varies according to the situation, but placebos are typically as effective as real drugs in over one-third of cases.

In one study, patients suffering pain from a wisdom tooth extraction got as much relief from a fake application of ultrasound as a real one. And warts that had proved resistant to other treatments were successfully eliminated when they were painted using a brightly coloured, inert dye, with the promise that they would be gone once the color wore off. They were.

The Placebo Effect even extends as far as conditions that require surgery. Patients requiring a procedure for angina were separated into two groups. All were anaesthetized in the normal way, but just one of the groups actually underwent the operation. The members of the other group only had their skin cut, to make them believe the procedure had taken place. Those operated on showed a useful 40 per cent improvement, while those who had the placebo surgery had an astonishing 80 per cent recovery rate.

Such studies show clearly that our beliefs can determine the way things turn out. They're not mere 'thoughts', they're instructions. Believing something sends a psycho-neurological message through your entire mind/body system that seeks to make it happen.

Another example of the power of beliefs can be found in the story from Abraham Maslow. A patient wouldn't eat because he believed he was a corpse. After spending much time and energy trying to convince his patient he wasn't really a corpse, the psychiatrist finally asked him if corpses bled. The patient said he didn't believe they did, so the psychiatrist asked him to participate in an experiment that involved pricking the patient with a pin. The patient started to bleed, and in astonishment said, 'Wow – corpses do bleed after all!'

The language of beliefs and values

The expressions people use often reveal their beliefs and values. The words 'can' and 'can't' in particular are a clear indication of a belief. The same is true when ideas are presented dogmatically, with no room for debate. When beliefs are deeply held, they often lead to black and white thinking. Words such as 'right' and 'wrong', 'appropriate' and 'inappropriate', 'good' and 'bad', 'should' and 'shouldn't', and 'important' and 'unimportant' tell you immediately that someone is talking in terms of their values.

Where do beliefs and values come from?

Beliefs and values are not innate. We don't arrive as babies with them all neatly organized. We acquire and develop them as we strive to make sense of the world. But where do they come from? The following are some of the factors:

- ▶ **Imprint experiences:** *Significant experiences during the imprint stage, up to the age of seven, often result in limiting or empowering beliefs.*
- ▶ **The culture we grow up in:** *Our parents play a large part in shaping how we think. Many of us follow the same religion as our family. And how often do you see small boys wearing the same football team colours as their father?*
- ▶ **Unconscious modelling:** *As we grow up we naturally copy not just the behaviours of others but their values and beliefs as well.*
- ▶ **Feedback from others:** *Parents often tell children what they can't do, not what they can – rather than praising success they criticize failure. As a result, people establish negative perceptions of themself.*
- ▶ **Repetitive experiences:** *The more we think about something or are exposed to it, the more credible it becomes, and over time it can be established as a belief.*
- ▶ **Peer groups:** *Other people we meet have different values and beliefs from us, and sometimes we change to fit in with them, or discover attitudes that seem to suit us better.*
- ▶ **Reference experiences:** *Sometimes all it takes is a one-off life event to change what people believe is possible, for good or ill. Imagine how you would feel after delivering a successful presentation in front of 80 people and coming out brimming with confidence.*
- ▶ **Role models:** *We often take on the values and beliefs of those we admire. Princess Diana influenced many people with her perceived characteristics of compassion and charity. Reading about someone who has completed the London Marathon*

at the age of 80 may be just the trigger we need to start
running ourselves.

▶ **Organizational culture:** *It can be hard to settle and thrive if*
your values and beliefs are at odds with those of the company
you work for.

▶ **The media:** *Increasingly we live in a 'media landscape' created*
by newspapers, the radio and television, which plays a large
part in shaping our beliefs and values.

Beliefs change

Beliefs and values are not fixed. We often act as if they are facts
when in reality they are only our perceptions. They may guide our
thinking and our behaviour, and we may hold on to some of them
for long periods, but they can and do change naturally over time.
When you were five, for example, you probably thought Father
Christmas and the Easter Bunny were real.

Exercise

Think of three things you used to believe and don't now.
What happened to change your mind?

Limiting beliefs

Beliefs can be positive driving forces in people's lives but they
can also be disempowering and limiting. When Emma started to
learn to play the piano she found she couldn't play a tune fluently
straight away and became disheartened. She began to think of it as
difficult and told other people she would never be able to play well.
Not long after she gave up.

's had the experience at school of being told by a teacher couldn't draw, sing, dance or whatever. We believed them, ...d stopped trying. Yet a moment's reflection will reveal those beliefs to be untrue. We can all draw, sing and dance to a degree, though admittedly not as well as Michelangelo, Pavarotti and Nureyev. 'People can, and do,' observes L. Michael Hall, 'believe all kinds of utterly idiotic things.'

One of the reasons that we don't realize our beliefs are illogical is that they're largely self-fulfilling. When you believe something, you act in a way that validates it. That's true whether it's a positive or negative belief. The life we create and the experiences we have are determined to a significant degree by what we believe. When we believe we can't do something, our behaviour will be such that we 'fail', perhaps by not trying hard enough or by sabotaging ourselves in some way.

Existing beliefs can also prevent us considering evidence that would contradict them. Someone who believes they're unattractive, for instance, might discount a compliment – you look fantastic! – on the basis that the person was trying to flatter them for some reason and was insincere.

Many limiting beliefs originate from a vacuum at the capability level, in other words people don't know how to do something. If they do learn how, their beliefs often change spontaneously. If, after a few goes, people continue to struggle to grasp how to do something it's easy for them to slip into believing it's not possible. What they say to themselves and other people reinforces this. Limiting beliefs hold people back or prevent them from doing things.

Exercise

Which beliefs are working well for you?
Which are not serving your best interests?
What stops you believing something else?
What needs to happen for things to change?

HOPELESSNESS, HELPLESSNESS AND WORTHLESSNESS

In their research into beliefs, Dilts and DeLozier discovered there are three main ways that people limit themselves: if any of the three apply, it may be difficult to change a limiting belief.

▶ **Hopelessness** *is when we don't believe it's possible to achieve something – there is no hope.*
▶ **Helplessness** *is when we believe something's possible but we don't believe we are personally capable of doing it.*
▶ **Worthlessness** *is when we don't believe we deserve to attain something – we're not worthy of it.*

Insight

In my (Amanda's) experience discovering a limiting belief is the first step to changing it. The second is knowing whether your limiting belief is based in hopelessness, helplessness, worthlessness, or a combination of these three. Once you find out where you're stuck you can ask yourself, 'What would need to happen for me to believe it may be possible after all?' and to know that you're capable of achieving it – and deserve to!

Choosing beliefs

Sometimes, when they're examined in the cold light of day, and it's obvious they make no sense, beliefs change spontaneously. You don't, however, have to wait or leave it to chance. You can choose new beliefs at any time. As Anthony Robbins says, 'You're not just a leaf on the wind'. Sometimes all you have to do is think of the beliefs that would empower and assist you in achieving your goal, and act as if you have them already. If that doesn't work, and the issue seems deep rooted, you may need to use an NLP belief change pattern.

BELIEF CHANGE PATTERN

NLP offers many ways of challenging and changing beliefs. The following example, devised by Richard Bandler, provides an

opportunity to transform an old belief into one you would
rather have, using the submodality distinctions we discussed
in Chapter 5.

Steps

1 *Think of a belief you would rather not have because it limits
you in some way.*

2 *Identify the submodalities relating to this belief. What is your
internal representation of it?*

3 *Next, identify something you're in doubt about. By doubt we
mean something you're unsure about, something that may or
may not be true. Explore how you represent this internally.
What are the submodalities?*

4 *Use contrastive analysis to identify the differences between the
old belief and doubt. Belief and doubt, for instance, may be
in different spatial locations.*

5 *Test each submodality that you've noted as being different by
exchanging the submodality relating to the old belief with its
counterpart in doubt. Change each one back to the way it was
originally before moving on to test the next.*

6 *Ask yourself what new belief would you like to have instead.
Make sure you state this positively and that it's described as
something you want rather than something you've already
achieved. Before pressing ahead stop and reflect for a moment
about the possible consequences of having this new belief.
How will it affect other people or other areas of your life?
Make changes to your new belief to account for these.*

7 *You're now ready to change your belief to doubt. Leaving the
content the same, change one or more of the most powerful
submodality differences you found before in Step 4. If, for
instance, you see an internal moving picture like a film you
might change it for a still photograph.*

8 *Now go on to change the content from the old belief to the
new one using another submodality shift. One way to do this
may be to move your representation of the old belief off into
the distance so that you can barely see it. Then have it return
as the new belief.*

9 *Change doubt to belief by reversing the submodality changes you made in Step 7 and keeping the content the same. This might mean exchanging the still photograph for the moving picture. If you sense any resistance to the change you need to redefine your new belief. Go back to Step 6 and make sure you have expressed your belief positively and have dealt with every possible consequence.*

10 *Test by checking that your new belief is automatically represented by the new submodalities.*

Understanding values

The importance of values cannot be overstated. Just imagine what it would be like if nothing mattered to you. Why would you want to do anything? What would be the point? People who have a strong sense of what's important to them usually have a real sense of purpose that acts like a propulsion system, which moves them towards it.

Stop and think for a minute. All the things you want to do are ways of actualizing your values. At the highest level, these are likely to be things such as security, making a difference, independence, living life to the full, acceptance and helping others. Values are essentially generalizations about what does or doesn't matter. And behaviour flows directly from them. If someone values fairness, for instance, they may also believe that people should treat one another equally, and act that way themself. If they don't follow up with this behaviour they feel uncomfortable with their actions.

In his book *First Things First*, Stephen Covey advocates using your personal values as the basis for how you allocate your time, being guided, as he puts it, by the compass rather than the clock. By this he means prioritizing based on your personal mission, vision and values – what's most important to you.

Criteria and criterial equivalence

It's also crucial to think about what the criteria, or standards, are for values being met. Criteria, are what people consider important in a specific context. You have criteria for everything you do, whether you're conscious of them or not. They're the ultimate reason you do things, the tangible pay-off you get. At work they might include success, challenge and teamwork, and at home sharing, intimacy and support. When you're buying a house your criteria will include the number of rooms, the location, the size of the garden, its state of repair, and so on.

Just as important is knowing what your evidence procedure is by which you'll know when criteria have been satisfied. You might, for instance, have 'affection' as one of your criteria and the corresponding criterial equivalence, as it's called, is 'being hugged by someone I care about'. If someone you care about doesn't hug you, you may feel the criteria has been violated rather than honoured. When criteria are violated this often results in friction between the people involved. For relationships to be effective it's essential that people recognize that others have different values and criteria. Two people can have the same value but different evidence for judging whether the value has been satisfied.

When examined, the behavioural evidence procedures for criteria sometimes prove to be outmoded or even nonsensical. Someone might have 'love' as one of their criteria for a romantic relationship, and a criterial equivalence for love of 'knowing what I'm thinking and feeling without having to ask'. Although surprisingly common, this can be a recipe for disaster.

Exercise

1 Think about a particular area of your life, such as work, home or a loving relationship. What's important to you? Make a list of your criteria.

2 Next to each one add your own personal definition of what it means – your criterial equivalence. If your criterion was 'honesty', for instance, you might add something like 'being straightforward with people and speaking your mind'. Someone else might define 'honesty' as 'telling the truth at all times'.

Hierarchies of criteria

Some criteria are more important to us than others. One person, for example, might value their family more than money and be willing to sacrifice a well-paid job to spend more time at home. Someone else might do the opposite, with their income and the security it represents coming first. We may not be consciously aware of how we've prioritized our criteria, but it will be evident in our actions, by what we put first. What takes precedence will, to a degree, depend upon circumstances; when talking about values and criteria it's essential to have a frame, a context.

Exercise: Establishing a hierarchy of criteria

Refer back to the list of criteria you created earlier. Now rate them in order of importance with 1 high and 6 low. Sometimes it helps to ask yourself, 'If I could only have one of these which would it be?' Then repeat this question with the remaining items until you have created an order of priority.

Changing values and criteria

Most of us never chose our values and criteria. We sort of ended up with them by accident rather than by design. But they can be changed. If you criticize your children more than you like because one of your most valued criteria is compassion, it may be time for a review. Take care, though, as re-prioritizing your values is one of the most powerful and pervasive changes you can make and you need to consider the consequences carefully.

'More than any other change in the plethora of techniques, values hold the key.

More than any other element in our personal and professional lives, values are the basis of and have the most effect on our behaviour. They drive our purpose as a human being, by motivating us towards or away from that on which we choose to spend time, resources and energy. At a more conscious level, and clustered around each value are our beliefs, by which we make come true our constructed world.

Values then become a key tool by which to make the maximum impact on a person's world. By modelling and exploring the areas of life where results are least satisfactory, the client, student or coachee can be enabled to discover and let go of their deepest most repressed issues. By teasing out from the unconscious those deeply held unuseful core beliefs behind the related values, the individual is then liberated from their unusefully constructed world to a new dawning of enlightenment. Aligned, congruent and free to evolve mentally, emotionally and spiritually, wholeness and balance are restored.'

Dr Susi Strang Wood and Craig Wood MSc have more than a decade of experience in the area of personal development and consultancy. They are leading providers of NLP trainings, leadership, staff development, and change management programmes within the United Kingdom and Europe.

www.drsusistrang.co.uk

NLP has beliefs – but no values

Of course, NLP itself holds certain beliefs – the presuppositions you were introduced to in Chapter 2. Although they were conceived individually, taken together they represent a reasonably coherent belief system. However, neither the founders of NLP nor those who have since developed it further have ever claimed the presuppositions are true. Only that they are useful.

In fact, NLP has no value structure whatsoever. As Robert McDonald points out in *Voice of NLP (Issue One)*, 'The word "good" is considered unacceptable in NLP, because it involves making a judgement. It's no more valuable in NLP to shoot people than to embrace them. It all depends on your goal. We're not going to call it good we're just going to call it useful or unuseful.'

NLP in action

▶ *Take an area of your life such as work and identify the values you hold in relation to it. Prioritize these values to create a hierarchy.*

▶ *Become aware of your limiting beliefs by paying attention to the number of times you talk about things you can or can't do.*

▶ *Become more aware of your own and other people's beliefs by listening to language used in everyday conversation.*

▶ *Choose a belief you would rather not have and exchange it for something new using the Belief Change Pattern technique.*

TEN KEY POINTS TO REMEMBER

1 *Beliefs are assumptions and presuppositions we have about ourselves, other people and the world in general.*

2 *Values act like a compass or principles we use to decide how to live our lives.*

3 *The language we use often reveals our beliefs and values – 'can' and 'can't' are a good example of this.*

4 *We acquire and develop beliefs over time through the experiences we have in our lives.*

5 *Beliefs can be positive, empowering, forces in our lives and they can be limiting and hold us back.*

6 *The Belief Change Pattern developed by Richard Bandler provides a way of transforming an old belief into one we would rather have.*

7 *Values are generalizations about what is or isn't important to us.*

8 *Criteria are what we consider important in a specific context or situation.*

9 *Criteria are typically organized in hierarchies – some are more important to us than others.*

10 *Re-prioritizing your values is one of the most powerful changes you can make.*

7

···

Well-formed outcomes

In this chapter you will learn:

- *why outcomes need to be well-formed*
- *about the well-formedness conditions*
- *how to create a well-formed outcome*

Goals and outcomes

Most people have goals or objectives, things they're trying to do or achieve. Maybe we sit down after Christmas and come up with a list of New Year Resolutions, but all too often we give up on them or forget about them by the middle of January.

In NLP, the term 'outcome' is used in preference to goal or objective. The *Collins English Dictionary* defines outcome as 'something that follows action; a result or consequence'. The difference between a goal and an outcome may not be immediately obvious, but is significant. A goal is always something we want, while an outcome is what we get as a result of our actions. It's not, however, necessarily something we desire. For clarity and precision, 'desired outcome' is generally used in NLP to designate an outcome that we're seeking to accomplish. Desired outcomes are central to NLP. Many of the techniques and patterns are focused on achieving defined objectives. In fact, it has been said that if you don't want anything, NLP probably has nothing to offer you.

The reason those New Year Resolutions wither on the vine or never take root in the first place is because they're often, in NLP parlance, 'ill-formed' – they're not specific or have unforeseen consequences which prevent them from flourishing.

'Well-formed' outcomes

In business, people often use SMART – an acronym for Specific, Measurable, Achievable, Realistic and Time-bound – to sharpen up their goals. This is a valuable and worthwhile process, but has its limitations. Goals can still end up fuzzy and not fully thought through. In NLP, it's considered essential that outcomes be 'well-formed', that is, they meet a series of rigorous criteria or 'conditions' designed to increase the likelihood of their success. These are:

1 *State the outcome in positive terms.*
2 *Ensure the outcome is within your control.*
3 *Be as specific as possible.*
4 *Have a sensory-based evidence procedure.*
5 *Consider the context.*
6 *Have access to resources.*
7 *Ensure the outcome preserves existing benefits.*
8 *Check the outcome is ecologically sound.*
9 *Define the first step.*

Let's take a look at them all now in depth.

1 STATE THE OUTCOME IN POSITIVE TERMS

Many people express their goals in negative terms: 'I don't want to smoke', 'I don't want to feel nervous when presenting', 'I don't want to worry about the future'. But there's a problem with this way of thinking because of how our minds work. When we use negative language we end up focusing on what we don't want, which has the opposite effect to what was intended.

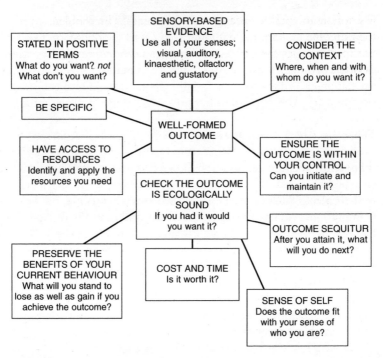

Well-formed outcomes.

If someone says 'Don't think of a guitar', the only way you can remember not to think of it is to think of it. You have to hold it in your mind and then cancel or delete it. For that reason, NLP insists that all outcomes are stated in positive terms. So 'I don't want to feel nervous when I'm presenting' is revised to 'I want to feel confident when I present', on which the mind can focus without distraction.

It might sound as if this is just playing with words, but framing outcomes positively really is a crucial step in achieving them.

2 ENSURE THE OUTCOME IS WITHIN YOUR CONTROL

It's also essential that the outcome is under your control. If it requires other people to do certain things, or not do certain things, it's not an acceptable outcome in NLP terms. The problem with the outcome, 'I want my daughter to do well at college' is that it's not totally under the person's control. It's dependent on the action of other people. 'I want to provide reading materials to support my daughter's education', or 'I will help my daughter in every way possible' are both outcomes that are well formed in this regard.

The essence of this condition, as Steve and Connirae Andreas express it in *Heart of the Mind*, is that 'the goal is stated in a way that means you can get it yourself no matter what other people do'.

3 *BE AS SPECIFIC AS POSSIBLE*

Many outcomes are vague and woolly, such as 'I want to do something interesting' or 'I want to be rich'. NLP requires that outcomes be defined in sensory specific language, that is in terms of what can be seen, heard and felt. When we refine an outcome by clarifying the detail the whole thing becomes more vivid and real. The more specific we are the less likelihood there is of ending up with something we don't want.

You want to be rich? How rich, specifically? You want to do something interesting? What, precisely?

If you were helping someone with their outcomes and they say they want a new job, you might ask: What kind of job? Any job or a specific job? What sort of work would you like to do? Do you want to work alone or as part of a team? What hours would you like to work? You keep 'drilling down' until you reach a sensory-based description.

With a larger outcome it may be necessary to break it down into a series of smaller outcomes. In the example of getting a new job, there may be other actions that need to be taken first, such as undertaking a course of study, buying a suit, passing an exam, networking with the right people, and so on. If at any point you get stuck, the question 'What stops you having this outcome?' will be useful in making the outcome clear and specific.

Outcomes that are too small, however, or which seem unimportant, may not be motivating enough. If that is the case it may be necessary to 'chunk up' to a higher level outcome – a 'meta-outcome'. The outcome 'cleaning the car once a week' may seem trivial, but when it's linked to 'keeping the car in good order so it can be sold for the highest price', it will probably seem more worthwhile.

4 HAVE A SENSORY-BASED EVIDENCE PROCEDURE

This well-formedness condition is linked to the last one. Having defined your outcome as specifically as possible, you need to put in place a sensory-based evidence procedure. If you were working with someone else, you would ask them, 'How will you know when you've achieved your goal?' and expect the answer to be in terms of what someone would see, hear, feel, taste or smell. This degree of specificity is required because people often have evidence procedures that are abstract, and as with many things, 'the devil is in the detail'.

Imagining you've achieved the outcome already can be a useful way of clarifying the evidence procedure. Suppose you want to be an effective team manager. When you achieve your outcome what would you see around you? What would each team member's face look like? What sort of things would they be saying to each other and to you? What would you say to them? How would it feel to be an effective manager? What would a detached observer see, hear and feel in that situation?

5 CONSIDER THE CONTEXT

It's also essential to consider where, when and with whom the outcome is wanted. Does it relate to the whole of their life or just part of it? An outcome that works well in one context may not fit in another. Someone may want more challenges at work and more relaxation at home.

If someone wants to be honest and direct, do they want it in every situation? With their boss? With their partner? All the time?

That sounds like a recipe for conflict. Perhaps the context in which the behaviour will operate needs to be specified more clearly. And the people involved. One useful question is, 'When don't I want this outcome?' This will allow appropriate boundaries to be established.

6 HAVE ACCESS TO RESOURCES

One of the goals of NLP is to support people in moving from their 'current state' to a 'desired state'. To achieve this they usually need 'resources'. These may be internal, such as skills, knowledge, understanding and courage, or external, such as money, contacts or equipment.

If, for instance, the outcome was to run a marathon, what resources do they have, what can they do, already? Perhaps they regularly run ten miles. They've got quality footwear that can take the extra pounding. They have a friend who wants to do it as well, and will train with them. And so on.

What resources are they lacking? Well, they've never before actually run 26 miles. But two years ago they completed a 40-mile walk, and that confidence can be transferred to support the latest outcome. They don't know enough about 'pasta loading', which is supposed to help sustain energy, and they need to find out.

The aim of this condition is for the person to assess realistically whether they have, or can get, the resources needed to achieve the outcome.

7 ENSURE THE OUTCOME PRESERVES EXISTING BENEFITS

Many people are motivated and committed to achieving an outcome yet still don't attain it or it doesn't last. This is often because their current behaviour provides benefits that will be lost if they accomplish what they set out to do. In NLP, such benefits are known as 'positive by-products' or 'secondary gains'.

People who drink too much coffee, for instance, or who are regularly late for meetings, get something from those behaviours, or they wouldn't continue with them. These could be stimulation from the caffeine and a desire to make the best use of time respectively. But there's no 'one-size-fits-all'. Positive by-products are specific to each person and situation.

Sometimes these 'positive' aspects to 'negative' behaviours are not obvious, but it's essential they're taken account of if the outcome is to stand a chance of succeeding. Once we're aware of these positive by-products we sometimes come to the conclusion that they no longer apply. If, for instance, you started smoking at 14 so you could fit in with your friends you may not feel the need to do this when you are 30. If you want to retain the benefit, the new behaviour will either need to deliver the same secondary gains or plans must be made to provide them in some other way, perhaps by means of additional, associated outcomes. If you don't take action they will sabotage your progress.

8 CHECK THE OUTCOME IS ECOLOGICAL

NLP places great importance on 'ecology', on taking into account the effect of any change to the wider systems of which a person is part. Each outcome we set and achieve, no matter how small, will create a ripple effect on the world around us and the people in it.

If you're a manager and you put lots of energy into working on a big project you'll have less time to spend with your staff – and your family and friends. You may have to put interests and hobbies 'on hold'. And you may not have as much time to get to the gym, so your health and fitness could suffer.

Ecology is about the consequences for the system as a whole. And this well-formedness condition involves thinking carefully and deeply about the advantages and disadvantages in following any course of action.

Do you want the outcome no matter the price? Maybe you want to be better qualified to improve your career prospects. Are you prepared to spend six years studying for an Open University degree and to invest several hundred pounds a year doing it? Money is a consideration few of us can ignore when it comes to making sure our outcomes are well formed. What will it cost to achieve it? What impact will this have on how you spend your income now? Is it worth it?

And does the outcome fit with your sense of who you are as a person and what's important to you? Some outcomes can literally change the way we think about ourselves. Does this take you in the direction of becoming the person you want to be?

There are four classic NLP questions that cover the important ecology issues:

▶ *What will happen if you achieve this outcome?*
▶ *What won't happen if you achieve this outcome?*
▶ *What will happen if you don't achieve this outcome?*
▶ *What won't happen if you don't achieve this outcome?*

Insight

When I (Steve) was younger I used to play chess at an advanced level. One of the many skills I developed at this time was the ability to think ahead and plan several moves in advance and the possible consequences of each option available to me. What I've noticed is that many people don't do this in life and then wonder why their carefully created plans go awry. Asking the four classic NLP questions is a great starting point to getting what you want.

9 DEFINE THE FIRST STEP

Turning an outcome into reality requires action. And even the longest journey begins, as an ancient proverb says, with a single step. Defining that first step is a final and important part of the well-formedness process. If you don't take that step, you probably won't take the others that follow afterwards. Once again, be specific: what precisely will you do, and when will you do it?

Outcome sequitur

What would having this outcome do for you? After you attain your outcome what will you do next? In *The Encyclopedia of Systemic NLP* and *NLP New Coding* Robert Dilts and Judith DeLozier define 'outcome sequitur' as what happens after the outcome has been achieved. An outcome is often a step along the way towards a more long-term effect. By exploring the consequences of actually having achieved the outcome we can make sure we get what we really want.

> **Insight**
> In my experience (Amanda's) this final, crucial step in creating a well-formed outcome is sometimes missed out even by experienced NLPers. It's a shame this happens because it can be an extremely empowering and motivating force in moving you forward to achieving your outcome. For me personally, writing my first book on coaching was the result of an outcome sequitur.

NLP in action

▶ Take one or two of your goals and find out if they still apply after turning them into well-formed outcomes.
▶ If the opportunity arises, help someone else clarify their outcomes by using the well-formedness conditions.

TEN KEY POINTS TO REMEMBER

1 *In NLP it's important that outcomes are well-formed, which means they meet a series of 'conditions' or criteria that increase the chances of success.*

2 *Outcomes should be stated in positive terms. If you use negative language you'll end up focusing on what you don't want.*

3 *Make sure your outcome is under your control, so you can get it no matter what other people do.*

4 *Be as specific as you can – avoid vague and woolly language.*

5 *Have a sensory-based evidence procedure to make sure you get the outcome you want.*

6 *It's essential you specify the context in which you want the outcome – it may not be desirable in all contexts.*

7 *Access resources both internally and externally to help you achieve your outcome.*

8 *Identifying any positive by-products of your current behaviour and preserving them is crucial to success.*

9 *Check the outcome is 'ecological' by taking account of the effect the change will have on other areas of your life.*

10 *Define the first step to make sure you take action and start the process of change.*

8

States and emotions

In this chapter you will learn:
- *about states and how they affect behaviour*
- *how to become more aware of your own state and change it easily and effortlessly*
- *how to recognize the positive intention in 'negative' emotions*
- *how to support other people in changing their state*

The state we're in

In everyday conversation it's not unusual to describe someone as being in a 'state' of some kind – a state of panic, a state of boredom, a state of bliss. The term is also used in a more general way: 'he's in a right old state', 'look at the state of her'.

The *Collins English Dictionary* describes state as 'the condition of a person'. In NLP, 'state' has a similar, but more specific meaning: 'a gestalt of the neurological processes (mind and body) within an individual at any one time ... the ongoing mental and physical conditions from which a person is acting' (Dilts and De Lozier, *Encyclopedia of NLP*).

Tony Robbins suggests that state is the 'sum of the millions of neurological processes happening within us – the sum total of our experience – at any one time'. In short, it's a heady cocktail of everything that's going on in the body and the mind.

One of the best ways to understand states is to experience them. How do you feel right now? Put down the book for a moment and allow your attention to go 'inside', into both your mind and your body. What state would you say you're in right now?

▶ *Perhaps you're in a state of curiosity, as you think about what's coming next.*
▶ *Or a confused state, as you get to grips with all these new concepts.*
▶ *Maybe it's a state of excitement, as you become increasingly aware of how much richer your life will become as you learn NLP.*
▶ *Or some other state entirely – what would you call it?*

Now think back over the last couple of days. What other states have you been in? List as many as come to mind.

In a typical day most of us go through a range of states, some of which we experience as positive and enjoyable (happiness, love, pleasure, confidence), and others which seem negative and unpleasant (frustration, tiredness, anger, sadness). Some are fleeting, lasting just a few seconds or minutes. Others are more enduring, and we have them for most of the day, or even longer. Our state is constantly changing. Not all states have names. Sometimes we're just 'in a good mood' or we 'feel out of sorts'. On other occasions we feel as if we got out of the wrong side of the bed. Nothing goes right. The whole world's against us. Other times we can't put a foot wrong. Everything we touch turns to gold.

Mostly, though, we're somewhere in-between, until something happens to change it. For many people life is like a roller-coaster. Sometimes they're up, sometimes they're down, as their feelings get tossed around by the experiences life throws at them. Their boss either gives them a hard time because they haven't completed a task, or praise for a job they did well, and they feel lousy or elated.

What would it be like if you could choose your state, rather than have it controlled by what happens to you? Well, with NLP that's possible. It's simply a matter of using your brain in a way that gives you what you want.

Behaviour arises from state

The state we're in is important because it not only affects how we feel, it also determines how we behave and our ability to perform well. When we feel confident, we act with boldness. When we feel apprehensive, we act timidly. When we're in a 'negative', unresourceful state, we struggle with things we find easy to accomplish when we're feeling strong and resourceful. Although we're still the same person, our state makes all the difference.

Have you ever tried to do something, such as write a report or find the solution to a problem, and found it virtually impossible, only to have another go later, perhaps after a good night's sleep, and find it easy and effortless? That's the power of state, and one of the reasons certain states are highly sought after. Not only are they enjoyable, they're also empowering.

State awareness

Many people, however, are unaware of how they are feeling much of the time – and one of the most valuable things we can periodically do is ask ourselves how we feel and what state we're in. Knowing what state you're in is the first step to changing or enhancing it.

Just allowing your attention to 'go inside' for a moment, perhaps closing your eyes as you do so, will let you get more in touch with your experience. How's your breathing? Fast or slow? Deep or shallow? Is your body tense or relaxed? Can you feel any discomfort anywhere? How are you mentally? Tired or bright? Quick or slow? Do you have anything on your mind? Or are you without a care in the world?

Once you've taken stock in this way a few times, you'll develop the ability to know what's going on for you virtually instantly. Most of us have a limited repertoire of states, just a handful we use regularly, and one – our 'baseline' state – that feels most natural.

Reflect for a few moments on what your baseline state might be – perhaps a time when you were on your own or doing something ordinary. What is the state you go back to more often than any other? Maybe you're chilled or anxious, playful or grumpy. If someone who knows you well had to describe you in one word, what would they say? How would you describe some of your friends and colleagues?

Success isn't the key to happiness – happiness is the key to success.

Albert Schweitzer

How we create states

Most of us experience states as 'happening' to us, and think of them as being outside of our control. In fact we create them by the way in which we perceive the world. We're able to choose our state and are able to run our own brain, rather than have it running us.

In NLP, the mind and body are thought of as one system, directly influencing each other, with changes in one impacting on the other. When we alter any aspect of our neurology and physiology, such as rate of breathing, blood pressure, temperature, muscle tension and posture, there's a corresponding variation in our mental state. And the thoughts we have – that is the way in which we represent the world internally – have a powerful influence over our neuro-physiology. It's a cybernetic loop.

When most people look at someone they love or hear a favourite song they get a warm feeling inside. And when they look at an unpleasant photograph or hear footsteps behind them in the street at night the feeling they get is uncomfortable. These are examples of how external stimuli create or change our state.

People vary in how they perceive, interpret and react to different situations and that makes an enormous difference to the state they end up in. Say you get up in the morning, go outside, and find your car's been stolen. How will you react? Some people will fly into a rage while others will be philosophical. It's the same with virtually anything. Many of us can tolerate quite a lot of upsets and take a while before we reach the point where the proverbial straw breaks the camel's back. Most of us also know individuals who get upset and stymied by the smallest thing, while others brush aside adversity as if it were nothing.

Insight

One of the most empowering things about NLP, is knowing we create our own emotional state. Instead of 'blaming' others when we feel sad, frustrated or angry, we can choose how to respond to experiences and events. This doesn't mean stuffing emotions down inside – that is unhealthy and to be avoided. It simply means choosing the best state for the outcome you want. We are masters and mistresses of our own emotions.

Changing state

If you like your baseline state, and your other familiar states, there may seem no obvious reason to change them and it may even seem strange to think about doing so. But you can if you want to. And given the choice wouldn't you rather be in a high performance 'peak' state or a relaxed state given the choice?

NLP places great emphasis on being able to manage state, because when you're in the right state for the situation you're more likely to achieve your outcome. In business it's important to be able to keep calm under pressure, while athletes need to remain focused when there's lots of activity going on around them.

Some people use cigarettes, alcohol, drugs, sex, food, shopping or TV to change their state. But while 'looking for love in the fridge' can be effective in managing the symptoms, it's a sticking-plaster solution. The best way of altering your state is by changing your neuro-physiology or the way you think about things. What does this mean in practice? Try these simple exercises.

Exercises

Put on your grey-tinted glasses. Imagine all your plans and hopes and dreams turning to dust with nothing working out the way you want it. Make it as vivid as possible.

How do you feel now? Very different probably. You may feel down and even depressed. Perhaps your energy is low, there may be a knot in your stomach, and your body may have slumped.

Now just move around for a few seconds and think about something else. In NLP this is called 'breaking state'. It's an essential part of many change patterns because it stops one step in the process contaminating another. When working with someone else, asking a question about an unrelated subject, for example 'how did you get here today?', can help change state.

Then put on your rose-tinted glasses, and imagine all your plans turning out for the best. Things could not be more fantastic. It's like a dream come true. Enjoy the experience in your mind using all the representational systems, amplifying it by means of the appropriate submodalities.

(Contd)

How do you feel? Energized? Excited? Exhilarated? What's your posture like? How's your breathing?

Now 'break state' by moving around and thinking of something different.

In Chapter 14 we look at 'reframing', which is another way of changing state because when a frame (or the way we think of something in a particular context) changes so does the meaning, and our response to it. This in turn affects the way we feel.

One of the easiest ways of changing state is by changing your physiology: in fact, this exercise has been demonstrated to be one of the most effective 'treatments' for depression. Try it for yourself:

Exercise

1   Bring to mind a memory that makes you mildly uncomfortable. Say 3 to 5 on a scale of 1 to 10 where 10 is the highest. Fully associate into it, so you can really feel it in your body. Now, trying to hold on to that uncomfortable feeling, dance, jog, hop or jump around the room. If you're like most people, you'll find it hard to stay uncomfortable.
2   Break state by counting slowly up to 10.
3   Now think of a calm, safe place, where there's nothing to do, for instance lying on a beach or under a shady tree on a sunny day. Fully recall the memory. Next increase your rate of breathing, bring it high in your chest. And try to hold on to that feeling of calm. It's not easy. Perhaps impossible.

The point of these examples is to show how quick and easy it is to change states. You don't have to be the victim of your moods and emotions, you can choose how you want to feel at any moment in time.

Ecology in state change

This is not, however, to suggest that you ignore your emotions and simply look on the bright side. Most of us would rather not have grief, frustration, guilt, fear, disappointment and so forth, but jumping around to get rid of them may not always be the best option. Many emotions are, in the words of Tony Robbins, action signals, which contain a message about something in your life that needs attention. A feeling of overload, for instance, often means that you're trying to deal with too many things at once, and need to re-evaluate what's important to you. What most of us regard as negative emotions are actually our allies – they have a positive intention that we often overlook. Once we allow ourselves to fully experience the emotion we can get in touch with what it's trying to tell us, and then if we take action, which may sometimes involve changing the way we think about things, we can be in control of choosing our own state.

The states of others

We are also incredibly sensitive to the states of others. Generally you can get a good idea what kind of mood someone is in just by looking at them. Recognizing the states of others is extremely important, especially in terms of rapport and communicating effectively with people in their map of the world. We'll be looking at the importance of Sensory Acuity and Calibration in Chapter 10.

Elicitation

In NLP elicitation is the technique for assisting someone else in moving from one state to another. If someone is feeling uncertain and they want to feel confident and self-assured the easiest way to help them is to ask them to recall a time when they felt that way. Once they bring the memory to mind they will re-experience it as long as they're associated into the experience.

Try it for yourself: recall a time when you felt relaxed and fully associate into that memory. When you're working with someone else it helps a great deal if you act as a model for the state yourself. If you want to lead them into a state of curiosity you need to demonstrate it too.

NLP perspectives
L. Michael Hall – Emotion/state

'At the heart of NLP are neuro-linguistic states. These mind–body states are a dynamic complex of thoughts, feelings, and physiological components or activities within our nervous systems – they are at the same time mental states, emotional states, and physiological states.

These components of our *mind–body* system experience give us two "royal roads" to state: mind and body. We can think our way into state and we can act our way into state, hence the classical elicitation questions, "Has there ever been a time when ...?" "What would it be like if you were X (relaxed, energetic, loving, etc.)?" "If you were feeling Y (confidence, joy, sadness, etc.), how would you be breathing, standing, etc.?"

As a mind–body dynamic, states involve both thoughts and kinesthetic sensations so we cannot have one without the other. An emotion or emotional state is the combination of sensations and a cognitive understanding.

The relativity of emotions arises because they weigh the difference between expectation and experience. We map our sense of things (our model of the world) and then use it to navigate the territory. How we go in the world compared to our map of the world creates our up and down (positive and negative) emotions. As the difference between these two phenomena, our model of the world and our experience of the world, emotions gives us a somatic register of this difference.

If we think about our inner map on one side of a scale and our outer experience in the territory as the other side, then when the scales tip downward on the *experience* side, then we feel that the world isn't living up to all that we had mapped and expected about it. So we feel bad. We were expecting, wanting, believing, and hoping for a lot more than we got. As this doesn't feel good, it elicits "negative" emotions (anger, fear, discontent, frustration, stress, upsetness).

When the scales tip upward on the *experience* side, then our experience of the world is higher than our *inner maps*. So we feel great. We receive more from the world than we expected. This elicits the "positive" emotions (joy, happiness, pleasure, delight, playfulness, contentment).

This relativity of our emotions does not tell us what is real, what exists "out there", or what is right or wrong. We can't trust our emotions to provide us that kind of information. We can trust them to tell us about the *relationship* between our mental mapping and sensory experiencing.

In our "positive" emotions we are valuing and attributing significance and so setting a frame of importance. This elicits an internal sense of desire and hope and if we

(Contd)

receive it, then joy, happiness, excitement, contentment, fulfilment, etc. Our nervous system then reflects this "sense" of valued significance. In our "negative" emotions, we are *dis-valuing* something, viewing it as hurtful, ugly, distasteful, undesirable, etc.

A state is always an *emotional* state and so never static or non-moving as the term "state" may suggest. Our states are dynamically alive and for ever changing. In our "e-motions" the *motion* that we feel is somatic energy, an urge to *move out* (ex-) to change things. In a so-called "dissociated" state we are still in our bodies and feeling things, typically we feel numb, weird, incongruent, disoriented and we conceptualize it as being out-of-our-bodies.

Our emotions can go astray in two ways. First, we can have an ill-formed, mis-informed, and distorted *model of the world* so that our inner frames of expectations, understandings, beliefs, etc. are erroneous. Second, we may lack the skills to translate into action what we have mapped.'

L. Michael Hall is a prolific writer with more than 30 titles to his name. He is recognized as a leading NLP Trainer and developer of many models, most notably the Meta-States and Matrix models. In 1996 he co-founded with Dr Bob Bodenhamer Neuro-Semantics as a field of study and as an International Society.

www.neurosemantics.com

The Meta-States model

The Meta-States model was developed by L. Michael Hall, PhD from his research in Korzbyski, Bateson, systems, and meta-cognition and recognized by INLPTA (the International NLP Trainers Association) as the most significant contribution to NLP in 1995.

A meta-state is a state-about-a-state structure so that what we are thinking, feeling, or somatically experiencing is about or above another state, i.e. *joyful* learning, *respectful* anger, *calm* fear. Meta-states arise from our special kind of consciousness – our self-reflexive consciousness. This reflexivity enables us to *reflect back* onto ourselves and our experience other thoughts and feelings. As a higher state, a meta-state sets the frame for the previous or primary state. As it does this, it classifies the previous state making it a member of the meta-state classification.

The Meta-States model is a meta-model that maps *how self-reflexive consciousness works* to move us to a higher level (as we go *meta*). We can now step back from our thinking and feeling and layer another level of reasoning (or logic). This creates our 'psychological' levels, levels that make sense from within – from the inner logic that creates the frames for our thinking-and-feeling. This classification process generates our embedded frames of meaning, called the Matrix in Neuro-Semantics.

Meta-Stating, *a verb*, is the process of applying one state to another to create a meta-relationship between the states. Meta-stating is a natural process for how we think with our self-reflexive awareness. As a competency, meta-stating is the skilful and elegant process of accessing a state, amplifying it, applying it, appropriating it into a particular context, and then analysing for ecology and fittingness. In meta-stating, we transcend our current state, including that inside of the next level state, to create an embedded set of frames.

Neuro-semantics

Integrating mind as our *semantics* or meanings and body as our *neurology* and physiology to recognize, diagnose, understand,

and design the *embodied meaning states* that incorporate our highest and best meanings. A field that studies and works with the mind–body system focusing on the synergy between meaning and performance. The design is to *perform* our best meanings and to add rich *meanings* to our current performances. *Synthesizing* meaning and performance gives us a holistic neuro-semantics state so that we can embody the robust meanings that we want to live and experience.

Neuro-Semantics focuses on three facets of human experience:

1 *Performing our richest and most inspiring meanings so that our highest values and principles can be made real in our lives as we embody meaning.*
2 *Adding the most robust meanings to our current performances in order to enrich the quality of our performances.*
3 *Suspending and releasing old meanings which we have already embodied, meanings that do not enhance or empower us.*

NLP in action

▶ *Monitor your state for the next few hours and get a sense of how often it changes.*
▶ *The next time you're feeling a little low in energy recall a time when you felt full of beans – associate into the experience. Amplify the feeling by adjusting the appropriate submodalities.*
▶ *When you experience an emotion you would rather do without get in touch with the positive intention.*
▶ *Guide someone else to change state using the elicitation process.*

TEN KEY POINTS TO REMEMBER

1 *Our state is the sum total of what's going on in our body and mind at any one time.*

2 *The state we're in affects the way we feel, our behaviour and our ability to perform well.*

3 *Knowing what state we're in is the first step to changing or enhancing it.*

4 *Most of us think of states as happening to us, but in reality we create them by the way we perceive the world.*

5 *One of the most effective ways of altering our state is to change the way we think about things.*

6 *Paying attention to the positive intention behind 'negative' emotions can make it easier to change our state.*

7 *Recognizing the state of other people, and responding to it, can help us gain rapport.*

8 *Elicitation is an NLP technique for helping someone move from one state to another.*

9 *A meta-state is a way of thinking about the levels of states that we experience all the time.*

10 *Neuro-semantics focuses on: performing our richest meanings so that our highest values can be made real; adding robust meanings to our performances to enrich their quality; and suspending or releasing old meanings that do not empower us.*

9

Anchoring

In this chapter you will learn:
- *about anchors, anchoring*
- *how to anchor experiences and states*
- *about well-formedness conditions*
- *how to stack, chain and collapse anchors*
- *change techniques that use anchoring*

When you see a police car in the rear-view mirror of your car it's likely that you'll slow down or check your speedometer regardless of whether you're driving too fast or not. The image of the police car in the rear-view mirror is, in NLP terminology, an anchor which triggers an automatic behaviour in many of us.

Virtually anything we can remember or perceive can act as an anchor: the smell of freshly baked bread, the memory of a house we used to live in, the touch of a loved one, etc. Many people report that when they hear a piece of music they can recall where they were when they first listened to it, who they were with and how they felt at the time.

The process by which an internal response became paired, or associated with, an external or internal experience is called anchoring. In the same way that a ship's anchor holds the ship in place, an anchor becomes a reference point for a particular experience.

Anchoring is similar to behavioural conditioning, which Pavlov made famous. Over a period of time Pavlov rang a bell when he was about to feed his dogs. He subsequently discovered that if he rang the bell without feeding them they still salivated, indicating that an association had been established. The difference between this stimulus–response concept and the NLP approach is that it takes account of the fact that human beings have a range of mental processes that are more complex.

Insight

When I (Steve) first encountered the idea of anchoring, I was – to be perfectly honest – rather sceptical. Having an honours degree in psychology I was familiar with Pavlov's famous experiments with dogs, and with the behaviourists' stimulus-response research but I found it hard to believe, when first reading about anchoring, that an emotional state could be paired with something as simple as a touch on the arm. But it can. And more. Anchoring is extremely powerful, and can be used in a wide range of situations.

Everyday anchors

Anchors are naturally occurring. Things we see, hear, feel, taste and touch in our everyday lives spontaneously evoke memories, and often feelings as well. While some anchors are neutral – you see a blue car and it reminds you of one you used to own – many trigger some kind of emotional reaction.

A particular voice tone could remind us of a critical parent. A lake might remind us of a time we nearly drowned. Phobias are examples of extreme 'negative' anchors. A spider, confined space or something equally innocuous has become associated with danger, and produces a fearful response.

Sometimes anchors are set as the result of a single, traumatic experience. But more often, like the bell and Pavlov's dogs, they are established through repetition, and strengthened over time. If every time you went to do something you got shouted at, you would quickly learn not to do it and that association, that anchor, would persist.

Anchors are learned programs and they're state dependent. Pavlov's dogs had to be hungry for the stimulus to have any effect in the first place. Anchors can be unlearned too and NLP has devised many methods of cancelling them, some of which we'll consider later in this chapter.

Many anchors originate in childhood. Often the original experience that created them has long since been forgotten, but the emotional response continues.

Other anchors set off positive feelings. Looking at a photograph from a holiday brings back thoughts of happy times, while holding a brooch that belonged to a grandmother can be a reminder of the smile on her face.

People fire off anchors in each other all the time. If you get a response that seems disproportionate, either in yourself to what someone else said or did, or from someone else to what you said or did, there's likely to have been an anchored response behind the emotion.

Words, too, are anchors. When we read or hear a word such as 'table' it may bring to mind various tables that we've seen before. Advertising is based on anchors. The aim is to create an association that encourages you to buy certain products. Aftershave may be sold on the basis that men wearing it will be fighting off a host of beautiful admirers.

Using anchoring

Many of the anchored responses we have are useful to us. They allow us to function effectively in the world without having to consciously think too much about what we're doing. We don't have to remember to press our foot on the brake pedal when we see the brake lights on the car in front of us light up. It's an automatic, anchored response. Perhaps you've had the experience of 'braking' when you've been a passenger, and the driver didn't seem to respond quickly enough.

Anchors, though, don't have to be left to chance. You can set them – intentionally, systematically – in support of your desired outcomes. If you want to be in a particular state or feel a specific emotion in a future context, you can create an anchor that achieves that, as we'll demonstrate in a moment.

And in the hands of a skilled practitioner, a person's memories, states, emotions and other experiences can be anchored kinaesthetically onto their body and utilized to remedy problematic behaviours. Many of the most powerful and transformational NLP techniques involve the use of anchors.

Some management trainers use spatial anchoring. When they stand in a certain place in the room they invite questions. When they stand in the middle of the stage they impart information. Trainees get used to this and respond accordingly. In fact, people use spatial anchors in all kinds of ways. Some of us have a quiet room in the house where we can relax or a sacred area of the garden where we feel a spiritual connection.

How to set an anchor

To create an effective anchor it's essential to follow a set of five well-formedness conditions – use a unique stimulus, calibrate (by paying precise attention to changes in state – there is more on this in the next chapter) so it's set at the highest intensity, make the anchor pure, time it precisely and consider the context.

UNIQUENESS OF STIMULUS

It's essential to choose anchors that give clear and specific signals to the brain. Effective anchors combine all representational systems.

Kinaesthetic anchors are often used by NLP practitioners when working with others so that people can re-access a particular state simply by touching a part of the body. The most common places are knees or wrists. As Robert Dilts and Judith DeLozier say in the *Encyclopedia of NLP*, 'Shaking hands or touching a person's shoulder are much less unique stimuli than a touch on the middle digit of the little finger'. Choose a place that can easily and precisely be returned to when needed. Combining a kinaesthetic anchor with an auditory anchor such as a tone of voice will make this more effective. When you're working with someone else it's essential that you seek permission before applying a kinaesthetic anchor. This is especially the case when a male is working with a female or vice versa. Many people close their eyes when they access a state so it's best to have this conversation before you start. Reinforcing an anchor by repetition helps to strengthen it, but the quality of the initial anchoring experience is what makes it effective.

INTENSITY

To create an effective and enduring association, the anchor needs to be set just before a person's state reaches its highest intensity. Intensity refers to how vivid and strong the state feels inside. If, for instance, you are working with someone and want to anchor a resourceful state such as confidence, you ask the person to recall a time when they felt confident. To experience the intensity of the remembered state the person will need to be associated into it – seeing, hearing, feeling, tasting and smelling what they did at that time. As the person recalls the state, use your sensory acuity to determine the point of highest intensity.

PURITY

Purity is about ensuring that when a state is anchored nothing contaminates the experience. When an anchor is fired we feel precisely what we did at the time the anchor was created. This means that if someone was wondering whether they had chosen the best experience to anchor or was feeling sceptical about the whole process when the anchor was created they will access uncertainty or scepticism when the anchor is fired at a later time. When you're working with someone else be precise about your language so that only one state is elicited – the one you want to anchor. If you're anchoring a state of confidence, for instance, don't ask the person you're working with whether or not they're sure it's a good example of it. If you do they may say 'Yes', and at the same time start to doubt whether they have the best example. To be sure the right result is achieved, calibrate the person as they move into the state to be anchored.

TIMING

For an anchor to be effective the timing has to be just right. Apply it a second or so before it reaches its highest point and then release it when it's at peak intensity. Let go the moment it starts to decline otherwise another slightly different state from the one you intended will be anchored – a reducing rather than increasing response. When applying a self-anchor it's easy to gauge this yourself. When working with someone else there's a need to calibrate the precise moment to start creating it and to let go.

CONTEXT

Many anchors are context-dependent in that they only work in the environment in which they were created. This is because the surroundings contain cues that can affect the anchoring process or even become part of the anchor. If it were possible to revise for an examination in the room the exam takes place, the environmental anchor of the room would aid recall. Whether or not the environment feels safe also plays a part. This may be a deciding factor as to whether someone pays full attention to the resourceful state they're attempting to anchor or not.

This series of steps will help the anchoring process work effectively.

1 *Clarify the outcome you want to use an anchor for and decide on the state you would like to anchor.*

2 *Elicit and anchor the desired state using the well-formedness conditions.*

3 *Test for effectiveness by firing the anchor again and monitoring the response.*

When working with someone else start by establishing rapport and explaining the process.

Resource anchoring

A resource anchor allows a specific state to be accessed when needed. If, for instance, you're about to attend an important meeting it would normally be useful if you were confident and articulate. The steps to take to create a resource anchor are detailed below.

Steps

1 *Identify a situation where you want to feel more resourceful.*

2 *Choose the resource you want in that kind of situation. In the example above you might choose confidence.*

3 *Recall a time when you experienced that state. See what you see, hear what you hear and feel what you feel. Check in with yourself and mentally note the subtle details relating to being in this resourceful state. When you've done this thoroughly stop thinking about it and break state.*

4 *Select three anchors, one kinaesthetic, one visual and the other auditory. The kinaesthetic one could be a place on your body that's unlikely to be touched very often, such as an ear lobe. The visual anchor can be as simple as recalling what you were seeing at the time. The auditory anchor can be anything you like, such as the word 'confidence'. You don't have to say it out loud.*

5 *Begin to fully re-experience the resourceful state. As it comes to the peak connect the three anchors as explained in Step 4.*

6 *Break state by saying or doing something that has nothing to do with the anchoring process.*

7 *Repeat Step 5 several times and each time improve the experience by adjusting the submodalities associated with it until they reach the optimal level.*

8 *Test the association by firing the anchors. If you return to the resourceful state you're done; if not repeat Steps 5–7 again until you can easily achieve it.*

9 *Identify several situations where you would like to have access to this resourceful state. Imagine being in each state and as you do so fire your anchor to create an automatic association to them.*

Circle of excellence

We all have the resources within us to achieve what we want. The experiences we've had in life are all stored away in our unconscious mind and can be retrieved to support our current endeavours. Circle of Excellence is a technique that allows us to access these resources. You could use it to increase your confidence in public speaking and making presentations, or whatever. The process is most often carried out with two people and can be used on yourself. The version described below doesn't require anyone else's involvement.

Steps

1 *Think of a situation where your current or anticipated behaviour does not give you the outcome you want. You may, for instance, have a presentation to do in the next few weeks and want to feel confident.*

2 *Mentally 'lay down' a circle on the floor wherever you wish. Make it whatever size you like. Give it a colour and a soft humming sound too if you wish. Don't step into it yet.*

3 *Reflect for a moment on the resources that would be useful to you in the situation you've selected.*

4 *Recall a time when you had those resources, taking each one in turn. It can be three different times or a single time when you had all of the required resources. You are seeking* *really good examples of each resource. It's common to have at least three resources and it could be more. If you want to make an effective presentation you might, for instance, choose confidence, feeling calm and clearly articulating a message. Sometimes people can't recall a time when they had a particular resource. If this happens to you, think of someone you know who has the resource and pretend you're them. You can include the visual anchor of this person in place of your own memory.*

5 *When you've identified a resource, step into the circle and relive that experience. Taking the example of confidence, vividly recall a time when you were really confident. Relive it, seeing what you saw, hearing what you heard and feeling what you felt. Repeat this process for each named resource, stacking one on top of the other.*

6 *Think of a specific time in the future when you want to have those resources. If it's confidence in presenting, for instance, see and hear what will be there just before you want to feel confident.*

7 *Now step back into the circle. Access all those resources, take them to where they're needed, and feel the difference. Imagine the situation in your mind's eye. You can add an additional auditory or kinaesthetic anchor at this stage such as hand clapping or squeezing a finger and thumb together.*

8 *Step out of the circle again. Now imagine a time in the future when a similar experience may happen and become aware of how different it is with these resources.*

9 *Finally, test to make sure it has completely worked by recalling the original situation. Check how it feels now. If you have any doubts you may need an additional resource in which case you should repeat the process adding this in.*

Stacking anchors

It's possible to pile one anchor on top of another, creating a stack of resourceful experiences. In his book *Unlimited Power*,

Anthony Robbins describes the state he accesses for firewalks, sky-diving and other challenges. Each time he experiences the point where he feels most resourceful he makes a 'unique fist'. What this means is he has stacked the powerful feeling associated with all those past experiences on top of one another. The fist is the anchor. A great way to practise this is to start anchoring an empowering state whenever the opportunity arises. It can be anything that makes you feel good or uplifted in some way. The same well-formedness conditions still apply. All you do is anchor each resource in turn using a kinaesthetic self-anchor in the same place. When you fire the anchor you'll feel empowered.

Chaining anchors

Chaining is a form of anchoring that's used to link together and allow movement through a sequence of different states easily and automatically. The aim is to progress from the current state to a desired state by creating a series of anchors that lead in that direction. It is a form of pacing and leading because the change is achieved through a series of incremental steps.

This can be used when someone is stuck in a particular state and it feels to them like too big a step to leap straight to the desired state. It can be used, for instance, if someone is experiencing a state of anger and wants to experience a state of love, or if they're experiencing fear and want to be ready to deal with a situation. The sequence of steps for anger to love might be: anger – resignation – acceptance – love, and for fear to readiness: fear – concern – anticipation – readiness.

To achieve this, kinaesthetic anchors are created using points on the body to denote each step in the sequence of states. The current state of fear, for instance, is accessed and then anchored to the person's wrist. The second state of concern is anchored to their forearm, anticipation to the upper arm and then readiness to their shoulder. Each anchor is created and tested in turn. The first anchor is then used to trigger a sequence of graduated states leading towards the positive state. Each anchor is fired in order with the next anchor in the chain being fired just before the previous one reaches its peak. This means the previous state acts as a trigger for the next one in the chain. This needs to be repeated several times to make it operate automatically.

Sliding anchors

Sliding anchors can be used to intensify or diminish a state by sliding the kinaesthetic anchor beyond the peak intensity level of the original state. Most kinaesthetic anchors are either on or off. Sliding anchors are analogue. This means they move along say an arm from the wrist up to the shoulder. The benefit of using sliding anchors is that they give much more control over the intensity of the experience. To try out a sliding anchor first of all think of a pleasant experience. Using all the usual well-formedness conditions, anchor this experience to your wrist with a finger of your other hand. Move your finger slowly up your arm. As you do so become aware of the increasing pleasure you feel. Move it still further and feel the experience become even more pleasurable than before. By the time you reach your shoulder your experience will be approaching bliss!

Extinguishing anchors

There are various ways of cancelling or extinguishing anchors. A common method is desensitization. If someone has a phobia of snakes, for example, you can gradually increase their exposure to them, starting by showing them pictures through to having a snake on the other side of the room. Doing so diminishes the power of the anchor to evoke the response. Another extremely effective way is collapsing anchors.

Collapsing anchors

If two opposing states are anchored and fired simultaneously, the negative state will collapse into the positive state. The human nervous system cannot deal with two incompatible states at the same time. To collapse an unwanted anchor, first access and then anchor the unwanted state and a desirable state. Next fire both anchors at the same time. For it to be effective the positive anchor needs to be stronger. If not it is possible to stack further positive resources to strengthen it. This action sometimes results in a brief period of confusion, which is followed by the desirable state.

Steps
1 *Identify both the problem state and a positive state to overcome it. To check you have the balance right ask the person to rate the negative state on a scale of 1 to 10. Do the same with the positive states. When you come to anchor the positive states ask them to rate these and aim to end up with at least two numbers higher on the positive side.*
2 *Access the positive state by recalling the pictures, sounds, feelings, tastes and smells associated with it. Anchor the state using the well-formedness conditions. Stack further positive states if required.*
3 *Break state by saying or doing something that has nothing to do with the anchoring process.*
4 *Test the positive anchor to make sure it's in place. One way you can be sure is to look for physiological evidence of the desired state. If the state is 'confident' the person should appear confident.*
5 *Access and anchor the problem state.*
6 *Break state by saying or doing something that has nothing to do with the anchoring process.*
7 *Test the negative state with the same care that you took in Step 4.*
8 *Keep testing and reinforcing each anchor in turn, until you're satisfied they're both firmly established and the positive anchor is stronger.*

9   *Break state by saying or doing something that has nothing to do with the anchoring process.*

10 *Fire both anchors at the same time. Hold them for as long as necessary; this can be several minutes. As a precaution remove the negative anchor before the positive one.*

11 *Note the physiological change after a period of confusion. Test by asking the person either to access the problem state or by using the negative anchor.*

12 *Ask the person to think of a situation in the future when they might have expected to experience the problem state. If it doesn't fully work you could consider stacking some additional resources on the positive anchor.*

Future pacing

Future Pacing is like mentally rehearsing a future experience to ensure the behaviour you want is anchored, and will occur naturally in the specified contexts. This is achieved by associating a new behaviour to specific cues in a future situation. Later, when the situation arises, that unconscious link will trigger the change to a new behaviour. If the new behaviour were to be patient with the boss, an association could be made to an image of the door to the boss's office. Future Pacing is the final stage of most NLP exercises. This often involves asking the person to imagine a time in the future when the resource will be needed. If you look back over the last few exercises you'll see we've included it.

Insight

Future pacing may seem like a relatively small, unimportant step that you might skip if you were short of time.
But actually it's a must have, not a nice to have. If you don't future pace, the change might not stick – and the behaviour might not even be activated at the appropriate time. So, don't be tempted to leave it out. Always, *always* future pace.

Change personal history

Change Personal History is a technique devised by Richard Bandler and John Grinder for helping someone change their perspective and feelings about past experiences that are still affecting them in the present. It's not possible to change what has already happened but it is possible to change the meaning it now holds. The technique allows resources to be gathered through the use of anchors and taken back to a time in the past where they are needed. Essentially it involves searching back through our store of memories, either consciously or unconsciously, to find reference experiences that relate to a current behaviour or emotion. This search can also be achieved by means of a timeline. There is more information on timelines in Chapter 17.

Steps
1 *Identify the unwanted, unresourceful or problem state of the person you are working with. We suggest you ask them to choose a fairly simple issue while you get used to working with this technique. Ask them to experience it now and notice where and how they sense it in their body.*
2 *Create a kinaesthetic anchor by touching a shoulder, wrist or knee while the person is experiencing the problem state. Apply the usual well-formedness conditions. Make sure you're in a position to continue to hold the anchor comfortably.*
3 *While holding the anchor ask them to allow their unconscious mind to track back to a time when they had the same feeling in the past. Get them to continue doing this, stopping at various points along the way and associating into each one, until they have reached their earliest experience. Calibrate throughout.*
4 *When they've done that release the anchor and break state. Bring them fully back to the present.*
5 *Ask them what resources they would have needed, knowing what they now know, for the situation to have turned out as they would have liked. At this stage they're dissociated and reflecting on those past experiences. They're likely to identify the resources with words such as strength, calm, trust or confidence. The resource should come from the person and*

be something they control. Ask them to associate into a time when they had the resource they've named. (If necessary, access and anchor two different resources in different places.) If you used the left knee for the negative anchor, use the right one this time. Stack any additional resources with this anchor.

6 The next step is to collapse the anchors. Ask the person to recall the negative state and take the resources to where they're needed. Simultaneously fire the negative and positive anchors and hold both. As you do this ask them to come up through history with this resource, stopping at each past experience and noticing how it is changing and becoming more satisfying. If their eyes are closed keep the anchors on until they are open. Release the negative anchor before the positive.

7 Break state and bring them back to the present.

8 Test the change by asking the person to recall the experience and notice how the memory has changed. If there are any signs of the negative state go back and find the other resources that are needed. Calibrate.

9 Future pace. Ask them what they would see, hear or feel in a future context that would mean they knew they would behave differently. Calibrate.

NLP in action

▶ Create an anchor for a resourceful state, making sure you use the well-formedness conditions – unique, intensity, purity, timing and context.

▶ Think of an event that's coming up and practise the Circle of Excellence to ensure you're in the most resourceful state when it arrives.

▶ Each evening for a week reflect on the events of the day and identify an empowering or uplifting moment. Create an anchor stack that you can access whenever you need to in the coming weeks and months.

▶ Identify an unwanted anchor and eliminate it using the collapse anchor technique.

TEN KEY POINTS TO REMEMBER

1 *An anchor is a stimulus-response connection, in which two things are linked together.*

2 *Anchors occur naturally in our everyday lives – you hear your favourite song, and you feel happy.*

3 *An anchor can be established that triggers a particular state or emotion in a specified future context.*

4 *To create an effective anchor you need the five well-formedness conditions – uniqueness of stimulus, intensity, purity, timing and context.*

5 *A resource anchor allows you to access a specific state when you need it.*

6 *You can stack anchors to access a resourceful or empowering state.*

7 *You can chain anchors and allow movement from the current state, through different states, to a desired state.*

8 *There are various ways of extinguishing anchors, including desensitisation and collapsing anchors.*

9 *When two opposing states are anchored and fired simultaneously the negative state will collapse into the positive state, providing it is stronger.*

10 *Future pacing is a way of mentally rehearsing a future experience. This technique anchors the behaviour so it will occur in the specified context.*

10

Sensory acuity and calibration

In this chapter you will learn:
- *about the importance of sensory acuity and calibration*
- *the distinctions between observation and interpretation*
- *how to pay precise attention to changes in another person's state*

The most important thing in communication is to hear what isn't being said.

Peter Drucker

Being aware of what's going on around us is essential if we're to be effective in the world, but people vary in how much they take in. Some have highly developed and finely tuned observational skills, and pick up on every detail and nuance. Others seem lost in their own thoughts, and wouldn't even notice if a Yeti walked by carrying the Loch Ness Monster.

Of course, it also depends on what we're doing and how we're feeling. Have you ever driven along a road you know like the back of your hand and missed your turning because your mind was elsewhere? And travelled the same route on a different occasion and been acutely aware of every curve and twist of the landscape.

When taking a holiday in an exotic location our senses come alive as we delight in all the new sights and sounds, tastes and smells. Yet when we're at home we barely look up when we walk down the street. The good news is that we can develop our ability to observe fine detail, known in NLP as 'sensory acuity', through practice and by consciously paying attention to what's happening around you.

Imagine for a moment strolling down a country lane and being entranced by the delicate red veins threading through an autumn leaf the colour of gold. A drop of dew glistens in the watery sunlight as the leaf dances gently in the breeze, creating a delicate rustle that blends with the buzz of insects and birdsong in the distance. You feel the warmth of the sun on your skin and sense the ground under your feet.

As we open up our sensory channels, and our acuity develops, so our experience of the world becomes richer. We also get more detailed, accurate feedback on how we're doing in respect of achieving our desired outcomes.

Sensory acuity is equally important when it comes to observing people, especially their non-verbal behaviour, which research has shown is more important than what they actually say. Being able to observe and decode what's being communicated outside of conscious awareness will give you the edge in everything from sales and negotiation to leadership and coaching.

How to develop sensory acuity

A good place to start developing your sensory acuity is to become aware of the kind of things you notice already – you might think of it as carrying out a stock-take of your observational skills. The simple act of reflecting on your behaviour will expand your range anyway, because you'll automatically begin to consider what's not on your list that could be.

Exercise

What details could you observe that you're not currently observing? Reflect for a moment on some of the things you could pay attention to in human behaviour.

The list you came up with probably includes some of the following:

- *posture*
- *gesture*
- *breathing*
- *voice tone/volume/rhythm/pitch*
- *skin tone/colour*
- *facial expression*
- *eye movements.*

Another useful way to expand your range is to compare your abilities with other people you know. Do you know people who regularly comment on things they observe in the world around them, or who seem to be good at noticing human behaviour? What do others notice that you don't?

Insight

Developing your sensory acuity is, in my (Amanda's) view, an invaluable skill. The more aware you are of what's going on around you the better able you are to communicate effectively and build rapport with people. It's the subtle details that give us essential information about others. All it takes to become expert is knowing what to be aware of and lots of practice.

Observation and interpretation

One thing that's really important is to be able to keep your observation 'pure', to prevent it spilling over into interpretation. The starting point is to understand the difference:

- *Observation is simply what you notice with your senses: what you see, hear, feel, taste and smell.*
- *Interpretation is when you go beyond the sensory information gathered and draw a conclusion of some kind.*

The following exercise will give you an opportunity to practise distinguishing between observation and interpretation.

Exercise

Place a mental tick next to each item that contains specific sensory-based information. Place a mental cross next to anything that's an interpretation.

1   *The manager raised his right eyebrow slightly as he read the report.*
2   *Jerry squirmed in her seat as she waited for his reaction.*
3   *His lips narrowed and his nostrils flared.*
4   *Jerry's voice had a rhythmic quality to it when she confidently responded to his questions.*
5   *The pinkish colour gradually disappeared from the manager's face.*
6   *Jerry showed how unflappable she was.*
7   *The manager stood up, having regained his composure.*
8   *Jerry was clearly happy as she held out her hand.*

Answers

1   *'Raised his right eyebrow' is sensory-based information; 'read the report' is an interpretation of his behaviour.*
2   *'Squirmed' is an interpretation – more than a mere description.*
3   *This is sensory-based information.*
4   *'Rhythmic quality' is sensory based; 'confidently responded' is an interpretation.*
5   *The 'pinkish colour gradually disappeared' is sensory based.*
6   *This is an interpretation.*
7   *The first part is observation, the 'regained his composure' part is interpretation.*
8   *'Clearly happy' is an interpretation and 'held out her hand' is an observation.*

It's all too easy to start speculating about the reasons why people do what they do. In fact, it seems to be human nature. In NLP this is known as mind reading. Take the first question in the last exercise. Most people interpret non-verbal signals such as a raised eyebrow as having meaning. Just reflect for a moment on the range of inferences it would be possible to make about what the manager might be thinking or feeling. Maybe he was:

▶ *concerned about what he was reading*
▶ *surprised by something he read*
▶ *annoyed by the content or recommendations.*

In reality his raised eyebrow may have been none of these things. He could have been thinking about something else entirely, perhaps reacting to Jerry's behaviour or pondering over what he needed to do that evening.

Once you understand the difference between observation and interpretation, you can go on to do something useful with all the data you'll gather. Which brings us to calibration.

Calibration

We all notice patterns in human behaviour. When the boss walks into the room Bob starts working. Whenever money is mentioned everyone goes quiet. Kate takes a deep breath before she makes important announcements.

In NLP, noticing patterns of behaviour is called calibration, defined by Joseph O'Connor and Ian McDermott as 'Correlating signs you can see and hear with the other person's state'. It's the process of using sensory acuity to pay precise attention to changes in another person's state by detecting patterns in the nuances of their behaviour – the way they breathe, their voice tone or volume, skin colour, micro muscle movement, posture and gestures.

You can forget the 'one-size-fits-all' approach to body language taken by most books on the subject, in which looking away always means you're avoiding the issue. NLP doesn't see things like that at all. Although there are similarities between us, we are each unique individuals with our own pattern of responses. And calibration is the process of identifying the behavioural cues that go with or before a particular state – 'x' always accompanies or precedes 'y'.

The more well developed our calibration skills, the more connections we pick up. This doesn't mean guessing, it's essential you work from sensory specific evidence. If, for instance, you observe on several occasions that someone frowns and narrows their eyes when they don't agree with something, the next time they do those things, even if they don't say anything, you may be able to conclude they disagree.

How to calibrate

The good news is that we all have calibration skills that we use naturally on a daily basis. The bad news is that most of the time they operate outside of conscious awareness. We intuitively read other people's responses and then adjust our own behaviour. As with any skill the more you practice the easier it gets and the more proficient you become. Here are some of the things you might like to attend to when developing your calibration skills.

▶ **Posture:** *How does the person sit or stand when they're alert, relaxed, happy, sad, fearful, joyful, etc?*
▶ **Gestures and other body movements:** *What unconscious movements do others make? Do they tap their fingers on a desk? Do they 'jiggle' their foot as they speak? What gestures do they make with their hands?*
▶ **Breathing:** *Where do people breathe? Is it in the upper, middle or lower chest/abdomen? And how does that change according to what they're doing or their state or emotion?*
▶ **Voice:** *How and when do people's voices vary in terms of tone, volume, pitch, tempo, rhythm and quality?*

- ▶ **Skin tone:** *The colour of human faces can vary to a surprising degree, normally in line with emotional shifts. Blushing is one of the most obvious, and extreme, examples. When blood pressure goes up even slightly there are resulting changes in skin colour. What patterns can you detect?*
- ▶ **Facial expressions:** *There are thousands of configurations of facial movements and it can be surprisingly easy to become aware of many of them once you start paying close attention. Notice in particular 'micro expressions' that come and go quickly, or movements of tiny muscles around the eyes and mouth. How do these changes relate to the person's state?*

One way to develop your ability to calibrate is to ask a friend to recall a happy memory and then one where they were disappointed or upset. Observe the differences in their facial expressions, eye movements, etc. You should be able to identify clear differences between the two. Then ask your friend to think of another happy or disappointing memory without telling you which one they're thinking about. You'll be able to tell which pattern you're observing.

Calibrating others in change work

The success of any NLP intervention depends on the practitioner's ability to calibrate. When starting out in NLP it's easy to make the mistake of focusing on the process rather than the person. When you are working with someone you need sensory specific information to be sure the technique or intervention has had the desired effect – relying on the person's self report is not sufficient. In the last chapter, for example, we stressed the importance of being aware of the right moment to fire an anchor for it to be effective. To get this right requires a high degree of sensory acuity. According to Grinder and Bostic St Clair, 'Calibration is the most fundamental NLP skill without which it is literally not possible to do high quality work in the field of NLP'.

CALIBRATING GROUPS OF PEOPLE

We find ourselves working with groups of people in many situations, such as in meetings and training events. This is when calibrating shifts into another dimension. We're not only observing signals in individuals but also looking for patterns of behaviour within the group.

When working with a group you may identify certain states that are useful. If, for instance, you're presenting to a group you're likely to want them to pay attention. If you are delivering a training session it would be useful for the participants to be in a learning state. Calibrating with groups means using your sensory acuity to detect the non-verbal behaviours that indicate to you the group are in the desired state.

Of course, a group is made up of individuals and there will be differences in how they respond. This will also vary over time. If you are working with a large group it's possible to pick out certain individuals to calibrate. When you're clear how a person responds when he or she is bored, this person's behaviour can act as an indicator to you that you need to take some action to liven up the proceedings for everyone. The art of calibrating groups lies in observing how non-verbal responses change according to the interventions you and other group members make.

Calibrating your own responses

One of the most beneficial things you can do is to calibrate your own responses to what you're doing or considering. You might notice, for instance, a nagging feeling of doubt when something doesn't feel quite right. You may even be able to detect where in your body you experience this feeling of uncertainty. Or there might be an internal voice or some other sensory-based expression of incongruence. Some people also experience a feeling of alignment or a sense of being centred that suggests to them that they are taking the right course of action. In NLP this is known as congruence.

By tuning in to your own internal signals for congruence you are able to question an intended course of action rather than ploughing ahead without first resolving your cause for concern. We will expand on this topic in Chapter 14 where you will be introduced to the concept of 'parts' and how we sometimes experience internal conflict with part of us wanting one thing and another part wanting something else.

NLP in action

▶ Pay more attention to your environment. Spend at least five minutes a day for a week doing nothing except observing your everyday surroundings. Keep a record of what you observe and then add something new to it each day.

▶ Ask a friend to help you develop your sensory acuity. Practise the exercise we suggested earlier and this time expand your range by asking them to recall times when they were angry, delighted, sad, bored, joyful, fearful, amused and so on. Calibrate each one and then get them to test you by recalling a memory from the list at random without telling you what it is.

▶ The next time you attend a meeting or get together with a group of people, identify how the state of the group and individuals within it change with the passing of time and following various interventions. Alter your approach and see how this brings about a shift in them.

TEN KEY POINTS TO REMEMBER

1 *Sensory acuity is the ability to observe fine details.*

2 *You can develop your sensory acuity through practice and paying attention to what is happening around you.*

3 *It's really important to keep your observation 'pure' and not slip into interpretation.*

4 *Interpretation is when you go beyond the sensory information and draw a conclusion.*

5 *In NLP, noticing patterns of behaviour is called calibration.*

6 *We intuitively read other people's responses and adjust our behaviour.*

7 *You can develop your calibration skills by paying close attention to: posture, gestures and other body movements, breathing, voice, skin tone and facial expressions.*

8 *Calibration will enable you to check whether your intervention has worked – a self report is not enough to ensure high quality work.*

9 *Calibrating with groups of people means using your sensory acuity to make sure you and the group are in the desired state for the situation.*

10 *You can calibrate your own responses by paying attention to how aligned you feel with a course of action.*

11

Rapport

In this chapter you will learn:
- *how to achieve and maintain rapport easily*
- *about matching, mismatchings and pacing and leading*

What is rapport?

Have you noticed that when people are in conversation with colleagues at work, chatting over the garden fence or are out together having a drink in a bar they often adopt similar poses and postures? They make eye contact, chat easily, and are comfortable in each other's company. Perhaps they lower their voices conspiratorially at the same time, so as not to be overheard, or giggle uproariously together when someone tells a story.

In NLP this is known as *rapport*, which has been defined as the establishment of trust, harmony and co-operation in a relationship. The state or process of being in rapport with someone is often described as being 'in tune' or 'on the same wavelength' as them.

Rapport is usually achieved without us consciously having to try or even think about it. It's a natural phenomenon. When we're getting along with people we're in rapport most of the time. It's a fundamental part of effective communication and a vital component to building and maintaining successful relationships with others.

Unless you plan to live like Robinson Crusoe on an island, with no Man Friday, you'll need to get along with people, and this means having good rapport skills. If you want to be successful and popular you'll need to be able to connect and engage with others.

When we meet people for the first time and discover we share common interests it makes it easier for us to break the ice and establish rapport. We often know when we're in or out of rapport with another person by the way we feel inside. When we're in rapport it can feel like you're in 'flow' with the other person and when we're out of rapport it can feel awkward.

Robert Dilts describes rapport as a 'loop of mutual influence'. It's like a dance with two people moving effortlessly and gracefully across the floor in perfect step and harmony. But if one person treads on their partner's toes the rapport may be lost for a while, though it's often quickly recovered. When you dance with a new partner it can feel clumsy at first until you get to know each other's moves.

Because rapport is natural some people think it can't be learnt, but there are numerous ways that skills can be enhanced, and we'll be covering the most important ones in this chapter. In simple terms this involves behaving more like the other person, using your sensory acuity skills to pay attention to what they're doing and saying.

There are many applications for using rapport. It allows you to influence others to see things your way, resolve conflicts, negotiate win-win deals, coach other people to fulfil their potential, and enhance almost any interaction, both personal and professional.

Matching and mirroring

Only a small part of human communication is achieved through what we actually say. The rest is non-verbal: gestures, facial expressions, posture, eye movements, nods, breathing, and voice qualities such as tone, pitch and rhythm.

This means that one of the key ways we establish and build rapport is by reading these non-verbal communications and mirroring and matching them. In fact, body mirroring and matching to create rapport are among the earliest and best known NLP techniques.

▶ *Matching is the process of observing someone and then behaving like them, such as sitting in the same way or using similar gestures.*
▶ *Mirroring is precisely matching another person's behaviour – creating a mirror image.*

It's important to take care when copying someone's physiology. If you do it overtly it can look as if you're making fun of them and break rapport. There's a fine line between matching and mimicking. If the other person does something and you follow straight afterwards they'll probably notice. You might get away with it once, but if you do it repeatedly they're sure to pick it up. If you wait 20–30 seconds it's likely to go unobserved.

Here are some things you can match:

▶ *Whole body matching, where you adjust your stance or your whole seated body to match another person's. Note the angle of their spine.*
▶ *Upper or lower body matching, where you match either your upper or lower body to theirs.*
▶ *The way they move, slow and smooth or energetic and jerky. Some people move a lot, some move a little. Some move mainly on one side of the body or just one hand or foot. Others move both sides together.*
▶ *Head tilt or shoulder matching, to the left or right, forwards or backwards.*
▶ *Matching gestures, some people make large gestures, others small.*
▶ *Matching facial expressions, eye direction or even their blink rate.*
▶ *Breathing, patterns and rhythms.*

The next time you're in a café, restaurant, bar, open plan office or at a family gathering, take the opportunity to observe the people around you. What do you notice as people greet each other, converse and generally interact? Focus on one group and watch how things develop. See how many of the behaviours you can identify on the list we gave you. Who is matching who? How do you know?

Matching in practice

The next stage in learning about matching is to have a go yourself. It's a great opportunity to practise calibrating too. You can either take a risk and try matching in everyday situations or you may prefer to ask a friend if they'd be happy to help you in the early stages. If you choose the latter option don't tell them what you're doing. Just get them to discuss something they feel passionate about. As you listen to them, and acknowledge what they have to say, match their behaviour leaving a gap of around 20 seconds after they've done something before copying it. At this stage concentrate on the most obvious things: overall posture, hand gestures, foot movements, etc. You'll struggle if you try to match everything and copying things such as breathing patterns takes a certain amount of practice. At the end of the exercise ask for feedback. If you went too far they'll soon tell you if it felt like mimicry. If you get it right they'll have the sense you were really interested in them and what they had to say.

Initially it can feel strange matching others. But you quickly get used to it, and skilled at continuing to chat in a natural way as you do so. The biggest challenge is when the other person's non-verbal behaviour is very different from yours. If they make big gestures and you don't gesture much you may feel as if you're going outside your comfort zone. But stick with it, and you'll start to feel more comfortable in doing things you wouldn't normally do.

Cross-over matching

Cross-over matching is where you use one aspect of your behaviour to match a different behaviour in someone else. You could, for example, tap your foot in time with a series of head nods or synchronize the rhythm of your speech to a person's breathing rate. This is a great way of matching in a less intrusive way.

Psycho-geography

The physical relationship between people, their psycho-geography, is also important when you want to build rapport with someone. If two people sit alongside each other it creates the experience of being aligned. Metaphorically speaking, when we are on the same side we see things from the same perspective. This can be especially useful when negotiating or for handling conflict. Contrast this to talking face-to-face or across a desk, when you can easily end up in opposition to one another, or literally seeing things from a different perspective.

Matching through language

It isn't just through body language that we can match others. There are many ways to build rapport with another person through the spoken word, such as using the same vocabulary, responding to their Meta Programs, and matching the sensory specific words they use, such as see, listen, feel. When you are able to speak someone else's language you inevitably build rapport.

The hypnotherapist Milton Erickson, from whom many NLP concepts are drawn, was asked to treat a patient who suffered from schizophrenia and spoke only in 'word salad'. The words he used were all real, but were arranged in sentences that apparently made no sense. Over the course of several meetings, Erickson identified a structure in the word salad. Once he'd cracked the code he used the same way of speaking himself over several meetings with the patient. Eventually the patient said 'Talk sense Doctor', and the door was opened to recovery.

You're unlikely to go that far when it comes to matching language, but one powerful way is to notice any metaphors they use and develop them. When someone says, 'I feel like I'm hitting my head against a brick wall', you might respond by asking more about the brick wall and what's on the other side of it. We'll be exploring the use of metaphor in Chapter 19.

Matching through shared beliefs and values

You can match all you like at the behavioural level with body language and voice tone but if your values and beliefs are different it will eventually affect the degree of rapport you have with someone. It doesn't mean you have to believe what they do but it's important to acknowledge and respect their views.

Voice

You can also match people in terms of their voice. This is particularly valuable when you're speaking to someone on the phone, where it's obviously impossible to match physical movement, but is equally valuable in face-to-face encounters.

Is their speech steady, all at the same pace, or are bits of it fast and others slow. Do they pause much? Are their sentences short? To the point. Just like this. Or do they wander about a bit, with lots of diversions, things said to one side, or expanding on areas of interest before finally, eventually, ultimately coming to an end.

Exercise

Take a moment to think what other aspects of the voice you could match.

You probably came up with things such as pitch, volume, tone, rhythm, speed, cadence and musicality. The next time you answer the phone, listen carefully to what the other person sounds like before saying anything yourself. If they speak fast, you speak fast. If they're quiet, you're quiet. Copy them, but once again short of mimicry. If someone has an unusual vocal style or strong accent, they could think you're making fun of them.

Insight

If you have a job that involves using the telephone a lot – which many of us do these days – you have endless opportunities to practise voice matching and hone your skills. Some call centre staff use this as a way of both relieving the monotony of their job and being more effective at the same time. Sales people who want an extra edge use it to build rapport with prospects. If you're in a customer facing role of any kind it will improve your effectiveness.

Pacing and leading

Having matched someone, and gained rapport, you can begin to influence them, taking them in another direction. In NLP this is known as Pacing and Leading. If you enter the other person's world, and do what they're doing for a while, then subtly change your behaviour, they will often follow. You might, for instance, match someone's breathing rate (pace) for a few minutes and then change yours (lead), either to calm someone down or increase their energy or feeling of excitement. The next time you walk alongside someone match their pace and length of stride for a while. Then make a subtle change perhaps by slowing down and notice how they change their speed to match yours.

What's important is that you don't try to lead too soon, or the person may not follow. The principle can best be described as pace, pace, pace and then lead. The longer you pace, the more likely you are to succeed.

Emotional rapport

You can also pace and lead others emotionally. This is especially effective when they're angry. Most people deal with such situations by being calm and quiet, but this often doesn't work because there's no pacing. A better approach when someone is angry is to respond using the same voice speed, volume and tone with 'I know you're angry, and I'm concerned about that'. What you are doing is matching your voice with their emotions. This will help them to fee heard, accepted and understood and you can then gradually change your voice tonality and lead them towards a resolution of the problem.

You can do a similar thing in many situations. If you want those around you to be happy, start by pacing their current state. If someone looks sad, match their expression and posture. Then by degrees change the way you hold your body and start to smile.

Breaking rapport

When someone in the office wants to chat and you've got a pile of work to get through it can be useful to break rapport for a while. You can do this by looking away briefly or changing your posture so you're not matching them. They'll often get the message without you having to say anything. There are other occasions where mismatching is also appropriate. If you want to convey disagreement, for instance, a simple shift in posture may be enough to emphasize your view and your autonomy before returning to a state of rapport.

Verbal and non-verbal conflict

Have you noticed that sometimes people shake their head while saying yes, and vice versa. There is incongruence between the verbal and non-verbal behaviour. The conscious mind is saying yes but the unconscious mind is saying no. Even though the non-verbal part of the communication may be out of the conscious awareness of both parties, the person being spoken to will often register and respond to that rather than the words said. It's easy to lie, but more difficult to control the non-verbal portions. When we're in rapport with ourselves verbal and non-verbal communication are aligned.

Are rapport techniques manipulative?

People sometimes express concern that rapport techniques are manipulative, that using these skills covertly involves hoodwinking people and taking advantage of them. At the end of the day it depends what you mean by manipulative. If your desired outcome is simply to improve communication or be more influential there's surely no issue. It's no different from dressing smartly and taking an interest in what someone else does.

▶ *Become an avid people watcher and notice what they do to achieve rapport.*

▶ *Take one item at a time from the list below and spend a day practising matching it with who ever you meet:*

   ▷ *whole body*
   ▷ *the way they move*
   ▷ *head tilt*
   ▷ *gestures*
   ▷ *facial expressions*
   ▷ *breathing*
   ▷ *voice*
   ▷ *language*
   ▷ *beliefs and values.*

▶ *Practise pacing and leading whenever the opportunity arises by matching and then subtly altering what you do to bring about a change in the other person's behaviour.*

TEN KEY POINTS TO REMEMBER

1 Rapport can be defined as the establishment of trust, harmony and co-operation in a relationship.

2 One of the best ways of gaining rapport is by reading non-verbal communication and matching other people.

3 Matching is observing someone and behaving like them whereas mirroring is precisely matching them – creating a mirror image.

4 Cross-over matching is where you match a different behaviour, such as tapping your foot in time to their head nods.

5 Psycho-geography is about the physical relationship between people. If, for instance, two people sit alongside each other it creates the experience of being aligned.

6 You can build rapport by matching language, such as sensory specific words and meta programs.

7 Voice matching is another way of building rapport, including: pace, rhythm, volume, pitch and tone.

8 Pacing and leading is where you match someone for a while then subtly change your behaviour – resulting in them following to maintain rapport.

9 You can pace and lead someone emotionally by at first matching and then making subtle changes which they follow.

10 There are times when you will want to break rapport. This can be achieved by mismatching.

12

Perceptual positions

In this chapter you will learn:
- *about first, second, third and fourth positions*
- *how to improve relationships with perceptual positions*
- *some useful techniques for understanding yourself and others better*

The value of multiple perspectives

There are times when other people don't see things from our perspective. They appear to be stuck in their own world view and can't seem to understand what things are like for us. And yet, to some extent, in certain contexts, we all behave this way at times because we are so immersed in our own map of reality.

When we're able to understand other people's maps of the world we can more easily create and maintain rapport, communicate better, demonstrate empathy for others, resolve conflict and, in a business setting, negotiate effectively, improve customer service and develop marketable products.

One of the principle ways in which New Code NLP departed from NLP as it was originally formulated was in its emphasis on 'multiple perspectives'. As part of their Triple Description model, John Grinder and Judith DeLozier highlighted the fact that systematically shifting from one perceptual position to another can make available information about a situation that may have been out of conscious awareness.

There are three main perceptual positions: first, second and third position. These involve seeing things from our own perspective (first), from another person in the situation (second or other), and from a detached viewpoint (third or observer).

When we want to expand our understanding of a situation, we can either use the other and observer positions in an ad hoc way, quickly 'trying on' those different stances or carrying out a complete Perceptual Positions exercise, the format of which is detailed later in this chapter.

First position

We naturally perceive our environment and the people in it from first position; it's where our sense of 'self' resides. We use words such as 'I' and 'me' to describe our experience, and have our own way of standing and gesturing that is personal to us. In this position we're associated, seeing through our own eyes, hearing through our own ears (plus our internal dialogue) and are aware of the feelings in our body. If we can see ourself in our mind's eye we are dissociated, and not in first position.

WHEN TO USE FIRST POSITION

There are many benefits to using first position. When you're deciding on an outcome it's important to know what you want. It's the position from which people are assertive, expressing their view, and pursuing their own goals. Carrying out an ecology check from this position when considering outcomes ensures the action we commit to fits with our sense of identity.

THE DOWNSIDE TO FIRST POSITION

In first position we only think about how things affect us because all we are aware of is our own perspective. If we only operated from this position we'd become egotistical, narcissistic and insensitive to the feelings of other people, and could easily end up trampling on them.

Second position

To occupy second position you imagine stepping into the shoes of someone in a particular interaction and experiencing the world through their eyes. You take on their posture, breathe the way they do, and act as if you were them. You see, hear, feel, taste and smell their reality. Dissociating from your own thoughts, feelings and beliefs and associating into the 'other', you 'see' yourself through their eyes – and think of that person as 'you', not 'I'. As you do this you increase your awareness of what things might be like for the other person. The more you can take on their beliefs, values, Meta Programs and other aspects of their internal representations, the more accurate you will be.

WHEN TO USE SECOND POSITION

By adopting second position we obtain important new information about our relationship with the other person. We're able to develop empathy and compassion for them. We also gather useful data about ourselves in the process. In our mind's eye we can look at ourselves, see our own facial expressions, add body language, hear our voice, and get a sense of what it's like to be on the receiving end of our own behaviour. This means we have increased choice about how to interact with them, which is especially useful when we can't understand why they are behaving the way they are.

THE DOWNSIDE TO SECOND POSITION

Those who get 'stuck' in second position can become easily influenced by others, and prioritize their needs over their own. Accepting other people's version of things can lead to a loss of self-confidence and hold us back from fulfilling our potential. When we continually put ourself last there can be a tendency to take on other people's problems, which leaves us emotionally drained.

Third position

In third position we see, hear and feel what an interaction is like from an external perspective. From this viewpoint we're able to stand back and perceive the relationship between ourselves and others. This places us outside the communication process and allows us to act as a witness to what takes place. In third position we are associated but detached from the interaction, which allows us to feel resourceful and analyse what's happening. The information we gather can then be taken back to first position.

WHEN TO USE THIRD POSITION

The objectivity we get from standing back or taking a helicopter view can be extremely valuable. When we're in the situation our emotions can get in the way of noticing what's going on, particularly when there's conflict or aggressive behaviour. Third position is sometimes also called 'Meta' position, and features in many NLP patterns and change techniques, providing an opportunity for the person to stand outside their own experience when that's required.

THE DOWNSIDE TO THIRD POSITION

The downside of using third position is that we can become detached. Not only will we lack feelings, we will come across to others as emotionless, a bit like a robot.

Perceptual Positions pattern

The Perceptual Positions pattern provides a systematic way of harvesting insights from first, second and third position. This is an especially useful activity to carry out when there are problems or conflict in a relationship. This exercise can be repeated as many times as necessary – each cycle brings new information. The end result is usually subtle changes in your behaviour, which improve the situation.

Steps

1 *Select a relationship you want to improve in some way. To start with we recommend you choose something small. As you become more experienced at using the technique you can progress to larger and more significant issues.*

2 **First position:** *Begin by considering the situation from your own perspective. Re-experience it through your own eyes, as if you were looking at the other person. Listen to what they might have to say to you. See the expression on their face. Become aware of how you feel. Use first person language when you speak as if you were actually talking to them; you can do this inside your head or out loud.*

3 *Break state by doing something different for a few moments, perhaps by shaking it off.*

4 **Second position:** *Now imagine you're inside the other person's skin. Become as aware as you can of how this person experiences life. Take on that person's posture, gestures and voice tone. Set aside your own beliefs and values. Replay the interaction from this person's viewpoint. Pay attention to the thoughts and insights that surface as you observe the 'you' over there. Use second person language to describe what you experience, i.e. refer to yourself as 'you'.*

5 *Break state.*

6 **Third position:** *Next, move to a detached place where you can observe both first (self) and second (other) position. Once again replay the event as if you were watching and listening to a film. Be curious about what unfolds before you. Note the learning you gain from this perspective.*

7 *Return to first position, bringing the insights from the other perceptual positions with you. Pay attention to the difference in your experience.*

8 *Repeat the cycle as many times as necessary. Ending with first position helps to consolidate the changes you make in how you will respond in the future.*

Fourth position

Taking fourth position involves experiencing the whole system at one time – the other three positions combined and interacting with one another. The language used in fourth position is 'we' or 'us'. When we're in fourth position we experience sameness or oneness with all the other members of the system. It is an essential ingredient for effective teams. Robert Dilts describes this as 'a felt sense of "sameness" and identification with all members of a system'. And, as he points out, 'effective leaders are able to identify with the whole system they are influencing'.

Meta Mirror

In 1988 Robert Dilts developed the NLP Meta Mirror technique, which makes use of fourth position. Using it allows us to improve our understanding of the way we interact with others and ourselves by looking at a problematic relationship. The way the person is treating us is often the way we treat ourselves, hence the use of the term 'mirror'.

Steps

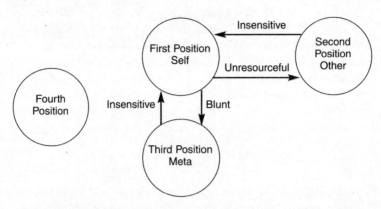

1 *Starting in first position picture in your mind's eye someone you want to have a better relationship with. Make sure you're associated into the experience. What are you seeing, hearing and feeling? Identify what it is that makes it difficult for you to communicate with them. You may, for example, find them insensitive.*
2 *Break state.*
3 *Now step back to a Meta (or third) position where you are dissociated from the situation, as if you were watching yourself. Identify the way you respond, for example, unresourceful. Recognize how your behaviour prompts them to react that way.*
4 *Break state.*
5 *Reflect for a moment on what you have learnt from this. What changes do you want to make to the way you respond to this person? What could you do differently?*
6 *Break state.*
7 *Now move further away to fourth position and identify a word to describe how you react to yourself, for example, blunt. How is this reaction a mirror image of the other person's behaviour?*
8 *From fourth position imagine that first and third positions swap places; this means the way you reacted to yourself switches to where first position used to be and vice versa.*

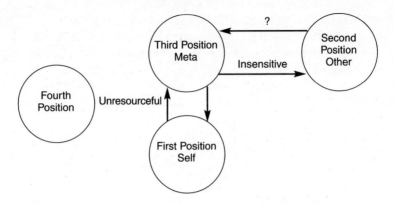

9 Next, step into the shoes of the person in second position and take a look at yourself from their perspective. What does your behaviour feel like? What can you learn from this?

10 Step back into the revised first position and take stock of how different you feel.

11 Continue to switch between the different positions until you feel congruent with the changes you have made.

NLP perspectives
Robert Dilts – The value of
exploring perspectives

'The basis for the various perceptual positions comes from the fact that relational experiences always involve more than one individual in the communication loop. The ability to understand the communication loop, and the ebb and flow of events that occur within the loop, is a powerful tool, enabling people to both improve communication and produce ecological outcomes. Even when the participants within the communication loop do not agree, their relationship is enhanced and the possibility of future co-operation is created when they are able to shift perceptual positions in relationship to the interaction.'

Robert Dilts has been a developer, author, trainer and consultant in the field of NLP since its creation in 1975. He is the author of 18 books on NLP including the *Encyclopedia of Systemic Neuro-Linguistic Programming* and *NLP New Coding*, from which this extract was taken.

www.nlpu.com

NLP in action

▶ *Think about someone you admire and in your mind's eye imagine them in front of you. Fully experience them from first position. Next step into their skin and experience what it is like to be them. Now step into third position and gain a different perspective. What do you learn from this?*
▶ *Think of a relationship you'd like to improve or to have more choice in, then follow the steps of the Meta Mirror process.*

TEN KEY POINTS TO REMEMBER

1 *Systematically shifting from one perceptual position to another can make available information that is out of conscious awareness.*

2 *We naturally perceive our environment and other people in it from first position.*

3 *First position is useful when you are deciding what you want to achieve. When you assertively express your views you are in first position.*

4 *When you step into someone else's shoes as completely as possible and see yourself through their eyes you are in second position.*

5 *When you are in second position you can gather useful information about their perspective and develop empathy and compassion for them.*

6 *In third position you can see, hear and feel what an interaction is like between you and another person from an external perspective.*

7 *Third position is sometimes called 'Meta' position and it provides an opportunity for you to stand outside of your own experience and learn from it.*

8 *NLP's Perceptual Positions pattern can be used to help resolve problems or conflict in relationships.*

9 *Fourth position allows you to step outside of the whole system – of first, second and third positions. In this position we experience a feeling of 'oneness' or 'sameness' with the other members of the system.*

10 *The Meta Mirror is a technique developed by Robert Dilts that makes use of fourth position and allows us to observe how the way another person is treating us is often how we treat ourselves.*

13

The Meta Model

In this chapter you will learn:
- *how the Meta Model was developed*
- *the relationship between deep and surface structure*
- *the 12 Meta Model distinctions*
- *questions to ask to recover 'lost' information*
- *the importance of rapport when using the Meta Model*

The first NLP model was the Meta Model. It was developed when Richard Bandler and John Grinder modelled the language patterns used by successful therapists Virginia Satir and Fritz Perls. What they observed was that certain types of question had therapeutic benefit, in other words, people got better. By analysing the structure of these interventions Bandler and Grinder identified six patterns that they were able to use to replicate the results achieved by Satir and Perls. In addition, they tested many other syntactic distinctions from Chomsky's transformational grammar, in which Grinder was an expert, in the context of change work and six were found to be effective. Details of the 12 patterns thus produced were published in the first NLP book, *The Structure of Magic*, Volume I, in 1975.

What these challenges do is help people recover lost information, reconnect to their internal experience, and so reconfigure their cognitive maps. The problem is not that the world is impoverished. It's the representations that people make of it, and then mistake for reality, that are lacking. Once their internal model is enriched they're able to function more effectively in the world.

Deep and surface structure

The Meta Model, like the linguistic model from which it drew its inspiration, makes a distinction between deep structure and surface structure. It's a tool for understanding how thoughts are translated into words. Transformational grammar suggests that each utterance or sentence can be analysed at two levels – surface and deep structure.

The surface structure represents the actual order of the words in a sentence. The following two sentences, for instance, have the same surface structure even though the words are slightly different: 'The walls were painted by a new decorator' and 'The walls were painted by a new technique'. The deep structure of the two sentences is different because they don't have the same meaning. Now take these two sentences: 'A manager wrote the project report' and 'The project report was written by a manager'. In this case the deep structure is the same even though the order of the words is different. The deep structure represents the basic grammatical relationships from which a sentence is derived.

In NLP this deep structure of what we seek to communicate is our complete internal representation, the mental images, sounds and feelings stored at the neurological, unconscious level of the mind. What we actually say or think is the surface structure. This is a greatly reduced version of our actual experience because in the course of moving from the deep structure to the surface structure three processes take place: distortion, deletion and generalization. However, these processes are a double-edged sword. While they make it possible for us to adapt, survive and grow, they can, if we're not careful, constrain us from maximizing our potential.

Elements of the Meta Model

DELETION

It would be impossible for us to pay attention to every stimulus around us. Our brain would be completely overloaded. In fact, George Miller and others have found that on average we can hold only seven (plus or minus two) items in consciousness at one time, though our unconscious mind has a greater capacity than that. As a result, at any particular moment we are tuning in to certain aspects of our experience and filtering out others. This reduces it to a level we can handle. That's how, for instance, you can see and hear what's happening on a TV when there's lots of activity in the room or people speaking loudly.

DISTORTION

The process of simplifying an experience inevitably leads to distortion. Sometimes we don't have all the information, and jump to conclusions that are unwarranted. But that doesn't mean it's a bad thing. Distortion is also a creative process, allowing us to imagine or fantasize about things that haven't yet happened, or come up with discoveries and inventions.

GENERALIZATION

Our ability to generalize is also essential when it comes to coping in the world. Using previous experiences that are similar as a starting point allows us to learn quickly. Imagine if every time you went to open a door you had to figure out how to do it. Sometimes, though, our minds make generalizations that aren't an accurate representation of reality. One element of an experience comes to represent an entire category. We have a bad experience when having our car serviced and come to the conclusion that all mechanics are rude. At its most extreme this can lead to all-or-nothing thinking, where situations or people are seen in black and white.

When we're not writing books, we spend our time helping people to improve their communication skills in various ways, and have found that it is often this lost information that causes confusion and misunderstandings. Once you start to pay attention to the language you and other people use you'll realize just how much deletion, distortion and generalization goes on. This allows you to ask questions to fill in the gaps, making your life, and other peoples', easier.

Challenging Meta Model 'violations'

Deletion, distortion and generalization are essential processes in the transformation of deep structure experience to a surface structure communication. Most of the time they work effectively in reducing the volume of information to manageable proportions while still representing the external world in a useful way. But not always. Sometimes problems occur. And the purpose of the Meta Model is to identify deletions, distortions and generalizations that are problematic by analysing the surface structure statements.

For each of the 12 distinctions that are defined by the Meta Model there are a series of challenges that aim to recover some of the information lost in the transformation from deep to surface structure. By asking certain kinds of questions when faced with a particular type of violation, the person is required to access the information that has been lost. Sometimes all that is needed for the issue to be resolved is for the person to fill in the gaps in their internal representation. And if that isn't sufficient on its own, the process usually points the way to an effective solution.

You'll notice that most of the questions begin with 'how' and 'what'. There are no 'why' questions. That's because the aim is to get more information, and most people respond to 'why' questions by explaining, justifying and defending. An added benefit of using the Meta Model is that the discussion is at a sensory specific rather than abstract level, which can all too easily result in the questioner creating their own fantasies or hallucinations about what's going on.

Below we've listed typical violations of the 12 distinctions, what the aim of the intervention is in each case, and given examples of what kinds of question to ask.

Challenging deletion

There are four principle ways in which information is deleted in the progression from deep structure to surface structure and as you might imagine the focus of any intervention is to recover what's been left out. People often say things such as 'people don't care' without specifying who those mysterious people are. In fact, we did exactly that in the last sentence! Verbs are often used that don't fully explain what's going on, and comparisons are made that are far from clear.

SIMPLE DELETION

Violation:	An important element, such as an object, person or event, has been left out of a statement.
Objective:	To recover the element that's been omitted.
Example:	'I'm sad.'
Response:	'Sad about what?'

COMPARATIVE DELETION

Violation:	A comparison is implied in the statement but it doesn't say what it's being compared to.
Objective:	To establish what the comparison is being made against.
Example:	'It's better to go along with things.'
Response:	'Better than what?'

LACK OF REFERENTIAL INDEX

Violation: The noun, object, person or event isn't specified.
Objective: To clarify what is being referred to in the statement by recovering the noun.
Example: 'They are kind to me.'
Response: 'Who, specifically, is kind to you?'

UNSPECIFIED VERBS

Violation: A verb is not clearly defined.
Objective: To define more precisely what's being done.
Example: 'I explain things badly.'
Response: 'How, specifically, do you explain things badly?'

Challenging distortion

We have a tendency to believe that our perspective on the world is accurate and the only one that's right, when in reality it's not only partial but distorted in a variety of ways. Sometimes, for instance, we think we know what people are thinking or feeling, when actually it's just a guess. In NLP terms, we're mind reading. It's not unusual for people to make cause and effect connections between different experiences that are not justified by the evidence, or even present their own judgements as if they were accepted as fact. One pervasive form of distortion is where a process, a verb, has been turned into a thing, a noun. This is called nominalization. Grieving becomes grief. Communicating becomes communication. The problem with this is that 'things' are 'fixed' and 'static'. But once the noun has been returned to its verb form, it becomes evident that change is possible.

CAUSE AND EFFECT

Violation: A causal relationship is implied by the statement.
Objective: To clarify the causal relationship.
Example: 'He really drives me crazy!'
Response: 'How, specifically, does he drive you crazy?'

MIND READING

Violation:	Where someone claims to know what someone else is thinking.
Objective:	To identify the thinking underlying that assumption.
Example:	'She thinks I'm lazy.'
Response:	'How do you know she thinks that?'

COMPLEX EQUIVALENCE

Violation:	Two different experiences are said to be the same thing.
Objective:	To establish the validity of the relationship.
Example:	'I failed my exam – I'm a compete loser.'
Response:	'How does failing your exam make you a loser?'

LOST PERFORMATIVES

Violation:	A statement expresses an opinion dressed up as fact.
Objective:	Identify the criteria used to make the judgement.
Example:	'It's not right for women to work when they have children.'
Response:	'Not right according to whom?'/'Who says?'

NOMINALIZATIONS

Violation:	A verb has been made into a noun.
Objective:	To turn the statement into a process statement.
Example:	'There's too much confusion.'
Response:	'What's confusing you?'

Challenging generalization

Everybody generalizes all the time – like we just did! Management never tells the truth; I always help other people; time is a great healer. Such statements are rarely true, and when examined carefully sometimes prove to have no basis in fact, yet important decisions and actions are based upon them. Examining them can determine when they can be relied upon and when more subtle distinctions about the nature of the world are required. Some of the generalizations people make were established when they were much younger. Some were handed down by parents or teachers, without them having been considered or challenged. Many will have been useful back then, but have no value now, indeed they limit the person. 'Don't talk to strangers' may be valuable advice for a toddler, but makes little sense when as an adult the person goes to a networking event and they don't know anyone. Many people have things they 'can't' do, such as 'I can't speak in public' or 'I can't dance'. These, too, are a kind of generalization and such beliefs can impose significant constraints. Other people are driven. There are things they 'must' do, such as earning a certain salary or getting to the top of the ladder. Once again, reviewing the beliefs that underpin such statements can open up new, and liberating, choices.

UNIVERSAL QUANTIFIERS

Violation:	A broad generalization using words such as 'all', 'every', 'never', 'everybody', 'always'.
Objective:	To check for counter-examples.
Example:	'He's never on time.'
Response:	'Never?'/'Not even once?'

MODAL OPERATORS OF NECESSITY AND POSSIBILITY

Violation:	Statements that limit behaviour, using words such as 'can', 'can't', 'should', 'must', 'ought', 'necessary'.
Objective:	To identify the thinking behind the statement.
Example:	'I must go to the gym three times a week.' (necessity)
Response:	'What would happen if you didn't go?'
Example:	'I can't delegate.' (possibility)
Response:	'What stops you?'/'What would happen if you did?'

PRESUPPOSITIONS

Violation:	Something is implicitly required to make sense of the statement.
Objective:	To clarify the processes presupposed in the statement.
Example:	'If they cared for me they'd behave differently.'
Response:	'How do you know they don't care for you?'

Putting it all together

When you first start working with the Meta Model it can be a challenge tracking all 12 possible violations, and you may find it easier to focus on just one or two at a time. When you've got the hang of them you can do another couple. A good way to practise is by listening to the radio, where there's no visual element to distract you, and you can have this book to hand if you find it helpful. Interviews with politicians often provide lots of good material, especially when they're trying to hide something. When you hear them say something bland like 'Things are getting better', you might find yourself shouting, 'Which things specifically are getting better than what?' Over time you'll develop the ability to monitor all the violations at once.

When using the Meta Model in real-life interactions, such as during an interview, meeting or coaching session, you can't challenge every violation. You'd end up asking dozens, maybe hundreds of questions, many of them leading to irrelevant, unimportant information. All things being equal, the best order in which to challenge violations is distortions first, followed by generalizations and then deletions. Most importantly, though, questions should be oriented around the outcome for the interaction. If, for instance, you're speaking to someone who wants to gain clarity about which of three courses of action to follow, the Meta Model questions you'd ask will support that goal. If you're working as a therapist with a person who has a problem with anger, the tack you take may be very different.

One useful approach, suggested by L. Michael Hall in his book *The Secrets of Magic*, is to ask: 'If I made a mental videotape from just these words, would I have a clear and detailed movie or would I find vague and unfocused areas?'

Such a model will help guide you towards what to ask to fill in the gaps. Here's a practical example. A member of your team or a colleague says to you: 'I can't get that project completed by Monday. There's never enough time. No one wants to help. They could make my life so much easier. This means I'm in big trouble.'

What violations are there? And what questions would you ask? Take a moment to reflect.

Well, there's quite a lot to go at. 'I can't' is a modal operator of possibility that could usefully be challenged. The 'never' in the second sentence is a universal quantifier. Underlying 'No one wants to help' is some mind reading, and the 'No one' and 'They' suffer from a lack of referential index. 'They could make my life' suggests cause and effect and the 'easier' involves a comparative deletion. However the final sentence, 'This means I'm in big trouble' – a complex equivalence – is probably a good place to start working with this person.

Exercise

To give some practice, here are a number of statements with Meta Model violations. What are they, and what challenge would you make in each case?

1 *They should be seen and not heard.*
2 *Everyone's against me.*
3 *We must all pull together.*
4 *She is driving me up the wall.*
5 *You don't care about me.*
6 *I have to achieve success.*
7 *She's smarter.*
8 *They want to see me fail.*

9 *Time and tide wait for no man.*
10 *He's late again, he's got no respect.*

Answers

1 *Lack of referential index – the noun object 'they' isn't specified. This is also the case in a number of the other examples – who are 'they'?*
Modal operator of necessity – what would happen if they were seen and heard? Lost performative – who says?
2 *Mind read – how do you know people are against you? Universal quantifier – everyone?*
3 *Modal operator of necessity – what would happen if we didn't pull together?*
4 *Cause and effect – how, specifically, is she driving you up the wall?*
5 *Mind read – how do you know I don't care?*
6 *Modal operator of necessity – what would happen if you weren't succeeding? 'Success' in this example is also a nominalization – what's important to you about succeeding?*
7 *Comparative deletion – Smarter than who?*
8 *Mind reading – how do you know they think that?*
9 *Universal quantifier – time and tide never wait? Lost performative – who says?*
10 *Complex equivalence and nominalization of 'respect' – how does him being late mean he's not respecting you?*

Challenging with rapport

Great care needs to be taken when using the Meta Model. It's all too easy to be over-zealous in your questioning so it comes across as interrogation. This sometimes happens when people go home after studying the Meta Model on an NLP Practitioner course and start using it on everyone they meet.

- *A friend says, 'He forgot my birthday, he doesn't care about me', and their response is 'How specifically does him forgetting your birthday mean he doesn't care about you?'*
- *Or they're chatting to a colleague who says, 'I can't relax' to which they reply, 'what would happen if you did?'*
- *And in the middle of a loving conversation a partner or spouse says, 'I'll always love you', and their response is 'Always?'*

It may sound like a joke, but it really does happen. But normally only once or twice. The shocked reaction of those who have been subjected to the Meta Model normally discourages people from using it so thoughtlessly. If you don't want to come across as confrontational, aggressive and intimidating, think carefully how you phrase your questions, and make sure you have plenty of rapport first. And be clear what your motives are. If your aim is to show the other person they're not expressing themself clearly or they're not making sense, you might want to think again unless they've asked you to help them in that way.

Of course, there will be times when you genuinely don't understand what someone is saying, or you need more information. In those situations the Meta Model challenges are perfect, providing you ask them in a spirit of curiosity, respect and caring. Preface your questions with something along the lines of, *'I'm a bit confused*, how specifically...', *'I'm curious*, what does...', *'Just so I understand*, how can...' and they'll be received more easily.

And while the Meta Model can be used in a structured way, by asking one question in sequence after another, the approach is normally informal, so much so that people don't register any 'technique' or pattern at all, just a conversation in which they get to clarify their thoughts.

Recognizing your own violations

The Meta Model, then, is a great way of getting quality information from people in everyday life, and a powerful, precision tool if you are in a role that involves helping others, such as a trainer, coach, therapist or counsellor. But it's not just for interpersonal use, you can also apply this to yourself with considerable benefit.

Recognizing your own deletions, distortions and generalizations will enable you to be a more effective communicator. By using language with precision you'll be able to express yourself and your thoughts and feelings with great clarity, and thereby increase your influence.

But there's more to it than that. The language you use reflects your internal representation – what's in your mind – and if that language is confused and unspecific, that means your thoughts are too. The good news is that working on your linguistic skills will change the way you code your experience, improving the clarity of your thoughts.

Managing your internal dialogue

It's not just the things you say to other people that matters. Of at least equal and arguably greater importance is what you say to yourself – your internal dialogue. Many of us have a voice in our head that comments on what's going on or even tells us what to do. It's extremely powerful because it operates insidiously, much of the time out of conscious awareness. As you become aware of it, and what it says to you, you might notice a number of Meta Model violations that you could usefully challenge.

Summary

The Meta Model is at the heart of NLP, and although many other models and processes have been developed over the years it remains one of the most powerful and versatile tools available. When you want to elicit high quality information it's absolutely perfect – and an essential part of everything from creating well-formed outcomes to helping people think more effectively.

TEN KEY POINTS TO REMEMBER

1 *The Meta Model was developed by Richard Bandler and John Grinder when they modelled the language patterns used by Virginia Satir and Fritz Perls.*

2 *Surface structure is what we actually say and is a greatly reduced version of our actual experience. Deep structure represents what we seek to communicate – our complete internal representation, mental images, sounds and feelings stored at the neurological, unconscious level.*

3 *It's impossible for us to deal with every stimulus around so we filter out much of the data through deletion, distortion and generalization.*

4 *There are 12 Meta Model distinctions, and a series of 'challenges' that recover information lost in the transformation between deep to surface structure.*

5 *There are four main ways in which we delete information in the progression from deep structure to surface structure: simple deletion, comparative deletion, lack of referential index, and unspecified verbs.*

6 *We tend to think our perspective on the world is accurate when in fact it's distorted. There are five ways we distort information: cause and effect, mind reading, complex equivalence, lost performatives and nominalizations.*

7 *Generalization takes the form of: universal qualifiers, modal operators of necessity and possibility, and presuppositions.*

8 *When you're learning to listen out for the 12 violations, it's easier to focus on a few at first. Over time you'll find it becomes second nature to identify them.*

9 *If you were to challenge every violation people make you would need to ask endless questions. To be effective you have to be selective and establish rapport.*

10 *Recognizing your own violations will help you to become a more effective communicator.*

14

....

Frames, framing, reframing and parts

In this chapter you will learn:
- *why frames are important within NLP*
- *the value of 'reframing' and know when to use it*
- *about 'parts' and discover how they can be reframed to bring about change*

The meaning of any experience in life depends upon the frame we put around it.

Anthony Robbins, *Unlimited Power*

Understanding frames

In NLP the word 'frame' is used to describe and define the boundaries or constraints of an event or an experience. A frame is another way in which we filter our perceptions of the world based on our internal representation of it. It's a kind of mental template. Like other filters, frames generally operate outside of conscious awareness – we have habitual, automatic ways of thinking about things that derive mainly from the beliefs we hold.

The way in which we frame something determines to a large degree the meaning we attach to it. A critical comment from a stranger is likely to affect us less than one from a boss or spouse, while our reaction to an ornament getting smashed may depend on how precious or valuable it is to us.

In everyday language we often speak about time frames as well. Having a limited time frame in which to complete a task is generally more stressful than a longer time frame but is more likely to focus attention and motivation on getting it done.

However, as we'll see later in this chapter, when the frame changes the meaning changes with it and 'reframing', as it is called, is an easy yet powerful way of helping people break free from limiting beliefs.

While there are many different types of frame, NLP has identified a number to which it ascribes particular importance. We have already discussed some without them having been mentioned as such. We will now describe them, with the addition of some others, to produce a coherent model.

OUTCOME FRAME

An important frame you've already been introduced to is the outcome frame. One of the requirements of the well-formedness conditions for outcomes is that they're framed positively, with people describing what they do want rather than what they don't want. Formulating an outcome frame, rather than a problem frame, focuses attention on achieving solutions rather than learning more about what's not working at the moment.

ECOLOGY FRAME

We've also discussed the ecology frame on a number of occasions. An ecology check features in virtually every NLP pattern and process, and is crucial in assessing what effect any change will have on all of the systems to which the person belongs, such as family, co-workers and friends. Another aspect of the ecology frame is that account is taken of the positive intention behind the current behaviour and the gains the person is getting from what they are currently doing.

EVIDENCE FRAME

Another frame that you are probably familiar with by now is the evidence frame. As well as being a crucial element in the conditions for well-formed outcomes, it's an integral part of the whole NLP approach. The aim is to ensure that everything is grounded in reality by using a sensory-specific evidence procedure wherever possible. This means stating in clear and unambiguous detail what will be seen, heard and felt when an outcome has been achieved.

AS-IF FRAME

The as-if frame enables people to enrich their perception of what's possible for them. By pretending – acting 'as if' – they've already achieved their outcome or already have the resources required they can step outside their beliefs about themselves and allow their imagination full reign. By doing so they often discover that what seemed out of reach can be realized after all. Someone who has a project to complete, but isn't sure how to carry it out, might go into the future to a time when they've done it and look back at the steps that got them there. Or someone who considers themself to be shy could pretend they're confident, which will stimulate the neurology that supports that goal. In many NLP processes the as-if frame takes the form of a visualization and, as we'll see in Chapter 16, acting as-if is one of the first steps in modelling someone else's behaviour.

CONTRAST FRAME

One of the things that NLP seeks to do is find 'the difference that makes the difference' and one of the ways it does that is through the contrast frame. When considering a particular course of action, for instance, asking 'How is this different from the current situation?' will provide additional information through a contrastive perspective. Another option is to ask 'What's the alternative?', which leads to the creation of other choices, which can then be evaluated.

AGREEMENT FRAME

In situations where there is a disagreement, or there are differing points of view, and a resolution is sought, the agreement frame can be a valuable resource. What often happens in meetings and negotiations is that the various parties get locked into discussing or even arguing about the areas where they are in conflict. This can be a futile waste of time. A better approach is to find points of agreement and build from there. So a couple struggling to decide where to go on holiday might first agree that they *do* want to go on holiday, that they want to go somewhere that's *sunny*, and that they want to go for *two weeks*. 'Chunking up' to a higher level – a 'meta-outcome' in NLP terms – can help further. They may both want the holiday to be relaxing, and options can then be explored that give them both what they want.

BACKTRACK FRAME

The backtrack frame is extremely useful in areas such as coaching and training, but also has value when it comes to chairing a meeting or facilitating a discussion. It involves repeating back to someone what they've just said, as far as possible using their exact words, phrasing, rhythm and tonality. It's not a summary, which usually distorts what someone means. The aim is first and foremost to check understanding – 'what you said was...' – but it also enhances rapport. To be able to backtrack effectively you obviously need to listen carefully to what others are saying.

Reframing

By nature people seek to make sense of the world. They attribute meaning to everything they encounter and every experience they have. Initially, as we are growing up, the frames we use are fluid but as we get older they start to become fixed. And by the time most of us are adults we have developed habitual ways of thinking about things. Some of these frames – viewpoints and perspectives that arise from beliefs we have about the world and our place in it – serve us well, allowing us to achieve our outcomes and live our lives to the full. But not always. Sometimes the frames we have developed limit us, and prevent us from hazving what we want.

We might believe, for instance, that only people who have achieved a certain level of education can be successful. In fact, we don't even believe such things, we come to accept them as true.

But nothing is intrinsically good or bad, positive or negative. Events or experiences don't, of themselves, have any meaning whatsoever, they have only the meaning we give to them. That meaning is determined to a large degree by the frame in which we perceive it. When the frame changes so does the meaning, and our response to it – the way we feel and how we act.

In NLP, this is called reframing, an important technique you can use with yourself and with others to free them from the shackles of rigid thinking and to have more choice.

A story from the introduction of *Reframing*, one of the classic NLP books, illustrates amusingly how this works.

A very old Chinese Taoist story describes a farmer in a poor country village. He was considered very well-to-do because he owned a horse which he used for ploughing and for transportation. One day his horse ran away. All his neighbours exclaimed how terrible this was, but the farmer simply said 'Maybe'. A few days later the horse returned and brought two wild horses with it. The neighbours all rejoiced at his good fortune, but the farmer just said, 'Maybe'. The next day the farmer's son tried to ride one of the wild horses; the horse threw him and broke his leg. The neighbours all offered their sympathy for his misfortune, but the farmer again said 'Maybe'. The next week conscription officers came to the village to take young men for the army. They rejected

the farmer's son because of his broken leg. When the neighbours told him how lucky he was, the farmer replied 'Maybe'.

At its simplest, reframing involves seeing things from a different perspective, in another light, from an alternative point of view. Reframing isn't something that NLP invented. It's something that most of us do on occasion, for example, seeing the funny side when it rains just after we've hung the washing out to dry, or looking back and realizing that being made redundant had actually been a good thing since it opened up new avenues.

But reframing can be used consciously and deliberately, making it extremely valuable in everything from coaching and other aspects of business to therapy and personal development. By asking a question or making a comment that invites someone to see things from a different perspective, the way they feel about it can be changed in a moment.

One thing that's important to understand is that reframing isn't about taking a Pollyanna approach where everything is wonderful. The aim is to achieve a more realistic perspective on reality. Reframes have to make at least as much sense to people as the way they thought about things before, and they have to match their view of reality. If the reframes don't ring true for them they will be ineffective and may even be considered rude or patronizing.

In NLP, a distinction is made between two different types of reframing – context reframing and meaning reframing.

Insight

For me (Amanda) reframing is a great way of turning negative thoughts into positive ones. This doesn't mean being unrealistic or ignoring potential problems. In fact it is often the best method for finding practical solutions that work. By changing the meaning you attach to something you gain a new perspective.

MEANING REFRAME (CONTENT REFRAME)

Meaning reframing, also sometimes called content reframing, is essentially what we've been discussing so far. There's nothing wrong with the stimulus – what actually happens – it's the response that's the problem. So you're not looking to change the event or behaviour, only the meaning that's attributed to it.

Meaning reframing is useful where, in Meta-Model terms, there is a cause-and-effect or complex equivalence relationship, such as 'I get frustrated when I have to wait'.

Humour is a great, natural way of content reframing. Jokes usually start with a particular frame and end with some kind of twist in the tale, which is really a reframe. Advertising is full of reframing. Using a certain brand of aftershave or perfume is supposed to mean the wearer is sexy or attractive. Politics arguably provides the best example of all. Politicians continually reframe the topics they debate in order to win support for their argument. Unemployment figures down on the previous month, for instance, can be presented as a healthy sign for the future or an insignificant reduction in relation to the large number of people who are still without a job.

CONTEXT REFRAME

The starting point in context reframing is the presupposition that every behaviour is useful and appropriate in some context. Pushing someone over will get you shunned by polite society and could save your life if you're attacked in the street. Procrastination may mean you'll never write that best seller, but what if you put off smoking a cigarette when you're trying to give up?

The secret to context reframing is to ask questions along the lines of 'When would this behaviour be valuable?' Asking this question allows the person to recognize that what they're doing is simply a behaviour. They can then go on to explore the context.

RECOGNIZING THE DIFFERENCE

It can be tricky at first recognizing the difference between context and meaning reframing, because the distinction is rather subtle, so here's a simple summary:

▶ *Identifying* where or in what situation *a behaviour or event would be useful is context reframing.*
▶ *Attributing a* specific meaning *to a behaviour or event is* meaning *reframing.*

Sleight of Mouth patterns

While it's useful to understand the difference between context and meaning reframing, in practice what's important is to be able to use them effectively. To make that easier, in 1980 Robert Dilts formulated what he calls Sleight of Mouth patterns, 14 types of verbal reframe that can be used conversationally to influence beliefs and the mental maps from which those beliefs arise. The patterns derive from modelling the language patterns of such diverse individuals as Jesus, Abraham Lincoln and Mahatma Gandhi, and together form a coherent set of questions and challenges similar to the Meta Model. You can use them in any situation where the person experiences a criterial equivalence or cause and effect relationship involving a belief, such as 'Money's hard to come by, so I have to work hard'.

We don't have space to discuss the patterns in depth but to give you a flavour we've listed a sample response for each of the categories. The examples given are intended to illustrate how each pattern can be used rather than how they should be used. Some are quite challenging, which means it's important to use an appropriate voice tone and to maintain rapport. Some patterns might seem familiar, reflecting as they do the NLP presuppositions and concepts such as Meta Programs. If you would like to learn more about conversational reframing, check out the book *Sleight of Mouth* by Robert Dilts.

Here are some examples of different perspectives or Sleight of Mouth reframes on the following:

'Money's hard to come by, so I have to work hard.'

1 *Intention – I'm doing the best I can to stay solvent.*
2 *Redefine – Money's a valuable commodity that's worth putting some effort into attaining.*
3 *Consequence – If you continue to work hard you may be left with just money.*
4 *Chunk down – What hard work do you have to do?*
5 *Chunk up – You need to earn money in this day and age.*
6 *Counter-example – My friend makes his money with minimal effort.*
7 *Analogy – Nothing worth having comes easy.*
8 *Apply to self – It must be hard work holding on to that belief.*
9 *Another outcome – The issue isn't whether you have to work hard, it's whether the return is worth it.*
10 *Hierarchy of criteria – Don't you think it's more important to have time with the family than earn a bit more money?*
11 *Change frame size – It may seem hard work now, but it will make things easier in years to come.*
12 *Meta frame – You only believe you have to work hard because you haven't found a better way of earning money.*
13 *Model of the world – It may seem like hard work in your model of the world but to some people work is fun.*
14 *Reality strategy – How do you know that money is hard to come by?*

Working with parts

Using frames and reframing means, to a large degree, working with 'parts'. In the NLP model we all consist of a multitude of sub-personalities or parts that were created to carry out a particular purpose. That is, they have a positive intention. Sometimes, however, parts get disconnected from the context in which they were intended to operate, or even 'forget' what they were trying to do in the first place. Others continue to run even when the reason for their existence has long since passed, becoming a nuisance in the process.

Many people, for example, start to smoke around the age of 13, to feel more grown up and to impress their friends. Yet many years later the part responsible is still active, which is one of the reasons why it can be difficult to give up smoking.

> **A part is not just a temporary emotional state or habitual thought patterns. It's a discreet and autonomous mental system that has an idiosyncratic range of emotion, style of expression and set of abilities, intentions and functions.**
>
> Richard Schwartz

You may find it useful to think of a part as a computer program that was installed at a particular time for a good reason but then continues to run when it's no longer needed. And sometimes programs, or parts, conflict. Part of you may want to work, another part play. Happily, using NLP, such programs can be updated or uninstalled if necessary or where parts are in conflict they can be organized in such a way that they operate in harmony rather than antagonism.

It's also good to remember that 'parts' is just a useful way of thinking about how we organize our internal experience. We don't actually have parts inside us.

Six-step reframing

One of NLP's best-known techniques, and one of the first patterns to be developed by John Grinder in 1976, is called 'six-step reframing'. It's used when someone is unhappy with an aspect of their behaviour which they'd like to change. This could be a habit such as biting their nails; some kind of impulse, such as butting in when someone else is talking during a meeting; or even a physical symptom, such as a chronic headache.

As you might imagine from the name, the pattern consists of six steps, and these need to be carried out strictly in sequence. The 'reframing' element involves separating the problematic behaviour from its positive intention, so that actions which on the surface appear to be negative are understood to have been trying to achieve something for the person. It's a context reframe, because although the behaviour would be appropriate in other situations, it's not producing the desired outcome here. Different ways of satisfying the positive intention are then generated, which don't have the undesirable effects of the original behaviour.

Six-step reframing is an extremely powerful and effective pattern, and one which needs to be used carefully. You can do it with yourself or with other people. The version here is for personal use.

Steps

1 *Allow yourself to relax fully and turn your attention inwards, thinking only about the behaviour you want to change.*
2 *Establish communication with the 'part' that's responsible for the behaviour by asking, in your mind, 'Please give me a signal if you are willing to communicate with me'. Be aware of anything that changes, such as internal sounds, images or feelings. If you get what may be a signal, but it's weak, invite the part to 'Please make the signal stronger if the answer is yes.' Thank the part for even the smallest response. If you have ignored a part for some time it may need some coaxing. (If you receive no signal after a number of times of asking, you may have to consider another approach to the problem.)*
3 *When you have a clear, unambiguous signal, the next step is to discover the positive intention behind the problematic behaviour. Ask 'What is it you are trying to do for me or communicate to me that's positive by means of this behaviour?' You may hear a voice in your head or simply 'know' the answer. Don't try to figure out consciously what*

it might be, just allow it to emerge. If the answer seems to be negatively stated, first thank the part and then simply ask again, 'What is your positive purpose?'

4 *Once you know what that purpose is, say 'Please go now to your creative part and ask it to come up with three new ways to satisfy the positive intention'. It may produce a symbol, sound or some other response that doesn't make much sense to your conscious mind. Just go with what ever comes up. Some people don't think of themselves as being creative and are surprised when they discover this part. Putting a limit of three on your request gives you a real choice and also prevents your creative part from continuing to supply you with an endless number of useful suggestions. It really is that creative!*

5 *Once you have those three ways, ask the part responsible for the problematic behaviour to confirm that it accepts the alternative choice(s) by using the same signal as before. Sometimes a particular choice is not acceptable, and you need to go back and generate more choices.*

6 *Finally, carry out an ecology check by asking whether any other parts object to these new choices being implemented. If you do find there are ecological concerns, you need to go back to Step 2 and repeat the process, making contact with that part and discovering its positive intention, etc.*

Insight

Six-step reframing is a technique I (Steve) use in many of my therapy sessions. Uncovering the positive intention behind a behaviour and finding an alternative that doesn't have the undesired side effect is one of the surest ways of eliminating many problems.

Negotiating between parts

Sometimes it's not a single part that's the problem, but two that are in conflict with each other. One part may want to get some work done and another sit and watch TV. One part may want to get married and settle down and another enjoy the freedom of being single. Both parts have a positive intention, but the outcome is often inner turmoil, with the parts effectively sabotaging each other.

In NLP there's a parts negotiation process that can solve the problem. It involves identifying the two parts, discovering their positive intentions, and finding a way of agreeing a truce between them. You can use this pattern on yourself or with other people.

Steps

1 *Identify the parts that are in conflict and separate them out spatially, perhaps placing one in each hand. It can be useful to give each part a name.*
2 *Ask each part in turn what its positive intention is, and what its meta-outcome is for the whole person. The information should be as sensory specific as possible, i.e. what someone would see when the outcome was achieved.*
3 *Get the parts to engage in a dialogue, ensuring that each part understands the other. The aim is to establish an outcome for the whole person to which they can both agree. This may involve chunking up a number of times to a higher level outcome.*
4 *Get each part to recognize some value in the other, however small, and appreciate its contribution. Then get each part to agree to at least some of what the other wants. If the parts have a long history of conflict, this may be as much as can be achieved initially. Sometimes you may be able to strike a deal that the parts will stop fighting and work together for a period of time.*
5 *Establish that both parts are satisfied with the outcome, and then carry out an ecology check by making sure that every other part is happy as well.*

NLP in action

- ► Formulate a number of statements and have a go at reframing them.
- ► Look for opportunities to make use of some NLP frames, such as the backtrack and agreement frames.
- ► Choose one or two sleight of mouth patterns at a time and make use of them in meetings and conversations.
- ► Use six-step reframing on some kind of problem with yourself.
- ► The next time you experience inner conflict use the parts negotiation.

TEN KEY POINTS TO REMEMBER

1 *In NLP a frame is defined as a boundary or constraint on an event or experience.*

2 *An outcome frame focuses on the positive, and what you do want, whereas a problem frame concentrates on what's not working.*

3 *An ecology frame assesses the effect a change will have on all the systems to which a person belongs, and an evidence frame ensures things are stated in sensory-specific detail.*

4 *The 'as-if' frame allows you to act as if you have already achieved your outcome.*

5 *NLP seeks to find 'the difference that makes the difference' and the contrast frame helps to achieve that. It allows you to consider how, for example, a planned course of action is different from the current situation.*

6 *An agreement frame allows you to focus on where two or more people agree, and build from there rather than placing energy and effort into areas of conflict.*

7 *The backtrack frame is where someone repeats back what another person has just said using the exact words and tone with a view to checking understanding and enhancing rapport.*

8 *Reframing involves seeing things in a new light or from an alternative viewpoint. The aim is to change the meaning that's attributed to the event or behaviour.*

9 *Robert Dilts developed 14 types of verbal reframe known as Sleight of Mouth patterns.*

10 *In the NLP model, we consist of a multitude of sub-personalities or parts. A part is like a computer program and sometimes parts continue to run when no longer needed or conflict with other parts.*

15

···

Other key NLP techniques

In this chapter you will learn:
- *about different types of NLP patterns and techniques*
- *how and when to use the New Behaviour Generator, Fast Phobia Cure and the S.C.O.R.E. Model*

NLP is famous for its amazingly fast, effective and safe techniques for curing phobias, improving confidence, and dealing with trauma and a host of other issues. Many of these patterns originated as simpler and quicker ways of carrying out therapy, and arose out of modelling. To demonstrate the diversity and flexibility of NLP in action we're discussing three different types of techniques in this chapter.

New Behaviour Generator

Are there situations where you would like to behave differently? Perhaps there's something you'd like to do but don't know how. Maybe you want to be more confident in a social setting. Or motivated to go to the gym. If so, the New Behaviour Generator holds the key to success. As the name indicates, it's a process that allows you to generate new behaviours – or, in NLP-speak, install a new strategy, program or part (depending on how you prefer to think of it) with a particular function.

When you use it you systematically create an internal sensory-specific representation of the behaviour you want. The reason it works so well is that our unconscious minds can't tell the difference between what happens and what we imagine because they share the same neurology. In practice it's a bit like a dress rehearsal. Using an 'as if' frame you create a new mental map of the behaviour you want. You try the new 'you' on for size and check kinaesthetically to find out if anything's missing or needs to be added. If there is you make a few adjustments. It really is that simple. Try it out for yourself using the process outlined below.

Steps

1 *Identify a behaviour you would like to have, and be clear what the outcome of having it would be for you.*

2 *See yourself, either in your mind's eye or as if you are standing in front of yourself, in the future carrying out the desired behaviour as you would like to.*

3 *Remaining dissociated – like a movie director – make whatever changes seem necessary to the action and soundtrack, so that the 'other' you performs the new behaviour easily and effortlessly. Continue making adjustments to your imagined scenario until you are totally happy. Be aware as you do so of the reactions of other people to the changes you've made.*

4 *In your imagination, step into that other you and, in an associated state, experience doing the new behaviour – seeing, hearing and feeling what it's like.*

5 *Carry out an ecology check to make sure that the new behaviour fits with your values and your sense of self.*

6 *If anything's not as it should be, go back to being the movie director and make whatever changes are necessary before stepping back into yourself.*

7 *Think of at least one future occasion when you will want to use the new behaviour, and imagine yourself performing in that situation.*

If you use this technique regularly you'll find it becomes almost second nature – you could find yourself using it on a daily basis. One way of getting it 'into the muscle' is to carry out a personal review at the end of each day. Ask yourself what went well and what didn't go as well as you would have liked. For the things that could have been better use the New Behaviour Generator. It's a powerful way of propelling yourself forward to where you want to be.

Fast Phobia Cure

based on the work of Richard Bandler

Spiders, snakes, heights, confined spaces, flying, thunderstorms or even public speaking – everyone knows someone who has a phobia. Maybe you're a sufferer yourself. *The Collins English Dictionary* defines a phobia as an 'abnormal, intense and irrational fear of a given situation, organism or object'. Typical symptoms include dizziness, heart palpitations and a sense of terror. When the stimulus appears – sometimes it only needs to be thought of – the person responds automatically with a strong physical reaction. Some phobias can be hard to live with, and many limit people in what they can do.

There are various schools of opinion on how phobias are formed but NLP has no real interest in causes. The main focus of NLP therapy is on how problems are handled in the present. The event itself has long since passed into the mists of time, so it must be the way the person is representing it internally that's causing the difficulty. When they're exposed to whatever makes them phobic they associate back to a picture they have of the memory, and experience all of the emotion again. It's a V–K circuit (see Chapter 18).

When you're dissociated, though, and looking at events as an observer, you can't have the bad feelings. And that's the principle at the heart of the Fast Phobia Cure, which uses double-dissociation to distance people from the emotions they felt originally. Although it's called a 'phobia cure', the pattern can also be used with any trauma or fear where the response to a stimulus is instantaneous. But it's not suitable for situations where anxiety or dread builds up over a period of time.

Steps

This is a powerful technique, and it's important to follow all of the steps in the order shown.

1 *Imagine you're in a cinema. Choose a seat somewhere towards the back while you wait for the film to start. See yourself up on the screen in a still black and white picture just before the original phobic incident took place, or if you can't remember, one of the most intense episodes you ever had ...*

2 *Now float back inside the projection room. (If you are phobic about heights, just walk there.) You are now in a safe, secure observer position and able to see yourself sitting in your seat in the cinema looking relaxed.*

3 *Remaining in the projection booth, continue to watch yourself as you allow a black and white film of the phobic incident to run on the screen. When it reaches the end, stop the film and turn it into a still picture.*

4 *Now leave the projection room and step into the still picture on the screen. Change the picture to colour and then run the film backwards as fast as possible – 1 to 2 seconds – experiencing it from inside. Repeat this process several times.*

5 *Try to access the phobic state by thinking about the stimulus. You should now have no trouble thinking about it. If some discomfort remains, do the process once again.*

Insight

Imagine spending most of your life afraid of heights – to the extent that you can't bring yourself to stand by a window in a high rise building of only three floors or loving the sea and not being able to bring yourself to step anywhere near a cliff top. That was true for me (Amanda) before I came across the Fast Phobia Cure. Since then I've had two life changing experiences. The first was the serene splendour of floating along peacefully on a balmy summer evening in a hot air balloon. The second was the exhilaration of a tandem sky dive over beautiful mountains and lakes in Queenstown, New Zealand. Many people prefer to hang on to their familiar phobias and end up missing out on some of the best things that life has to offer. Make sure that isn't true of you.

S.C.O.R.E. model

As you become more skilled at using NLP, the structures of the various patterns and techniques can start to feel like a straitjacket, with little room for manoeuvre. That's why the S.C.O.R.E. model was developed by Robert Dilts and Todd Epstein. Whereas the standard NLP model is a linear way to solve problems, moving from present state to desired state, S.C.O.R.E. is a much more fluid, intuitive approach. Instead of following a set procedure you can start from a number of different places depending on the context of the problem and how the person presents the issue. There are five elements that need to be considered in any therapeutic intervention, and they are symptoms, causes, outcomes, resources and effects, which make up the acronym.

▶ **Symptoms:** *As the name implies, these are the surface issues that indicate there's an issue or problem to resolve. The person, for instance, might say, 'I can't get on with my boss'. This is part of the present state.*
▶ **Causes:** *These underpin and trigger the symptoms. They are not always obvious at first. They are also part of the present state.*
▶ **Outcomes:** *This is the desired state. It's the new behaviours that replace the current ones.*
▶ **Resources:** *These are the tools and techniques we use to remove the causes. Almost any NLP technique can be employed such as anchoring, six-step reframing and change personal history.*
▶ **Effects:** *These are the longer term consequences or result of achieving the outcome, and part of the desired state.*

One of the ways you can use S.C.O.R.E. is to mark out areas of the room, one for each element. The simplest way is to use five pieces of paper with an element written on each one, e.g. symptoms.

The basic questions you ask are as follows:

▶ *What is the symptom?*
▶ *What is the cause?*

- *What outcome do you want?*
- *What would be the effect of achieving that outcome?*
- *What resource(s) would help you deal with the cause?*
- *What resource(s) would aid you in achieving the outcome?*

Before you ask a question get the person to move to the relevant area of the room. These areas act as spatial anchors. By doing this you separate out each part of the process, which helps the person to gain more clarity on their situation. You don't need to ask the questions in a set sequence. It's more a question of calibrating and listening to the person's response to each question. This will be your guide to where to go next. Often the person will instinctively know what area to explore once they are used to it.

The whole point is for the person you're working with to achieve their outcome. Along the way you can use all the NLP tools you have available to help them move towards their desired outcome.

NLP in action

- *If you want to become expert in using these techniques the best way is to practise whenever you get the chance.*
- *Experiment with the S.C.O.R.E. model with everyday problems you come across.*

TEN KEY POINTS TO REMEMBER

1 *NLP is famous for its amazing fast and effective techniques.*

2 *The New Behaviour Generator, as the name suggests, allows you to generate new ways of behaving.*

3 *This technique uses mental rehearsal – or visualization – to program the behaviour you want.*

4 *Visualization is effective because our unconscious minds can't tell the difference between what happens and what we imagine because it uses the same neurology.*

5 *The NLP Fast Phobia Cure enables many phobias to be cured in as little as five minutes.*

6 *The principle behind NLP's Fast Phobia Cure is that when you are double-dissociated from an event you can't have the bad feelings you would normally get.*

7 *This technique can also be used for trauma and fear providing the response to the stimulus is instant.*

8 *The S.C.O.R.E. model developed by Robert Dilts and Todd Epstein provides a fluid approach to resolving problems using NLP.*

9 *S.C.O.R.E. stands for Symptoms, Causes, Outcomes Resources and Effects.*

10 *You can use other NLP techniques at any stage when working through the S.C.O.R.E. model with someone.*

16

....

Modelling

In this chapter you will learn:
- *about modelling excellence in others*
- *how to model*
- *about implicit and explicit modelling*
- *applications of NLP modelling*

Modelling is the pathway to excellence.

Anthony Robbins

What would it be like if you could play the guitar like Eric Clapton or golf like Tiger Woods? Imagine being able to have any skill you want – and learning it quickly and easily, without having to slog away for years or waste time by trial and error. And what would it be worth if you could discover how the top performers in your company achieve their success, then replicate it? How would it be if your best salesperson, manager, negotiator, etc., could act as a template for the rest of the team, reproducing 'best practice' throughout the organization?

If that sounds like a pipe dream to you, think again. Right from the very beginning, with the studies Richard Bandler and John Grinder carried out on Perls, Satir, Erickson and others, the principle purpose of NLP has been the modelling of human excellence. And it has been demonstrated time and again that once you understand the thinking patterns and behaviours used by the most brilliant and talented in any field, you can learn to do what they can do.

Modelling has given birth to many fascinating and powerful techniques and processes, and a significant proportion of the major models, including the Meta Model and the Milton Model. These are often emphasized in books and on courses, with the result that some people mistakenly think of them as being NLP, when in fact, as John Grinder and Carmen Bostic St Clair argue passionately in *Whispering in the Wind*, modelling itself remains at the heart of NLP.

Understanding modelling

You may recall that one of the presuppositions we discussed way back in Chapter 2 is that, 'If one person can do something, anyone can learn to do it'. And although there are obviously exceptions – you may not have the build for a world champion weight lifter – it's essentially true. You may also recall another presupposition: 'Experience has a structure'. Put both presuppositions together and you have the rationale for modelling: once the structure that makes up the internal experience of an expert has been captured and encoded, it can be transferred to others, allowing them to achieve the same results. To be able to do this we have to break down what the person does into small enough chunks so we understand the deeper structure underlying their behaviour clearly enough to create a model that can then be explained to others.

Because modelling provides a short-cut to excellence there are many ways it can be applied. It's not about looking for someone who's superhuman, but it is about finding people who are skilled in a particular area – an athlete is not necessarily going to shine at mathematics or selling. There are many examples where modelling excellence has been applied in therapeutic work, sport, selling, negotiation, relationships, leadership, education, families and organizational development.

There are so many great role models around for anything you might want to excel at. Yet many of us appear to 'ignore' these rich, valuable, resources even when our attention is drawn to them and we know what can be achieved through modelling. When we run our Speak First courses we look at what role models such as Barack Obama do when presenting that makes them so successful – and learn how to do the same.

Natural modelling

People are natural modellers. From the moment we were born we started copying others, developing a multitude of skills and capabilities along the way. Somehow we internalize the rules of grammar and syntax simply by listening to our parents and siblings talk. In the playground and at home we watched others and imitated their behaviours. As adults wanting to learn a new skill such as playing a musical instrument, we look carefully at other people and do the same. NLP modelling is more purposeful and structured than natural modelling, which can be haphazard, and as a result produces accurate and reliable results.

Simple and complex modelling

The purpose of NLP modelling is, then, to be able to do something as well as an expert and to be able to teach others to do it as well.

The process by which the modelling is carried out will depend to a large degree upon what is being modelled. If it's something simple, with a largely behavioural element, it may be possible to model it in just a short while, simply by watching and matching. You may never have thrown a ball up against a wall, let it bounce and then caught it. But if you watched someone do it for a while and then had a go yourself, it wouldn't take long before you got the hang of it. It's the same with simple cognitive tasks: most people find it easy to assimilate a new way of remembering names, for instance, in just a few minutes.

However, more complex behavioural and cognitive tasks, which have a greater number of steps or perhaps a linguistic component, require a different approach.

If you wanted to learn how to play badminton, for instance, most of the basic skills could be absorbed by an alert observer in less than an hour, without the need for explanation. By carefully noting the position of the shuttlecock, the angle of the racquet and the way it's held, the stance and movement of the players, etc., it would normally be possible to play a game with an acceptable degree of competence. But to play with any degree of skill would depend upon having a more sophisticated internal representation of the game.

When you're learning how to model it's a good idea to start with simple behaviours otherwise you can easily feel overwhelmed, because there's so much more to think about, including:

▶ *Meta Programs*
▶ *representational systems and submodalities*
▶ *language patterns*
▶ *strategies*
▶ *beliefs and values*
▶ *the wider system.*

Implicit and explicit modelling

If you ever undertake NLP Practitioner training, you may find yourself following a fellow student around for 20 minutes, trying to walk and move like them. It's a simple but effective way of learning the principles and methodology of modelling. This is called implicit modelling, which involves acting like your model and building intuitions about what's going on for them. It's similar to the apprentice/master relationship in martial arts where the simple act of being with the master allows the apprentice to absorb what the master does.

But why not simply *ask* the person what they're doing and why? That may sometimes be useful, but one of the hurdles we have to overcome when modelling is that many people don't know what makes them successful. Or they may think they know, but are wrong. Once we become accomplished at doing something, we no longer have to pay attention to how we do it. There are four stages in acquiring a skill:

▶ *Unconscious incompetence, when we're not even aware of what it is possible for us to do.*
▶ *Conscious incompetence, when we know we don't know how to do something.*
▶ *Conscious competence, when we're aware we're doing something correctly.*
▶ *Unconscious competence, when the skill becomes automatic and we do it without thinking about it.*

To create a transferable model we have to uncover a person's unconscious competence (implicit phase), and become consciously competent and attain the result ourselves (explicit phase).

Implicit modelling, then, is an intuitive process of understanding the other person's subjective experience by putting ourselves in their shoes. By using second position we gain insights we wouldn't get in any other way. In contrast, explicit modelling is carried out in third position. It's a dissociated and deductive process of working out the specific structure of the role model's subjective experience.

It's important to select the right person and context, otherwise what you end up with may not be what you had imagined. If, for instance, you want to lose weight and choose a role model who has always been slim, you'll learn something useful about how this person achieves this. On the other hand, if you model someone who has been overweight and has now lost some weight, you'll learn how to move from where you are now to your desired outcome.

Below we detail the procedure for a full modelling process. Not everyone will have the time or, frankly, the interest to go to such lengths but it's a benchmark that should be aspired to whenever possible. However, it's worth bearing in mind that the aim of modelling is to create something useful rather than absolutely accurate. To that end it may sometimes be sufficient to use just part of the process, or all of it in a less rigorous way.

The process of modelling

Steps
1 *Identify an exemplar: someone who is excellent at the skill or behaviour to be modelled.*
2 *Implicit modelling phase – 'the unconscious uptake'.*
   Go into second position and attend to what the person does – the way they breathe, their physiology and their behaviour. Listen not only to what they say but the way they say it. Pay greater attention to micro-movements than larger gestures. Copy what the person does without judgement or assumption. Don't try to understand what they're doing. To model successfully requires a curious, open and intuitive frame of mind. Concentrate on the process not the content.
   Next, take on that way of being as if you were the person you've modelled. Then see if you can get the same result by being yourself. Step inside your own skin and experience it looking out through your own eyes and feel what it's like to do it their way. Continue to do this until you achieve broadly the same results as your exemplar.
3 *Explicit modelling – 'subtraction'.*
   Now you can discover explicitly what it is the person does that makes the difference. Your aim is to 'Clarify and define the specific cognitive and behavioural steps that are required to produce the desired results' (Dilts and DeLozier). You do this by 'subtracting' – systematically missing out behaviours until you discover the essential components. If you subtract something and it makes no difference to the results you achieve, it's not a critical element. You don't want to become the other person, you only want to take on what is necessary

*and sufficient. The purpose of subtraction is to make sure the
model you end up with is as clear and simple as possible.
In this phase of the modelling process you're moving between
first and third position. Your aim is to work out the sequence
of events. What precisely did they do? Identify the sensory
specific distinctions in their strategies. Upon completion, you'll
have information from first, second and third position.*

4 *Now you're ready to either use the model yourself or transfer
and explain it to others. The real test of any model is that
you're able to teach someone else how to do it. Be aware
that some existing competencies may be required, such as the
ability to mismatch or think logically, and if they are not in
place they may need to be developed before the 'student' can
take on the model.*

Values, identity and congruence

But what if the person is very different from you in terms of their
values and beliefs, etc? If you end up thinking and behaving like
them, won't that affect your sense of your own identity? The
simple answer is no, assuming you approach your modelling
project from the correct perspective. Your aim is not to *become* the
other person; it's to learn how to do something they can do. For
you to be able to internalize that capability and continue to use
it, you need to integrate it fully, so it feels like a part of you, not
something that's been bolted on. It's essential, therefore, to adjust
the values and beliefs of the exemplar to your values and beliefs,
otherwise you'll end up feeling incongruent, and what you've
modelled won't stick.

Indirect modelling

It won't always be practical to spend lots of time with your chosen
role model. It may not even be possible to observe them in action,

because they're extremely busy or at a distant location. But there are other ways of gathering information, such as interviewing them or reading about them. If you're able to speak to them you can ask lots of questions to understand their beliefs, values, state, Meta Programs, strategies, submodalities, and sense of identity. Glean every piece of information available. If you meet in person you can observe their physiology, breathing, etc.

Indirect modelling can also be effective where people are no longer alive, but there is information available about how they thought, felt, behaved and acted. Robert Dilts, for instance, modelled the patterns of Jesus Christ, Leonardo Da Vinci and Albert Einstein, among others, in this way.

NLP perspectives
Charles Faulkner – Modelling: the art and science of useful knowledge acquisition

'Modelling is the heart of NLP, a core competence and the methodology that created "the trail of techniques". A model is not a copy, just like a map is not the territory. A model is a representation; a picture, a description, or physical object that highlights essential features of the original – what makes it work. These features include: key elements and relations as well as their properties and dynamics. Whether it's a scale model car, a biological diagram, or the description of a business process, it's a model.

Model making is world making. A map or model highlights some features and hides others. This increases the significance of what is highlighted. For example, if Life is a Game – a model of life – it's easier to see what needs to be done than in life itself. Sports and games simplify experience. There are winners and losers, playing fields and positions, rules and time limits. The Business is a Machine model highlights the routine and regulated nature of work, and it hides the human and emotional. Neuro-Linguistic Programming uses a computer model to highlight how we process our experience – so we change it easily. Making sense of something is making a model.

We see what we already know; what we already have a model of. We like significance and certainty so much we use our models to make sense of other situations. We make analogies with our models to gain insights into new ones. So why not simply seek the right/best model and use it everywhere? Well, by way of analogy, imagine a tropical fish tank. One fish is long and cylindrical and darts through the water with ease – it's a model for speed. Another is a thin vertical foil and spins around a small space – the epitome of manoeuvrability. A third is round and naturally floats. Each is a model of one way of moving through a liquid. Most fish are some combination. Which model is the right, best or true? It all depends on their needs and environment. For you, it depends on your outcomes. Some models are more useful in certain situations than others. Keep all your models. Combine them to your advantage.'

Charles Faulkner, NLP Modeller, innovator and author, is NLP Comprehensive Director of Programs and Influential Communications' Senior Consultant. His modelling projects include: decision-making, software development, and famously top traders – featured in *The New Market Wizards* (1992) to *Trend Following* (2007). Other modelling in his ten plus titles include: *Metaphors of Identity, The New Technology of Achievement, Success Mastery*, the game Trimurti and Meaningful Influence.

NLP and benchmarking

Benchmarking is a well-known type of modelling commonly used in the business world. It's a study of excellence. Companies use it to find and share best practice. The whole idea of benchmarking is to find out which individuals or companies do something in a better or more efficient way. Real benchmarking doesn't just look at the surface structure of a process, it goes deeper and explains how to bring about a change. To carry it out successfully there has to be a clear outcome and clarity over where the company is now and where it wants to be. The next stage is to identify organizations with a reputation for excellence in the area where the improvement is required. Then information is gathered to find out precisely what people do in those organizations. Best practice can then be tried out and adopted.

NLP in action

▶ Think about skills you'd like to have and seek out those who have them. Ask if you can spend some time learning from them, either by using the Implicit Modelling approach, or simply by asking them about what they do.

▶ If you work in a company, identify the top performers in key areas, and find out what they're doing that puts them ahead of the pack.

TEN KEY POINTS TO REMEMBER

1 *The principle purpose of NLP, right from the start, has been to model human excellence.*

2 *People are natural modellers – from the moment we're born we start copying those around us.*

3 *When you're modelling a simple behaviour, it's often possible to watch for a while and then match the behaviour.*

4 *Complex modelling involves more involved behavioural and cognitive tasks with lots of steps. It may have a linguistic component, strategies, beliefs, values and so on that you also need to model to achieve the desired result.*

5 *Implicit modelling is an intuitive process of understanding the other person's subjective experience by putting yourself in their shoes.*

6 *Explicit modelling is carried out in third position. It's a dissociated and deductive process of working out the structure of the other person's subjective experience.*

7 *The process of modelling involves: identifying an exemplar, implicit modelling – the unconscious uptake, explicit modelling – subtraction to discover what the person does that makes the difference, use the model or explain it to others.*

8 *Your aim is not to become the other person. Once learnt you need to internalize that capability until it becomes part of you and you feel congruent about the change you have made.*

9 *Indirect modelling is where it's not possible to spend time observing your model in action. Instead you gather as much information as possible about them.*

10 *Benchmarking is a well-known form of modelling used in the business world. When it is done well it goes beneath the surface structure of a process and explains how to bring about a change.*

17

Timelines

In this chapter you will learn:
- *about time and the ways in which we code it internally*
- *how to identify your timeline*
- *about 'in-time' and 'through-time'*
- *how to make simple changes using timelines*

Have you noticed how, when you're doing something, you can suddenly find yourself thinking about something else? While you've been reading this book, for instance, you may have found yourself on occasions distracted by something in the text. Perhaps in Chapter 1 the discussion about elephants led you to recall riding an elephant as a child or watching the Disney film *Jungle Book*.

There are other types of diversion too. You might suddenly remember a job you want to complete or find yourself planning an upcoming event. In the space of a few minutes we can 'be' in the present (reading a book), in the past (riding an elephant) or in the future (completing a task). In the course of each day our subjective experience of time shifts countless times. There are moments when we imagine or even rehearse the future and others when we relive the past, even though it's only the present that's actually happening now.

Some people spend more time in the past. You may know individuals who love to tell tales about things they've done or talk about the good old days. Others are future-oriented: forever discussing their hopes and dreams. And some of us live for the present, experiencing life as it is now. Expressions like 'dwelling in the past' and 'living for today' give clues to the way we think about time. As well as past, present and future we also represent time in terms of short, medium and long term.

The way in which we internally represent time has a far-reaching effect on us, because it touches every aspect of our lives. We structure our daily activities around it, and to some extent it dictates to us.

Eliciting your timeline

The way in which people mentally code the pictures, sounds, feelings, tastes and smells of events in their past, present or future is known in NLP as a timeline. Each of us has a timeline that's as individual as our Meta Programs and submodalities – in fact, it could be argued that our internal representation of time is simply another kind of submodality. The best way to understand how timelines work is to become familiar with your own.

Exercise

Start by bringing to mind something ordinary you do on a regular basis, such as eating breakfast, getting out of bed or travelling to work. As you remember doing it yesterday, where do you intuitively sense that memory is in the personal space around you? If you think in pictures, you might even be able to see it. It could be to your left or right, straight ahead or behind, above or below.

Imagine doing the same activity for tomorrow. If you're like most other people, that picture will be in a different location, or you wouldn't be able to tell the past from the future. Think of them both at the same time, and notice where they are in relation to each other.

Now think of other times when you did the same thing: a month ago, a year ago, five years ago. Where is each located? You may find that all your other memories of carrying out this activity slot into place in a line. Do the same for the future: imagine yourself performing the activity in one month, a year and five years. Once again, they may appear to suggest a line.

Many people find their timeline is organized in a 'V' shape, in line with visual recall (past) and construct (future). This tends to tie in with their eye accessing cues. So if someone is 'wired the other way round', perhaps because they're left-handed, their timeline may be arranged accordingly. Some people have their future in front of them and their past behind them. Others have more unusual configurations, such as a future that heads up towards the sky or a past that goes down into the ground.

Once we have an overall sense of how we code time in terms of location, we can explore more of the submodalities relating to it. Does the timeline appear short or long? Is the past lower or higher than the future or vice versa? Does the timeline feel heavy or light? Are there sounds of any sort, or silence? Does it appear large or small – some people visualize stepping inside it almost as if it were a large tube. Some images are in colour, others are monochromatic. Some people have branches in their future, much like the limbs on a tree leading off in lots of different directions.

Exercise

Take a moment now to examine your timeline in detail. What submodality distinctions can you observe across the different sensory modalities? The better you understand the way you code time the easier it will be for you to make changes should you want to.

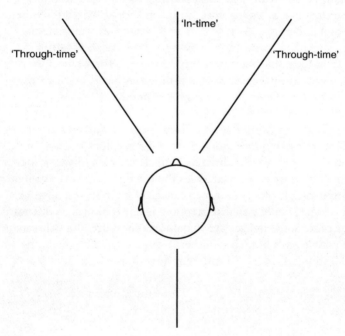

Timeline.

The language of time

The best way to find out how someone codes time is to carry out an elicitation process of the kind you did earlier. But often that's not necessary. When people talk about an event that happened in the past they'll sometimes point to it and you know exactly where it is. And the same is true for the future.

The words and expressions people use can also be revealing. They may say they've put a bad experience 'behind them', or that something happened in the 'dim and distant past'. If there's an event they'll 'never forget', you can be sure they've coded it in a particular way that marks it out. For some people, events in the future seem 'a long way off'. For others, time seems to just 'fly by'. Such descriptions are often a literal reflection of how they're representing time internally.

IN TIME AND THROUGH TIME

Whenever Emma's friends arrange to meet her they suggest a time that's half an hour earlier than necessary, because they're so used to her turning up late. She seems to be so wrapped up in what she's doing that time passes by without her realizing it. Emma doesn't appear to have a sense of urgency when she's working on a task or project. She finds it valuable when someone offers to help her monitor progress.

People who behave like Emma are associated into each life experience, living in the moment. They find it easy to be in the here and now and tend to enjoy living in a spontaneous fashion. They code their experience in a line that passes through their body, with the future ahead of them and the past behind. In NLP this is known as being 'in time'. The line can be reversed, with the past in front and the future behind, or the past or future lines can go off at an angle. But there will always be part of the line behind the person.

Pete has a reputation for being punctual. He dislikes being late for anything whether it's work or pleasure. He's quite matter of fact when it comes to arranging his schedule. Time's important to him and he likes to make sure he gets 'his money's worth' when he spends time doing something.

Such 'through time' people code time in front of them. This can be in a straight line running from left to right or, more usually, in either a 'V' or 'U' shape. Because they're on the outside looking onto their timeline they're dissociated from their experiences. They're aware of duration and tend to place a value on time. Unlike in time behaviour they're good at staying on track and like to establish deadlines for achieving tasks.

All people create combinations of memories, sometimes called gestalts or schemas, that collectively represent classes of things. We might, for example, have a gestalt for eating out at restaurants. All of our experiences of visiting a restaurant contribute to the way we represent it: such as a white linen tablecloth, a lit candle, a single flower in a vase, silver cutlery, and so on. This gestalt of memories is more noticeable in through time people because their memories are right in front of them and they're more influenced by them.

Ecology in changing timelines

Many NLP patterns and techniques involve working with the way people perceive time. Obvious examples relating to the future are well-formed outcomes and New Behaviour Generator, whereas Change Personal History and transderivational search primarily have a past orientation.

Timelines can be modified in two major ways. The first utilizes a person's existing timeline, with them going back or forward, changing events or adding resources. The second changes the way people structure time. This is achieved by finding out what a person wants and then reorienting the timeline to match their outcome.

However, it's important to think carefully about ecology before making any change. The main aim is usually to give people more choice, because their existing coding isn't working for them. If you're considering changing the structure of a timeline it's essential to assess the benefits the person gets from the way it is now. Having the future straight ahead, for instance, can be motivating for one person and stressful for someone else. Before altering a timeline it's important to have a well-formed outcome for making any change because there are pros and cons to different configurations.

Always emphasize the element of choice and ensure the person knows that any change can easily be reversed. Imagine a week has passed with the new timeline in place and check to find out what it feels like. This can be done by 'going inside' and asking the unconscious mind for any objections to altering it. Once we're aware of any incongruence relating to a temporary change we can either deal with the objection or revert back to the original configuration.

Timeline change options

There are various ways of using timelines to explore and change the way past and future events are represented.

One that's effective for many people is to mentally float above their timeline, having first created an anchor to the present – perhaps in the form of an imaginary cord – so they can't get 'lost'. From this position they can go back in time and drop back down into a memory or float forward and step into an experience they're yet to have.

Another option, which works well for those who don't find it easy to visualize, involves 'laying down' a timeline on the floor of the area where you're working. This is an imaginary line that spans the time from birth to death. It can be long or short, whatever feels right. As you step onto the line at a point that intuitively feels like the present, you can walk into the future or back into the past.

Both methods can be used to access the root cause of an issue that's affecting the person in the present or to gather valuable resources from the past that will help now or in the future. In the pattern Change Personal History, for example, the presenting issue is tracked back to the first time it occurred. Then the person identifies resources that would have been useful to them at that time and goes back in time to find them. When the resources are brought to the place where they are needed it changes the person's experience.

Insight

Many people find the idea of imaging their life as a line on the floor a little strange when they're first introduced to the idea. We find that clients tend to go along with it – as if to humour us at first – and are amazed afterwards at how effectively it works. In some cases they're incredulous. It's not until you try this out for yourself that you start to understand the many applications there are for using your timeline to help you achieve your outcomes.

Timelines and emotions

Tad James and Wyatt Woodsmall developed Time Line Therapy in the 1980s. Part of this work involved working with negative emotions such as anger, sadness, guilt and fear. For more information on their approach see *Time Line Therapy and the Basis of Personality*.

Changing the structure of a timeline

Although there's no right way of organizing time, not everyone has a timeline that works as effectively as they might like. Some people, for instance, code their future in the same place they access visual recall; for most of us visual memories are to the left. What can happen in this situation is that the person's future seems to them to be fixed in the way the past usually is. We generally think of the past as being permanent and the future as full of possibilities. To make a change all the person needs to do is try out a new timeline configuration. Changing the spatial representation of a timeline brings about a corresponding change in behaviour.

When the future is straight ahead of us we can be so future-oriented we ignore the present. Also, because the long-term future is out of sight, because it's hidden by what's about to happen, it can mean we don't consider future consequences. Changing the submodalities of the long-term future to make it appear bigger or brighter overcomes this by making it more visible.

When the past is behind us we may be less aware of it, and may repeat the same mistakes over again. Conversely some people have the past right in front of them and this can lead to them dwelling on it. This is fine if the past is full of happy memories and more of a challenge or even depressing if the opposite is true.

It's possible for us to change our timelines according to the context. If, for instance, a person usually codes time with their past behind them they could bring their past round to the front when they want to recall things more easily.

Some people easily identify part of their timeline and struggle to find the rest. They may, for instance, be able to locate their past and have no sense of a future, or have a past and future with no present. Others describe a mass or jumbled line.

Where there appears to be no future it can be useful to imagine where it would be if there was one. Then picture the future growing in length. Any change made need only be temporary and it's important to be sure your outcome for making the change is well formed. It's possible to add a future in great detail and end up being disappointed when it doesn't materialize in quite the way you visualized. One of the advantages of a future with many branches is that it increases your sense of having options and choices. If you want to add some specifics, populate your future with values or symbols of the kinds of things you want.

Being unable to locate the present can be disconcerting. This often relates to the configuration of the past and future; they may simply overlap each other, leaving no space for the present. Again a simple adjustment can bring about a change. Some people describe a mass or jumbled line. If they find this doesn't serve them they can visualize the line unravelling and then falling into place.

Location isn't the only change that can prove beneficial. Adding colour or light to the future equates to a bright and motivating future for many of us. Adding branches to the future can give a feeling of more opportunities and options. Making changes to any submodality will alter the experience in some way.

NLP in action

▶ Find out how you code your time by recalling various trivial events from the past few months and draw an imaginary line to link them together. Then do the same for some planned or imagined future events.

▶ Think of a future challenge you face and decide on the resources you will need. Float above your timeline and then back to a place or places where you had this resource in the past. Dip down into those events and experience that resource again. Bring the resource back with you through time to the present and into the future where it is needed.

▶ Change the structure of your timeline in some way, knowing that you can return it to its original location whenever you wish. Think of it as an experiment. Move your timeline around and notice what feels right for you.

TEN KEY POINTS TO REMEMBER

1 *In the space of a few moments we can 'be' in the present doing something, in the past recalling an experience, and in the future thinking about something that's going to happen.*

2 *Some of us spend more time mentally in the past, some people are more in the present and others in the future.*

3 *The way we mentally code pictures, sounds, feelings, tastes and smells of events in our past, the present or future is called a timeline in NLP.*

4 *Find out how you code time by recalling various trivial events from the past few months and draw an imaginary line to link them together. Then do the same for some planned or imagined future events. This should give you a sense of your timeline.*

5 *Some people are so 'associated' into each life experience they find it easy to be in the present that they often turn up late for appointments. In NLP this is called 'in time'.*

6 *Some people code time in front of them, and this is called 'through time'. They are dissociated from their experiences, are aware of how long things take and tend to place a value on time.*

7 *Before altering a timeline it's important to have created a well-formed outcome because there are pros and cons to different configurations.*

8 *There are various options for using timelines in change work. You can mentally float above the line, having created an anchor to the present, or visualize a line on the floor which you walk on.*

9 *You can move back in time to find the root cause of an issue or access a useful resource and go forward into the future to find out what making the change will be like.*

10 *If you want to change the structure of your timeline, you can regard it as an experiment. This allows you to put it back into its original location if that feels right for you.*

18

Strategies

In this chapter you will learn:
- *that strategies are sequences of representational systems and submodalities*
- *the NLP notation system for describing strategies*
- *two ways of eliciting a strategy*
- *how to design and install an effective strategy*

Have you ever thought about how many things you do in the course of a typical day? Just stop and reflect for a moment.

You probably came up with some big chunk answers: you get up, have breakfast, go to work, eat lunch, do some more work, go home, eat dinner, watch TV, read or go out, and then sleep.

But you can break that down into smaller chunks. Getting up involves dragging yourself out of bed, having a shower, getting dressed, etc. And each of those can be divided further: to accomplish the apparently simple task of having a shower you have to open the shower door or pull back the curtain, switch on the shower, squeeze out some gel, wash your body and hair, switch off the shower, reach for a towel, and dry yourself. That's already quite a lot of 'doing'.

But it's possible to go further. To squeeze out some shower gel you first have to locate the bottle and pick it up. Then you have to apply just the right amount of pressure to the bottle. When the gel comes out you need to be ready to catch it and apply it to your body.

As we continue to increase the magnification of the microscope, so other things come into view. To apply the right amount of pressure we must have a system for monitoring how much pressure we're actually applying, and some way of knowing when that amount is 'right'.

In NLP, such a system is called a *strategy*. As Tad James, of Advanced Neuro Dynamics, puts it, 'A strategy is what goes on in your head when you want to do something. All our external behaviours are controlled by internal processing strategies.'

Once you divide activities into their component parts it becomes obvious that over the course of any one day we do countless thousands of things. And for every one of those things we have a strategy. We have strategies for brushing our teeth, falling in love, buying a house, clapping our hands, listening to music, contributing to a meeting, digging a hole, scratching an itch, making love, being sad, being happy, sitting reading a book... and compiling lists of examples! We do, literally, have a strategy for everything we do.

The TOTE model

One of the key presuppositions of NLP is that experience has a structure. So what is the structure of our strategies? Since all of our internal representations are made up of pictures, sounds, feelings, tastes and smells, that too is how strategies are composed.

Much of the NLP way of thinking about strategies was developed out of the TOTE model proposed by cognitive psychologists in the 1960s. TOTE stands for Test, Operate, Test, Exit, which are the four essential elements of a feedback system. What the NLP founders and developers did was to modify the TOTE framework to account for the fact that our experience derives from the sensory coding of our representational systems.

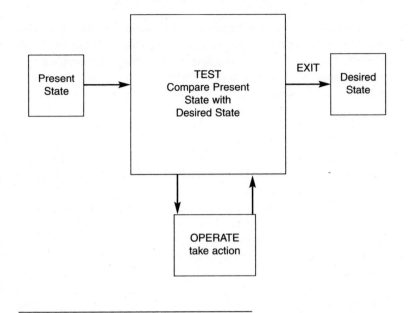

Strategy is about sequences

A strategy is a sequence of modalities and associated submodalities. And it's these chains of sensory systems that make up the structure of an individual's subjective experience at any one time. Strategies are the 'Programming' part of Neuro-Linguistic Programming. In computing terms, it's the coding that a programmer uses to write software packages. Simply by varying the coding, the way it's sequenced, programs as varied as Microsoft Powerpoint™ and Adobe Photoshop™ can be created.

It's the same with people. Different sequences of representational systems – different strategies – produce different results. A good example is spelling. Some people seem to have a natural talent, while others struggle with even simple words. You might think it's to do with intelligence or education, but in fact it's the strategies they're using. Almost without exception those who excel at spelling use the same strategy. What they do is make a picture of the word from memory, and then get a feeling of familiarity when it's right.

Most of those who have difficulty spelling do something different. Some use their auditory memory. They sound the word out to themself. This doesn't work because so many English words look different from the way they sound. Other people try to visualize the word, rather than remember it. But that will only be useful if you've never seen the word before, in which case you won't be able to recognize it.

Exercise: Work out your strategy for spelling

Take a word you know already such as 'learning'. How do you know how to spell it? Do you picture the word or sound it out to yourself?

Now choose a word that you don't know, perhaps something made up such as 'dognacious'. When you try to spell it, do you construct an image of the word first? If not, what do you do?

NLP strategy notation

To make understanding strategies and working with them easy, NLP has developed a shorthand notation, which was briefly discussed in Chapter 3. Although it looks complicated, it's actually very simple. The starting point is our five sensory modalities, which you'll be very familiar with by now, along with the VAKOG description:

V = Visual
A = Auditory
K = Kinaesthetic

O = Olfactory
G = Gustatory

In each of the modalities we can be focused either externally (e) on our real-time experience of the world, or internally (i) on what's going on in our mind. Seeing what's going on around you is Ve. Picturing something in your head is Vi. But that doesn't tell you whether the pictures are memories or imagined. So for greater clarity we use Vr for Visual Remembered and Vc for Visual Constructed.

It's a similar situation with the auditory modality. Ae is Auditory External, and Ai is Auditory Internal. However, there are three types of Ai:

▶ *Auditory Remembered – Ar – recalling sounds you've heard before*
▶ *Auditory Construct – Ac – imagining sounds you've never heard*
▶ *Auditory Internal Dialogue – Aid – talking to yourself.*

And in the Kinaesthetic modality, Ke is for feelings in the here and now, and Ki for internal feelings. Adding a superscript + or − indicates whether the feeling is positive or negative.

Notation in practice

Returning to the spelling strategy above, this is how it's written in NLP notation: Vr K+ Ae. The person remembers a picture of the word, feels that it's correct, and then reads it out.

Using the notation allows you to summarize any strategy in a way that's quick and easy to understand. Remember, NLP is interested first and foremost in process, not content. So most of the time you don't actually need to know what someone is thinking. What's important is how they're thinking.

Eliciting a strategy

But how do you find out what strategy a person is using? And why would you want to? To answer the last question first: strategies are one of the key ways in which we achieve, or don't achieve, our desired outcomes. Anthony Robbins calls them 'the syntax of success'. 'The man ate the chicken' is very different in meaning from 'the chicken ate the man'. The words are the same but the order has changed. If we can discover the way someone who excels is sequencing their thoughts, we can do the same, and achieve the same results. What we're talking about is, of course, modelling. To come back to the first question, there are two principal ways to elicit a strategy.

▶ *The first is to use the eye-accessing cues we discussed in Chapter 3 – but now pay attention to the sequence the person follows, rather than where they are at any one time. The starting point is to make sure the person is associated into whatever state applies to the strategy you want to model. Say you want to find out how somebody is motivated to go to the gym. You need to get them thinking about doing so, perhaps by remembering a time when they were motivated. As you get them talking, pay attention to the sequence their eyes follow. You'll have to watch carefully, because changes are often quick, and the time spent in any one position is usually fleeting.*

▶ *To build up your skills it's a good idea to find someone willing to help you practice, so you can get in close enough to see clearly what's happening, and go over things a few times until you've got the pattern.*

▶ *The second approach is to use a formal elicitation process, asking a series of questions to determine the sequence of their thoughts. Your aim is to be able to write down clearly and unambiguously every step of their strategy in sequence. Most people don't consciously know what their strategies are, and they'll be figuring them out as you go along, so you'll need to be patient if you're to* maintain rapport. Some effective strategies are short, just three to five steps, but others can run to ten or more stages.

▶ Once you have the bones of the strategy in the form of the modalities, you need to flesh them out by learning what the submodalities are because there are often crucial elements. There may be something particular about where an image is located in their mind's eye or the tonality of an auditory digital conversation that's crucial to the strategy.

Steps

You can use this process to elicit a strategy in yourself and others. In this case, a strategy is being elicited for being confident.

1 *Recall a time when you were totally confident.*
2 *Recall a specific time.*
3 *Go back to that time now and fully experience it.*
4 *As you remember it...*
   ▷ *What was the very first thing that caused you to be totally confident?*
   ▷ *Was it something you saw? (Or the way someone looked at you?)*
   ▷ *Was it something you heard? (Or the tone of someone's voice?)*
   ▷ *Was it the touch of someone or something?*
5 *After you saw, heard or were touched, what was the very next thing that caused you to be totally confident?*
   ▷ *Did you picture something in your mind?*
   ▷ *Say something to yourself?*
   ▷ *Have a certain feeling or emotion?*
   ▷ *Or did something else happen?*
6 *What was the next thing that happened as you were totally confident?*
7 *After you saw, heard or felt that, did you know that you were totally confident, did you picture something, say something, or have a feeling?*

Continue until the complete strategy has been elicited.

Designing effective strategies

Most of us never chose the strategies we use. They were developed by trial and error as we grew up. In the same way that we learned to walk by standing up and falling down a lot until we got it right, so we experimented with different ways of arranging our internal experiences until we came up with strategies that seemed to work.

When they did, we often stuck with them. By the time we get to be adults, most of us stop trying new strategies, and stick to tried and tested ways of thinking. Some are successful, and others less so. We may have hit upon a strategy that works reasonably well and stayed with it, when there are others that produce better results.

Part of the problem is that strategies are often generalized. Because they're effective in one context we use them in other areas as well, where they don't work anywhere near as well. Sometimes people end up with just one or two favourite strategies, for example, playing with their children the way they tackle a board meeting. You may be familiar with the saying, 'If all you have is a hammer, you'll treat everything as if it's a nail'.

Another complication is that strategies are invisible. We're not aware of them most of the time, even when they're not working. So habitual is our way of thinking that it doesn't even occur to us there might be another. One of the aims of NLP is to increase choice, and strategies provide a powerful means of achieving that. If the strategy being used to achieve a desired outcome isn't delivering results, it's relatively easy to change or replace it.

Many people, for instance, struggle with their eating patterns. Some are on the 'see-food' diet. They see food, and they eat it! There's no decision-making process in their strategy. They eat whether or not they are hungry and without concern for the consequences. By extending the strategy to include steps in which the person checks whether they're full or not before eating, and if it's food they like or which will be good for them, they'll have more choice about how they eat.

Well-formedness conditions for strategies

When designing a strategy, it's important to make sure it's well formed. Here are the conditions that must be met.

▶ *There's a defined representation of the desired outcome using sensory-specific language or NLP notation.*
▶ *All three major representational systems are involved.*
▶ *There's a logical sequence – there are no steps missing.*
▶ *It should involve the least number of steps required to produce the outcome.*
▶ *There should be no two-point loops because this means there is no exit point (e.g. V–K often found in worry and depression results in seeing something and then feeling bad, seeing something feeling bad – going on and on in a continuous cycle).*
▶ *It's not a loop, there is an Exit (the E of TOTE).*

Changing/installing a strategy

There are various ways of installing or changing a strategy. The easiest way, once you've designed one you think will work effectively, is to run through it several times to see if it works. Go through it step by step, using your eyes to look in the appropriate place at each stage. If it starts with a visual construct (Vc), look up and to the left. When you're saying something to yourself (Ad), look down and to the left. And when you want a kinaesthetic check of your feelings (K+), look down to your right.

If, for instance, you need to get a job done that has been outstanding for a while you might discover your current strategy is to: Ve (look at what needs done), Ki (feel bored with the idea of doing it) and Aid (tell yourself it will wait until tomorrow). If you want to install a strategy that will motivate you to complete a task you might start with Ve (looking at what has to be done) and then Vc (imagine what it will look like when it's completed). This could be followed with a Ki (for feeling good about the end result) and Aid (to tell yourself to get going on it).

The Disney creativity strategy

As part of his work on modelling strategies of genius, NLP developer Robert Dilts carried out an in-depth study of Walt Disney, based on articles and books written by him and about him. What this revealed was a structured, conscious strategy for creativity that can be used in a wide range of contexts.

For Disney there were three distinct phases that were necessary for success, which he called the Dreamer, the Realist and the Spoiler (Critic). In the Dreamer Phase you are wildly creative. In the Realist Phase you take a practical perspective. And in the Critic Phase you evaluate things constructively.

Most of us assume all three perspectives naturally, but this can sometimes cause problems, both when we're working on issues by ourselves and in a group setting. The main problem is that the Dreamer and the Critic often fight. Perhaps you've had the experience of doing something creative on your own and coming up with a fantastic, innovative idea, only to have another part of yourself immediately shoot it down in flames. The same can happen in a business context, with original ways of thinking generated by Dreamers getting strangled at birth by vociferous Critics. By separating out and sequencing the three perspectives this conflict can be avoided. It also ensures that all three viewpoints are represented, because it's all too easy to get so excited by an idea that you don't consider how best to implement it and where things could go wrong.

At a more detailed strategy level, the Dreamer phase involves coming up with constructed images (Vc) to give a 'big picture' of the options with no limits on what might be possible. The Realist phase tends to be more kinaesthetic, about getting a feeling for how the plan would work. And the Critic phase often has an auditory digital component, with the person asking themself questions such as, 'What's wrong here?'

The exercise that follows provides a structured process for using the Disney Creativity Strategy.

Steps

1 *Choose something you want to work with. It could be a problem you need to solve or an idea you'd like to explore.*
2 *You should also establish a 'Meta' position, from where you can view things from a detached, observer, third position viewpoint. Then allocate three locations for the Dreamer, Realist and Critic phases.*
3 *Anchor a strategy to each location:*
   ▷ *Recall a time when you were able to generate creative ideas and/or when you thought anything was possible, then step into the Dreamer location. As you fully associate into the memory, notice what you saw around you, what you heard and how it felt to be creative.*
   ▷ *Bring to mind a time when you were able to be realistic about how to implement a plan, and then step into the Realist location reliving the memory as fully as possible.*
   ▷ *Remember a time when you were able to offer positive and constructive criticism of an idea, then step into the Critic location, developing a full representation in at least the three primary modalities (VAK).*
4 *Thinking of your outcome, step into the Dreamer location and dream! Be open to every option no matter how crazy or unrealistic it might seem. Don't censor your thoughts at all. Brainstorm freely. Let your thoughts roam far and free. Then create movies in the cinema of your mind.*
5 *Step into the Realist location, and consider how the ideas the Dreamer has created could be implemented. Devise workable action plans with the first steps specified.*

6 Now step into the Critic location, and challenge in a positive way the ideas and the plan. What's missing? What wouldn't work? What's wrong? What would have to change to make it work? Be sure to keep the criticism positive.

7 Return to the Dreamer location, and dream once again, this time making use of the suggestions that came from the Critic.

8 Go round the cycle several times, until you feel it's complete.

Insight

I (Amanda) have often used the Disney Strategy with teams or groups of people who are working on a project together. It can be great fun to use it. People generally enjoy the creative dreamer phase. They often develop a greater appreciation of people who naturally look for what might go wrong with a task or project and the value this adds to the team's success.

NLP in action

▶ Think about your own strategies for doing things. Pay attention to what steps you go through when, for instance, making a major purchase such as buying a car or house.

▶ Find someone willing to work with you, and elicit their strategies by means of eye accessing cues and a formal elicitation process.

▶ Use the Disney Strategy before commencing your next personal or business project.

TEN KEY POINTS TO REMEMBER

1 *Strategies consist of the internal processing (sequences of representational systems and submodalities) that sits behind countless things we do every day.*

2 *The TOTE model stands for Test, Operate, Test, Exit, which are the four essential elements of a feedback system.*

3 *A strategy is a sequence of modalities and associated submodalities. These chains of sensory systems make up the structure of our subjective experience at any one time.*

4 *NLP has developed a simple strategy notation system based on VAKOG: V = visual; A = auditory; K = kinaesthetic; O = olfactory; G = gustatory.*

5 *The notation system allows you to summarize any strategy quickly and easily which is important for modelling others.*

6 *One way to elicit a strategy is through eye accessing cues. Another is to ask a series of questions to determine the sequence of someone's thoughts.*

7 *Most of us developed the strategies we use through trial and error and they are not always as effective as we might like. With NLP it is possible to re-design effective strategies adding new steps or replacing an ineffective strategy altogether.*

8 *It is important to follow the well-formedness conditions when improving or creating new strategies.*

9 *To install a new strategy run through it several times to test it. As you go through it step by step use your eyes to look in the appropriate place each time.*

10 *Robert Dilts modelled Walt Disney and revealed a strategy for creativity with three distinct phases – the Dreamer, the Realist and the Spoiler (or Critic).*

19

The Milton Model

In this chapter you will learn:
- **about the Milton Model**
- **how to use 'artfully vague' language**
- **about the relevance of the Milton Model in business**
- **the inverse Meta Model categories and other Milton Model patterns**
- **about metaphor and storytelling**

You are curious. And that means you can learn faster. As you become aware of your feelings you will relax. Because NLP is fascinating, isn't it? People always grasp things easily when they're comfortable. Could you reflect deeply on a memory? And as your mind wanders, all the way down, you know it's right now. Will you let go immediately, or in a moment? Fortunately it's no problem. They say, 'You can have whatever you want'. Understanding is valuable. Don't imagine it's not true. Reflecting on your experiences will make you realize what's important.

What was your reaction to that opening paragraph? Did it make perfect sense to you, or did it seem a bit strange? Are you perhaps tempted to call in the Meta Model police and arrest it for multiple violations?

The introduction was, in fact, carefully and methodically crafted using the Milton Model, a set of linguistic patterns developed by Richard Bandler and John Grinder in 1975 from their modelling of Milton H. Erickson, one of the world's leading hypnotherapists, and the founder of the American Society for Clinical Hypnosis.

Bandler and Grinder studied Erickson's therapeutic approach in great detail over a period of some months, using implicit modelling as described in Chapter 16. What they were fascinated to discover was that the language he used when treating clients was very different from that used by Perls and Satir, which had formed the basis of the Meta Model. In fact, it was almost as if Erickson were wilfully violating as many of the Meta Model patterns as possible.

Whereas Perls and Satir asked questions to help recover deleted information and reveal distortions and generalizations, Erickson would often tell stories that were vague and ambiguous. The Meta Model worked by helping the client develop internal maps that were more accurate and therefore more useful in achieving their desired outcomes. The Milton Model was equally effective but what was the secret of its success?

Being artfully vague

In their book *The Patterns of the Hypnotic Techniques of Milton H. Erickson MD*, Bandler and Grinder describe the language patterns used by Erickson as 'artfully vague'. He deliberately produced sentences that were open to a range of interpretations, in direct contrast to the specificity of the Meta Model. In essence, what he was doing was intentionally creating distortions, deletions and generalizations. This vagueness achieves a number of different and important things:

▶ **It's trance-inducing.** *Unlike many of his contemporaries and predecessors, Erickson favoured an indirect approach to hypnosis. Rather than go through a structured induction process, he preferred to lead his clients into trance in a more natural way. Because much of Erickson's language was general and unclear, clients had to go into their own experience in an* *attempt to make sense of what he was saying, and in so doing went into trance. Milton Model language provides a subtle and non-confrontational approach that's effective even with those who have an antipathy to hypnosis.*

▶ **It accesses the unconscious mind.** *Erickson's linguistic ambiguity also distracts the dominant hemisphere of the brain, which is responsible for language, so that the non-dominant hemisphere – the unconscious mind – can be accessed, facilitating therapeutic intervention.*

▶ **It stimulates a Transderivational Search (TDS).** *The unconscious mind is our storehouse of memories, resources and experiences, the deep structure that lies behind our consciousness. When clients are presented with vague, ambiguous statements while in trance, they're forced to carry out a TDS of this reservoir of learnings to make sense of what is being said. This has a similar effect to asking Meta Model questions, but at the unconscious level. What effectively happens is that the person is forced to make corrections to the violations at the deepest level of their mind.*

Some people worry about where the conscious mind ends and the unconscious mind begins but it's really not important. Bandler and Grinder addressed the issue directly in the book *Frogs into Princes*:

Don't get caught up by the words 'conscious' and 'unconscious'. They're not real. They're just a way of describing events that is useful in the context called therapeutic change. 'Conscious' is defined as whatever you are aware of at a moment in time. 'Unconscious' is everything else.

NLP and hypnosis

Milton Model language is valuable when doing any kind of change work with other people, including using specific patterns such as Change Personal History and the New Behaviour Generator.

Asking people questions, such as those in the Meta Model, engages people in reality processing. In NLP this is called 'uptime', where conscious thinking predominates. Getting people to focus on their experience, their internal representation, takes them into trance, or 'downtime' as it's sometimes referred to in NLP.

There are many myths about trance, but the most important thing to understand is that it's a naturally occurring state and one we go in and out of many times during a day. When we daydream, get lost in a book or television programme, think something through, drive without paying attention to where we're going, or space out playing a computer game, we're in a trance.

Is NLP, then, simply hypnosis by another name? Certainly, during many patterns and processes people clearly go into trance, and that can facilitate change. But as we've seen, there's a lot more to NLP than the Milton Model and trancework.

Insight

I (Steve) am a certified, trained hypnotherapist, and much of the time when I'm working with clients therapeutically I use NLP tools and techniques. They are particularly valuable with people who are fearful of 'giving up control' while in a trance. Although they are mistaken in their concern – it's one of the great myths of hypnosis – I use NLP visualization to help them 'go inside'.

The relevance of the Milton Model to business

What if you have no interest in therapy, and your aim is to be more effective in business? You may be tempted to turn to the next chapter, thinking the Milton Model has no relevance to what you do. You can't, after all, go around hypnotizing customers or putting your colleagues into a trance. But to take that view would be to misunderstand the value of the Milton Model, which is essentially about how language can be used to influence and persuade.

In his article 'Beyond Milton', Joseph Riggio explains it this way:

> **In a business context, the Milton Model is used extensively in public speaking, especially in politics where a presentation needs to be meaningful and positive to the listener, yet must lack any specific information which may lead to embarrassment later on. If you listen to a political interview, you'll often hear Milton patterns such as 'things are already much better and in relative terms will certainly be different in the future'.**

Inverse Meta Model categories

Let's start by looking at the aspects of the Milton Model that are the inverse of the Meta Model. As you read them reflect on how you will apply each one sooner or later.

SIMPLE DELETIONS

Deliberately leaving information out of a communication results in the listener asking questions and seeking answers. Consider: 'It can now be told'. What can be told to whom by whom in what way, and why only now? We don't know, it's not clear.

Examples:

'This makes sense.'
'It's easy.'

COMPARATIVE DELETION

If, when making a comparison, you don't indicate what's being evaluated against what, you create confusion and stimulate a transderivational search for the missing information. In the examples below we don't know what the starting point is: 'More than what?'and 'Better than what?'

Examples:

'They want more.'
'You can feel better.'

LACK OF REFERENTIAL INDEX

When it's not clear who is doing something, people have to draw upon their own experiences to understand a statement. In the first example, who precisely knows and in the second, which people?

Examples:

'They know all the answers.'
'Someone is coming.'

UNSPECIFIED VERB

When verbs aren't specified, the listener is required to fill in the details themself to make sense of the communication. Verbs that can work in this way include 'experience', 'feel', 'understand', 'sense' and 'learn'.

Examples:

'You can understand how you will feel better.'
'It's easy to remember the learning from that workshop.'

CAUSE AND EFFECT – CAUSAL LINKAGE

People naturally think in causal terms, with one thing following on as a consequence from another. 'The deadline's approaching and I need to work hard', or 'The telephone call made me late for the meeting'. Presenting ideas in the form of two statements that are linked can be extremely persuasive, moving the person in the direction of the desired behaviour. If the first is verifiable in experience the unconscious mind will often accept the linkage as true, even when there's no basis in fact. As the NLP trainer Tad James is fond of saying in his workshops, 'It doesn't have to be true, it just has to be plausible.'

CONJUNCTION

This is the simplest and weakest kind of linkage, where any two phrases are connected using words such as: 'and', 'but', 'for', 'yet' and 'so'.

Examples:

'You can notice your breathing and begin to relax.'
'You are smiling so you can be sure of success.'

IMPLIED CAUSATIVE

A stronger linkage is created by an implied causative, which uses 'If... then...', 'during', 'while', 'soon' or 'as you/so you...' to connect the statements.

Examples:

'If you consider these patterns then you can learn them easily.'
'While you weigh up these options you will be taking them in unconsciously.'

CAUSE–EFFECT

This is the strongest form of linkage, with the causality made explicit, using words such as 'makes', 'forces', and 'that means'.

Examples:

'The sound of my voice will make you feel comfortable.'
'This book has been carefully structured, and that means it's easy for you to learn NLP.'

Because the causal link is more evident when using implied causative and cause–effect patterns, it can be useful to use negative phrasing, because it's harder for the person to keep track of what's being connected.

Example:

'You won't be able to resist getting more curious as you hear what's coming next.'

MIND READING

Claiming to know what the other person is thinking can make suggestions more credible and strengthen rapport. Care needs to be taken to keep comments general to avoid a clash with their actual experience.

Examples:

'I know you are curious about what's going to happen.'
'There are new things you are learning right now.'

COMPLEX EQUIVALENCE

Two statements can be equated as having the same meaning by the way they're linked together. The easiest way is by using 'that means'.

Examples:

'You're learning NLP, that means you're interested in people.'
'You're approaching 50 – you're too old to start again.'

LOST PERFORMATIVE

Being able to present a judgement or evaluation as fact, without saying whose judgement or evaluation it is, can be valuable in by-passing resistance. One of the simplest ways is to use the word 'It's'.

Examples:

'It's useful to understand the way lost performatives work.'
'It's essential to practise language patterns at every
opportunity.'

NOMINALIZATION

As we discussed in Chapter 13, nominalizations are abstract nouns
that have been created out of process words, such as 'happiness'
and 'curiosity', which derive from being happy and curious. These
are great words to use because they allow people to attach their
own meaning to them.

Examples:

'You can take satisfaction in your knowledge.'
'Insights, understandings and discoveries await you.'

UNIVERSAL QUANTIFIERS

Presenting communications as if they were universal generalizations
can make them more credible, especially to the unconscious mind,
which may not examine them closely. Key words to use include
'all', 'every', 'nobody', 'always', 'everyone' and 'never'.

Examples:

'People always learn more easily when they relax.'
'Nobody wants to resist discovering new things.'

MODAL OPERATORS

The two modal operators of necessity and possibility can be
used to suggest rules and orient experience in a particular
direction.

The modal operators of necessity – should/shouldn't, must/mustn't,
have to/don't have to – can be used to limit choice.

Example:

'And you don't even have to try, it can all happen naturally by itself.'

Use can/can't, will/won't, able/unable for the modal operators of possibility.

Example:

'You are able to come up with many creative ideas.'

PRESUPPOSITIONS

It's possible to elicit agreement indirectly by including assumptions or presuppositions in your statement or question. Because they're taken for granted, but not made explicit, they often don't get noticed by the conscious mind. There are various types of presuppositions, as follows:

Time presupposition
Words such as 'before', 'after', 'continue', 'as', 'during', 'when', 'since' and 'while'.

Example:

'You can deepen your understanding while you read this book.'

Ordinal presupposition
Using numbers and positions – 'first', 'second', 'third', 'another', 'last' – presupposes a sequence.

Example:

'We'll come to the third example in a minute...'

DOUBLE BINDS

Double binds utilize presuppositions to present an illusory choice – whichever option is taken leads to the desired outcome.

Examples:

'Shall we discuss things here or in your office.'
'You can understand all that you need to when you're ready or at a time of your choosing.'

Additional Milton Model patterns

AWARENESS (FACTIVE) PREDICATES

Using words such as know, realize, notice and aware presupposes that what's being said is true:

Example:

'Do you realize there are many ways of becoming more knowledgeable?'

ADVERBS AND ADJECTIVES

Slipping in an adverb here and there is a simple but powerful way of presupposing that something's happening by focusing on the nature of the experience. Useful adverbs include deeply, surprisingly, happily, luckily, readily and easily.

Example:

'You are going deeply into trance.'

COMMENTARY ADJECTIVES AND ADVERBS

Sentences can be structured so that everything after the first word is supposed. Useful words are happily, fortunately, usefully.

Examples:

'Fortunately this concept is easy to understand. Happily you've grasped it already'.

QUOTES

When you want to communicate something directly, but feel you can't for whatever reason, one option is to use quotes. As we tell a story or recount a conversation we often quote verbatim what was said, such as: 'Then he said to me, "You need to *make that change now*"'. While listeners will recognize the statement as being for the person in the story, their unconscious mind will register it as a command directed at them, especially when special emphasis is given to the words.

Examples:

'The doctor turned to his patient and said, "It's time you started to *take better care of yourself*".'
'The motivational speaker said "*You can achieve* whatever you want for yourself".'

EMBEDDED COMMANDS

An embedded command is a message or instruction that's hidden or embedded in a sentence. It works subliminally, because although the conscious mind won't recognize it, the unconscious mind will. Using commands in this way makes it possible to give suggestions indirectly. The effect is heightened if you use analogue marking – lowering the voice tone and increasing the volume slightly – when saying the words that make up the command. You don't have to be obvious when doing so, the unconscious mind is remarkably sensitive to subtlety.

Examples:

'I wonder if *you can learn* about these things *easily*.'
'*You can* say lots of things to help people *feel better*.'

Placing a person's name after a modal operator – 'can', 'may', 'must' – allows the sentence to be structured in such a way that the command sounds like it's directed at them individually.

Example:

'Everyone must, *Amanda, listen carefully.*'

EMBEDDED QUESTIONS

Words such as 'wonder', 'curious', 'know' and 'understand' have a particular value because they make it possible to ask questions to which no response is expected. A message can therefore be communicated in an indirect manner.

Examples:

'I'm curious why you feel that way.'
'I'm wondering if you can remember a time when you knew you could achieve anything.'

NEGATIVE COMMANDS

In Chapter 7 we discussed the difficulty the mind has when processing negatively phrased statements such as 'Don't think of a guitar'. To be able to *not* think of it, you have to *think* of it. Phrasing a command negatively is particularly effective with people who mismatch.

Examples:

'Don't pay close attention to this section.'
'Don't write that cheque until you're good and ready.'

CONVERSATIONAL POSTULATE

Openly requesting information or action can sometimes generate resistance but that can be avoided by using the conversational postulate. It sounds like a question but it's really a command!

Examples:

'Could you pass me that file.'
'Would you like to read the last sentence again.'

AMBIGUITY

Ambiguity is when words or statements have a double meaning, and are open to interpretation. In NLP-speak, there's more than one possible deep structure for a particular surface structure. Ambiguity therefore stimulates a transderivational search to find the most appropriate meaning. There are four types of ambiguity:

Phonological ambiguity
This is where words that look different when written down sound the same when heard. Such *homonyms* include: nose/knows; there/their; write/right/rite; knot/not; weight/wait; here/hear; your/you're; know/no. Ambiguity is by its nature trance-inducing.

Example:

'And what's it thinking, *your unconscious* mind, *right now*?'

Syntactic ambiguity
Ambiguity can also be created by the syntactic structure of a sentence.

Examples:

'Hypnotizing people can be difficult.'
'The revolting peasants need their hair cut badly.'

Scope ambiguity
Sometimes it's not possible to tell how much of a sentence a particular word or phrase applies to. In 'The fascinating shop and museum', for instance, does fascinating relate to both shop and museum?

Example:

'You are aware that you are sitting and starting to relax.'

Punctuation ambiguity

When using punctuation ambiguity the sentence that results isn't grammatical, it's simply two ideas that are connected by a word that joins them. The aim is to create confusion of the conscious, so the person goes into their experience to make sense of what's being said.

Examples:

'The sounds that you hear are the learnings you want.'
'That's an attractive watch my hand closely.'

PACING CURRENT EXPERIENCE

One of the most effective ways of establishing rapport with someone is to make statements that match their current experience. Doing so narrows the person's attention to what they're seeing, hearing and feeling, and encourages them to go inside. For that reason it's useful to incorporate visual, auditory and kinaesthetic statements that the person will recognize as true. You can then follow on with statements that lead them into trance. As a rule of thumb, give three pacing statements before trying to lead.

Example:

'And as you become aware of your breathing, hear the sounds in the room around you, and focus on the words on this page, so you can feel comfortable and relaxed.'

TAG QUESTIONS

You can distract the conscious mind, and so displace resistance, by adding a question at the end of a statement, don't you think? The communication then goes directly to the unconscious mind, which is what you want, isn't it? Useful questions to tag at the end include won't you?, didn't I?, and aren't you?

Example:

'You can recognize the value of such an approach, can't you? It's an elegant way of communicating, isn't it? But you could take it too far if you did it in every sentence, don't you think?'

SELECTIONAL RESTRICTION VIOLATION

This complicated sounding technique involves attributing feelings to inanimate objects, concepts and animals, which they could not have. One of the most famous examples of this technique is documented and analysed in *Patterns of the Hypnotic Techniques of Milton H. Erickson MD*. During a session focused primarily on pain control, Erickson talked to Joe, a retired farmer, about growing tomato plants. He told him, for instance, that tomato plants can feel relaxed and comfortable. Generally when people hear this type of statement they make sense of it by assuming it refers to them in some way.

Examples:

'That outcome wants you to have it.'
'The chair was pleased to have someone sit in it.'

> **What will it be like when you have made those changes now ... in the future ... as you look back and see what it was like to have had a problem ; as you think about it now, here sitting in this room?**
>
> Tad James

Metaphor

Although Milton Erickson was sometimes directive in his approach, most of the time he simply told his clients stories. As you might imagine, they were not just random stories. They were carefully chosen or created to fit the needs of each particular person. Over many years of practice and research Erickson refined his skills, and was able to facilitate spectacular changes with seemingly difficult cases. There are many fascinating books available that document his imaginative interventions.

Quite a lot of NLP thinking is based upon Erickson's work, and many of the presuppositions – that people have all the resources they need, that all behaviours have a positive intention, etc. – originated with him. The idea of using stories has also been adopted. This is known in NLP as metaphor, with the term covering a wide range of interventions, including analogies, jokes, parables, similes, fables and allegories as well as stories and metaphors.

As Carl Jung and others have shown, metaphor is the natural language of the unconscious mind, and when utilized effectively speaks directly to the deepest part of a person. It also communicates in a way that bypasses the conscious mind, making it more difficult to resist or sabotage the message.

METAPHOR IN THERAPY AND BUSINESS

Therapy is a natural home for metaphor, but its value to business is increasingly being recognized. But there are cultural differences. The kinds of stories that work in a company setting may not be the same as those that succeed in other contexts. In a therapeutic situation tales might be told of elves or fairies and these might not be well received in some board rooms. Instead they might prefer a heroic saga of fortitude and succeeding against all the odds. The real art lies in matching the story to your audience and subject matter. If the topic for discussion was diversity or empowerment the following short tale might work well.

This princess was different.
She was a brunette beauty with
a genius of a brain.
Refusing marriage, she

inherited all by primogenesis.
The country's economy
prospered under her rule.
When the handsome prince
came by on his white charger,
she bought it from him
and started her own racehorse business.

Zoe Ellis, 1988

Stories can be effective in many business situations. They're great for bringing to life a presentation or communicating with impact. It's just a matter of being creative. It could be used in conflict resolution, negotiation, coaching, team building and even performance review. There are trainers who specialize in business storytelling, and you can even go on a course and learn how to do it yourself.

USING METAPHOR

Metaphor can be used in a number of different ways. At its simplest, in a coaching or therapy session or a normal conversation, the person you're speaking to may start talking metaphorically. They might say, for instance, that they're 'getting out of their depth, and afraid of going under'. In some way that's real for them, it's a reflection of their internal representation of the situation. Metaphors are a way of talking about experience. If your response is about them being overloaded with work or having their back to the wall, your description won't be a match for their map. But if you were to ask them how high the water is right now, or if there's any way they could pull the plug out, you would pace their experience and begin the process of guiding them to a solution.

If one doesn't emerge spontaneously, asking someone to provide a metaphor for their problem can often be illuminating. While it may not come immediately to mind, they'll usually have one and it can be worth persevering to bring it out into the open.

An advanced approach to using metaphor is to compose a story that reflects the structure of the person's problem. Such metaphors are said to be *isomorphic* – they have the same shape and structure. The starting point is knowing the present state and the desired state – where they are now and where they want to be. It's important to elicit as much information as possible, particularly regarding all the characters, elements and locations in their problem situation. These, and their relationships, must be faithfully represented in the metaphor that's created. As far as possible this should reflect an interest the person has, to ensure it engages their attention. What is then required is a 'connecting strategy' that will take them from their present state to their desired state, which will be an effective solution in real life and can also be incorporated in the metaphor.

Once that's in place, all that remains is for the metaphor to be presented to the person, with them ideally in a light to medium trance.

Insight

Those wishing to explore the world of metaphor will find that lots of books have recently been published on the subject. One of the best in our view is *Metaphoria* by Rubin Batino.

NLP in action

▶ Seek out opportunities to use Milton Model language, and observe its effects.

▶ Focus on one or two of the Milton Model patterns at one time, to avoid spreading your attention too thin.

▶ Listen out for people's metaphors, and find ways of responding to them 'within' the metaphor.

▶ Start your own collection of stories for use in different situations.

TEN KEY POINTS TO REMEMBER

1 *Richard Bandler and John Grinder used implicit modelling of a leading hypnotherapist, Milton H. Erickson, and discovered he violated many of the Meta Model patterns used by Satir and Perls.*

2 *Milton Erickson used artfully vague language that encourages deletions, distortions and generalizations. It is trance-inducing, allows you to access the unconscious mind and stimulates a transderivational search.*

3 *Trance is a naturally occurring state that is often referred to as 'down time' in NLP.*

4 *The Milton Model categories include the inverse of the Meta Model, for example, deliberately leaving out information on simple deletions.*

5 *There are some additional patterns in the Milton Model including: awareness predicates, adverbs and adjectives, quotes, embedded commands, ambiguity and tag questions.*

6 *Embedded commands are messages or instructions that are hidden in a sentence. The conscious mind doesn't recognize them and the unconscious mind does.*

7 *Phonological ambiguity is where words that look different when written down sound the same when heard. They stimulate a transderivational search to find the most appropriate meaning.*

8 *When you match another person's current experience you build rapport and in the process narrow their attention to what they are seeing, hearing and feeling. This encourages them to 'go inside'.*

9 *Metaphor is the natural language of the unconscious mind. Because it bypasses the conscious mind it is more difficult to resist the message.*

10 *Working with metaphors can be a powerful way of entering another person's world and bringing about change.*

20

....

NLP in action

In this chapter you will learn:
- *how NLP has been applied in a variety of areas*
- *ways to make NLP an integral part of your life*

Now you've learnt how powerful NLP can be, it's time to consider how it's used and how you might put it into practice on a daily basis. There's no end to the ways you can apply NLP – at home and in the workplace. Read on to be informed and inspired to take action.

NLP and personal development

People come to NLP for many reasons, and one of the most common is personal development. And even if that's not their primary motivation – perhaps they just want to be able to connect with others better – personal development is one of the key benefits many people achieve. It's not unusual for those attending NLP workshops to make significant changes in their life – and, although it's not intended to be a 'self-help' book, the same may happen to you as a result of reading *Essential NLP*.

Sometimes this is as a result of the Well-Formed Outcome process. They ask themselves, perhaps for the first time in a long while, 'What do I want?' Many people spend more time deciding what car to buy or where to go on holiday than consciously designing their life. Once they get in touch with what they really, specifically want, then change and personal development is perhaps inevitable.

As part of that process they may well get more in touch with their values, starting to live in a way that's more aligned with them. Many also become more aware of their beliefs, inevitably challenging those which seem to limit them – choosing empowering beliefs instead.

NLP provides a range of tools for expanding your self-awareness and your awareness of others – becoming more emotionally intelligent in the process. People learn to manage their emotions better, taking control of them rather than – as is sometimes the case – being victims of them.

But it's often the 'P' part of NLP that makes the most important difference. They change their 'Programs', sometimes installing new ones, sometimes updating them to the latest version, and sometimes uninstalling programs that no longer work or serve them. As a result they develop more effective strategies and habits which make them happier and more effective.

NLP perspectives
Steve Andreas – Transforming
Your Self

'Long ago people realized that someone's self-concept – how they think of themselves, and what they think they can accomplish – is a major factor in their success, or lack of it. As Henry Ford said, "Whether you think that you can, or that you can't, you are usually right."

Your self-concept is something like the keel and rudder on a sailboat, providing momentum and stability in a sudden storm, and allowing it to move against the wind. Without keel and rudder, a boat is blown here and there, completely at the mercy of winds and tides that shift – and rocks that don't. But with rudder and keel, you can move against adversity, using its energy to go where you want to go, avoid obstacles, and persevere through unexpected troublesome events.

What I have modelled is the knowledge of exactly how our self-concept works – what it is made of, and how it functions. Like our other concepts or ideas, it is based on selecting a certain set of experiences from the incredible variety of different experiences we have had, and then collecting these experiences, so that they become a strong and durable "package" of experience.

Since this is something that we learn how to do almost completely unconsciously and randomly, there is a considerable variation in exactly how a particular person does it, and how effective it is. Although discovering this structure requires eliciting experience that is usually unconscious or preconscious, it is relatively quick and easy to do when you know what to look for and how to ask. Once this structure is known, it is easy to offer someone a variety of simple changes that will make their self-concept much stronger and effective, more positive and congruent.'

Steve Andreas is author of *Transforming Your Self: Becoming Who you Want to Be*, and *Six Blind Elephants*.

http://www.steveandreas.com/

NLP in presentations

To be successful in business you need to be able to present your ideas with impact. Whether it's in a meeting with one or two people or to a crowd of 20 or even 200, at some point in your career you'll be asked to communicate to a group. Being centre-stage can be a nerve-wracking experience for many, and NLP can be a great help when it comes to managing nerves.

One of the simplest ways of altering your state is to change your physiology – because mind and body are one system. By standing straight and as if you're confident you start to feel self-assured. Reframing is another good way of dealing with anxiety. If we're worried about making a mistake or think an audience is out to get us we're bound to be anxious. By exchanging these negative thoughts with something positive such as 'the audience is on my side' or 'if I miss something out I can add it later or deal with it in the question and answer session' you start to feel calmer.

State management also applies to the audience. If you want your audience to experience an emotion you have to experience it first. When you feel passionate about a topic it comes across in your voice tone and body language. The audience will pick up on this and your enthusiasm for the subject becomes infectious. Being aware of the mood people are in is important when you're presenting. It's one of the ways you know whether or not you're getting your message across. If they're alert and looking interested, keep going. If they start to shuffle around in their seat or appear bored, you know you need to change your approach. Most presenters pick up these signals as a matter of course, but NLP trained speakers have enhanced skills in sensory acuity and are highly aware of the importance of doing something different if what they're doing isn't working.

There are many NLP skills and techniques you can apply to improve your success in presenting. If you want to model excellence there are lots of well-known people around to learn from. Bill Clinton is considered one of the most charismatic speakers of our time. He is a master of the 'power pause' and can captivate an audience for long periods of time. Barack Obama provides another great example of how rhetorical techniques can add power and memorability to your key messages.

An up-and-coming UK politician well worth noting is Nick Clegg, the leader of the Liberal Democrat party. While not as well known as the others, he uses stories to help make his key points stick.

From the world of IT check out the CEOs at Apple and Cisco – Steve Jobs and John Chambers respectively. You'll find many clips of well-known speakers like these on YouTube. By listening to their voices, observing their body language, and paying close attention to the words they say, you can pick up lots of ideas for improving the way you present. Think of someone you know who is a good presenter and ask them questions to elicit their success strategies and uncover the beliefs they hold that make them effective.

Learning to present well is extremely worthwhile, liberating and personally satisfying. If you take time to model excellence and improve what you do you will reap rich rewards.

NLP in sports and fitness

Time spent on the field, track or pitch or in the ring, gym or hall will only get you so far. It's essential, but on its own it's not enough. Sport is not just a physical battle – there's also a mental battle, and that's the one that can be really challenging. Physical fitness has to be matched by mental fitness.

How do you keep going when your muscles are beyond aching? What's the secret of holding your nerve at a crucial moment – such as downing a putt for a birdie or converting a try that could win the game? How do you stay motivated when you're staring defeat square in the face? Why is it sometimes easy to be 'in the zone' and why does it sometimes seem impossible?

Self-belief and self-confidence are absolutely essential for success in any kind of sporting endeavour. If you don't think you're going to win you probably won't. The tennis player Billie Jean King once said that 'more matches are won internally than externally'.

This is, of course, where NLP techniques come into their own, and why they're so widely used by professional sports psychologists when they're working with their clients – and why they're equally effective for amateurs. Using NLP it's possible to discover and challenge beliefs that are limiting, replacing them instead with positive beliefs that are empowering. When Roger Bannister broke the four-minute mile barrier (see page 77) it was his belief that it was possible which enabled him to do it when others had failed.

Visualization techniques, such as the New Behaviour Generator, are commonly used to install new habits at the neurological level. This can involve recalling and re-accessing peak experiences in the past, stepping mentally into the body of a role model, or acting as a film director and creating a movie in which the person has all the resources they need. Submodality adjustments can be made to counter intrusive or negative internal dialogue. The aim is generally to 'program' the sportsperson to enter a state of mental flow so that everything happens easily, effortlessly and automatically – in which the unconscious mind takes control and the conscious mind avoids sabotaging things. Similar techniques can also be used to maintain motivation when the going gets tough.

Those who would like to know more should track down a copy of *NLP and Sports* by Joseph O'Connor. It's currently out of print, but can be found – it's highly regarded and much sought after, so grab a copy when you see it.

NLP in health and well-being

One of the presuppositions of NLP is that the mind and body are one system – the thoughts we have affect what goes on in our body and vice versa. And this has been proved to be the case on countless occasions. You need only consider the placebo effect to know it to be true. A whole new discipline has, in fact, grown up that deals with this relationship: psycho-neuro-immunology.

You can heal your body and keep it well by thinking positive thoughts. Candace Pert has demonstrated beyond doubt in her book *Molecules of Emotion* that experiences can be stored at the cellular level, and many health therapists and practitioners believe that a significant proportion of illnesses and diseases have a psychological component. *Your Body Speaks Your Mind* by Debbie Shapiro is just one of many excellent books starting from this perspective.

The reverse is also true: you can help to keep your mind healthy by looking after your body. Many people find that a gentle jog or a visit to the gym at the end of a stressful day can act as a reset button that releases the tension and leaves them feeling revitalized. Research has even shown running to be one of the most effective cures for depression.

As well as visiting the doctor when you get something physical wrong with you, it can also be worthwhile considering things from a psychological perspective. In their ground-breaking book *The Healing Power of Illness*, Thorwald Dethlefsen and Rudiger Dahlke suggest that asking yourself questions about what your disease forces you to do or stops you doing can be the key to coping with it or curing it.

NLP can be a powerful tool in maintaining both your mental and physical health and well-being, with numerous tools and techniques to help you keep on track.

NLP perspectives
Arielle Essex – Talk yourself well

'When you think about all the commonly used phrases that refer to the body, it's no surprise that there is a direct link between how you think and how you feel. The language

(Contd)

chosen is no coincidence. Your unconscious mind not only runs your body but also stores old memories, beliefs and feelings. The body hears what you say and produces symptoms according to your requests! Listen more carefully to the words you use to describe an event. Phrases like the following simultaneously send directive messages to the body:

"I can't stomach this!" (ulcers and digestive problems)
"It makes my skin crawl" (skin rashes)
"I feel so unsupported" (back problems)
"It breaks my heart" (circulation problems)
"What a pain in the neck!" (headaches)
"I can't let go" (constipation)

Such organ language metaphorically describes inner tensions, conflicts, and deep seated issues that may need to be addressed. Although it may be a question of the "chicken or the egg", the new science of Psycho Neuro Immunology takes this relationship very seriously. Recent research has revealed that brain tissue found in many different parts of the body means memory and thinking power reside in different centres.

By using your sensory acuity to listen and pay attention to the language you use, you can positively improve your health and well being. Tune into the thoughts going through your head. Take your awareness to the parts of the body that relate to these thoughts and let the unconscious issues surface to be dealt with. Use whatever NLP techniques you need to resolve the conflicts, let go of old emotions, and change old limiting beliefs. Then break the habit of speaking organ language. Re-phrase the negative descriptions in your head before they come out of your mouth.'

Arielle Essex has been providing extraordinary coaching and training in health, life, business and career issues for more than 15 years, both in the UK and abroad. In 1995 she set up her own training business, Practical Miracles, in London, which has been providing top quality NLP and hypnosis courses ever since. After Arielle succeeded in healing her own brain tumour using NLP, she published her first book, *Compassionate Coaching*, in 2004, about how to self-coach yourself to health, happiness and success.

www.PracticalMiracles.com

NLP in relationships

Whether you're at work or at home, with friends or complete strangers, relationships hold the key to a successful and satisfying life. How well we relate to people often determines the opportunities that come our way and whether or not we're likely to get the job or partner of our dreams. Career prospects often depend on not just what you know but who you know. If you're good at getting on with people they're more likely to help you. How well you relate to your spouse, partner, children and other family members affects your happiness at home. It's not just people in your immediate circle that matter. Strangers can be thought of as friends you haven't met yet. Whatever the situation you find yourself in, your ability to connect will determine how effective your relationships are.

The key to getting on with people lies in being able to build rapport with them. When a child falls over we instinctively crouch down, our voice tone changes and we aim to enter their world to comfort them. This natural process is called Matching in NLP. By observing others closely, and flexing your body language and voice volume, tone and pitch to match theirs, you're more likely to make a positive connection with them. We do this unconsciously when we're with people we like. It's a fast-track way to make friends and improve existing relationships.

Matching representational systems deepens rapport too. Take these three sentences: 'I see what you mean' (visual), 'I hear what you say' (auditory), and 'I get your point' (kinaesthetic). If someone uses a lot of visual language it makes sense to use the same types of words in return. In essence the more the other person feels that you are like them the deeper the rapport will be. People gravitate towards those who seem familiar.

Intimate relationships can sometimes be bitter-sweet, they can be a source of bliss, of pain or somewhere in-between. People don't always see eye to eye with others at work, either, and rapport is the first step towards resolving conflict. As Anthony Robbins says in his best-selling book *Unlimited Power*, 'The way to go from discord to harmony is to go from concentrating on differences to concentrating on similarities'.

But connecting with people is about much more than body language and voice matching in difficult circumstances. By standing back, or dissociating from a situation, we gain new perspectives. The Perceptual Positions technique is invaluable when conflict arises because it helps us better understand what's happening from both sides.

Almost every area of NLP covered in this book will help you to improve the quality of your relationships in some way. We have selected just a few ideas to get you started. As you become more skilled at applying what you've learnt you'll find your interpersonal skills go from strength to strength.

NLP in therapy

Since NLP has its origins in therapy – beginning when Bandler and Grinder observed and modelled the work of family therapist Virginia Satir, hypnotherapist Milton H. Erickson and gestalt therapist Fritz Perls – it can be used to treat people with a wide range of conditions. The 'trail of techniques' that came out of

NLP's 'attitude and methodology' makes it possible to cure phobias in just a few minutes, neutralize emotional traumas from childhood and change the habits of a lifetime.

So powerful are these processes that some therapists use NLP more or less exclusively. Others draw upon other approaches, such as Cognitive Behaviour Therapy or Gestalt, both of which are similar in style and philosophy. The great advantage of NLP is that it's a form of 'Brief Therapy' – dramatic results and sometimes complete resolution of a problem can be achieved in a single session. And because there are so many different ways of working – submodalities, timeline, metaphor, anchoring, Meta Programs to name but a few – NLP can be applied successfully to the vast majority of the issues therapists commonly encounter.

Those who study NLP and start to use it for therapy also have another advantage: some understanding of hypnosis. Many NLP techniques, such as 'six-step reframing', are by their nature trance inducing, and the Milton Model explicitly provides language that is hypnotic. The power of hypnosis is that it gives therapists access to the person's unconscious mind, which is where the problem lies and where change needs to happen. Those serious about working this way should consider studying hypnotherapy, but even on its own, NLP is capable of producing stunning, awesome results.

NLP in business

Communication lies at the heart of every business. It's an essential ingredient for success that we cannot afford to ignore. Whatever your role, you'll benefit from learning more about yourself and how to interact with others more effectively. Rapport skills, for instance, help us to build good relationships with people we come into contact with on a day-to-day basis. In essence, NLP helps people become more effective communicators. People who work in any area of a business benefit from improved communication including finance, sales, operations or management. Meetings are more effective, teams work together cohesively, the right people are recruited and more business is won through a highly skilled sales team.

People who own a business or manage a team appreciate the importance of taking account of the needs of various stakeholders such as staff, clients, suppliers, partners and shareholders. In the hectic world of business, misunderstandings sometimes occur and, if left unresolved, they can cause tension, wasted time and loss of productivity.

Perceptual Positions is a great way of gaining insight into other people's 'maps' of the world. By moving from one perspective to another you make more information available to you about a given situation. We're often so immersed in first position that it's easy to forget how our behaviour affects others. Stepping into second position allows us to see ourself from another person's perspective. In third position we can stand back and learn without letting emotions get in the way.

While NLP's Perceptual Positions technique provides good preparation for handling challenging relationships, the meta model is an ideal tool to help you gain real understanding of any issue. It provides a way of accessing the real meaning or deep structure of what people say through active listening and questions. If we're equipped to handle difficult situations quickly we can minimize the impact these have on business results.

NLP perspectives
Robbie Steinhouse – Building the
four key business skills

'Often a promotion requires people to learn completely new skills which may move them out of their comfort zone. It's interesting to note the things people say at these moments. Their words are symptomatic of particular states – how you think and feel at any specific time. These states directly influence how quickly you learn, and become effective in, these new skills. The examples below illustrate common negative self-comments and accompanying states people experience when facing new business challenges:

Challenge	Self-talk	State
Management	"I am not a boss"	Fear of inadequacy (can also be aggressive)
Finance	"Finance is too complicated"	Fear of appearing foolish (can be manipulative)
Sales	"Salespeople are pushy"	Shame (aloof)
Operations	"You've got to do it yourself"	Overwhelmed (arrogant)

In order to change a state it's first necessary to accept it, however "negative" it is. Once you do this, you can then use that awareness to detach yourself and make decisions about what you want to do next.

It's essential to understand that your state originally had a positive purpose. A dislike of finance is often linked to childhood fears of learning mathematics, and thus looking stupid. Concerns about management and sales are often linked to a fear of rejection – too snooty or too pushy. The benefits you gained out of these states may have been protection and belonging. But now the task is to find positive, practical, adult alternatives. These will provide the same benefits without the negative side-effects of the outdated "protective" mechanisms.

Achieving this will almost undoubtedly involve changing "limiting beliefs", some of which may be quite deeply

(Contd)

embedded. NLP has a range of powerful techniques to effect this change, such as the Meta Model or Change Personal History.'

Robert Steinhouse is both a successful entrepreneur and a highly experienced NLP trainer and coach.

www.NLPschooleurope.com

NLP in selling

Much selling these days, especially for high-ticket items or services, is done in a 'consultative' way. This involves asking questions to understand what the customer wants and needs, identifying the gap, and then matching the wants or needs with what you offer. Consultative selling requires finely tuned listening and questioning skills, which studying NLP can help you to develop.

One of the secrets of success lies in identifying the person's 'criteria' – what's important to them – and emphasizing them in your sales pitch. This is easily done by asking questions such as, 'What do you look for when buying an X?' or 'What's important to you when choosing a Y?'. If you can establish what their 'hot buttons' are, and then press them, you're more likely to be able to make the sale.

Reflecting the language of the customer or prospect can be valuable when doing this. If you focus your sensory acuity and listen very carefully, you'll notice keywords they say time and again – 'reliability', perhaps, or 'quality'. Using the 'backtrack frame' to repeat what they actually said, rather than your translation of it, will allow you to communicate more powerfully with them. And if you can identify their preferred representational system, and use visual, auditory or kinaesthetic words and phrases as appropriate, you'll be speaking their natural 'language'.

Being able to identify a prospect's Meta Programs can be extremely helpful too. If they have a 'Towards' motivation you should place emphasis on how wonderful life will be for them when they've bought your product or service. If their pattern is 'Away From' you should highlight the problems they'll avoid. Using NLP can also enable you to recognize your prospect's Convincer pattern – the internal process they go through before they feel comfortable to buy. If they need to see something or use it before they're convinced, show them a sample, if appropriate, so they can try it out for themselves. If hearing or reading about something are convincers, put them in touch with a satisfied customer or client, so they can hear and/or read from a reliable source that the product or service is right for them.

One of the axioms of selling is that 'people buy people first', before they buy the product or service. However good you are at the technical aspects of selling – describing features (what the customer buys), advantages (what the features do) and benefits (what the buyer gains) – you have to be able to build rapport and win their trust first. Many successful salespeople have developed the ability to connect with others quickly and easily, using techniques such as matching and mirroring. The salesperson who embraces NLP is without doubt better equipped to win more business and create lasting relationships with customers.

NLP in coaching

Coaching has become extremely popular over recent years, both 'life' coaching for individuals and 'executive' coaching for those working in business. Most leading companies use it alongside training to help develop their staff, while the man and woman in the street may now choose coaching in favour of counselling or therapy when they have issues they need to deal with. There are many approaches to coaching but it's becoming increasingly apparent that when it's paired with NLP there are several key benefits.

One of the most important is speed. NLP techniques work quickly – sometimes astonishingly so – bringing about dramatic change sometimes in the very first session.

Another is the fact that NLP coaching is 'solution-focused' rather than 'problem-focused'. It doesn't dwell on what's gone wrong or going wrong. Instead it invites the client to focus on what they want, and develop effective strategies to achieve it.

Thirdly, NLP coaching is practical rather than theoretical. While there will inevitably be some exploration of the problem or situation, the aim is to get the client to take action, to do something different if what they're currently doing isn't working.

Finally, an NLP coach will encourage the person they are working with to think and act in a way that's aligned and congruent with their deepest beliefs and values – since that is when the plans they make will be truly ecological for them.

NLP perspective
Steve Bavister – Coaching and NLP were made for each other

'In my work as a business and executive coach I draw upon a wide range of models and techniques, but it's NLP that's central to my approach. In fact, in all honesty, I cannot imagine being effective as a coach without having the tools that NLP provides.

I rarely use NLP techniques as such – nothing "set-piece" such as Change Personal History – because I view them more as therapeutic interventions. What I find of most value is the Meta Model. Since asking powerful questions is at the heart of coaching, I need to be able to help the client go deeper into his or her own experience and find answers that don't trip glibly off the tongue.

That's what Meta Model questions do. They expose and challenge the deletions, generalizations and distortions that are often causing the client difficulty. As people become more aware of their mental processes, so they develop solutions to their problems.'

Steve Bavister is a coach, trainer, hypnotherapist and author of *Essential NLP* and *Teach Yourself Coaching*.

While it is possible to coach successfully without NLP, using the tools and techniques it offers will certainly make you a better, more effective coach.

NLP in negotiation

Negotiation is part of everyday life. When we buy anything, be it a new computer, a car or even a house, we have an opportunity to negotiate a better deal. At work whether you're in sales, finance, customer service, operations or part of a management team, you'll get better results if you're not afraid to ask for what you want while taking account of the other person's needs. Effective negotiation is all about achieving a win–win and maintaining a balance between getting the outcome you want and keeping the relationship intact. Communication and influencing skills are paramount for success – hence why NLP is invaluable. You may also need to be skilled in getting the other party to feel good about accepting a completely new viewpoint.

And yet many people don't even attempt it in the first place. They'd rather pay the full price than ask for a discount in a shop. If you have any limiting beliefs around negotiating or asking for a better deal, you're likely to be settling for less than you deserve. If this is true for you it will be worthwhile spending some time considering what the positive intention is behind your behaviour. Maybe there's a conscious or unconscious part of you that holds back.

One of the most powerful ways that NLP can liberate us is through exploring our limiting beliefs. The Belief Change Pattern is a good place to start if you're new to this. If you enjoy negotiating most of the time, and it's a core part of your job, you may want to consider whether or not your beliefs limit you when there are large sums of money at stake or there's a lot riding on the outcome.

You'll need all of the Four Pillars of NLP to achieve a great result in any negotiation. Preparation and planning are vital as are sensory acuity, behavioural flexibility and rapport. NLP allows you to move away from the traditional approach to negotiation and towards understanding a more powerful set of strategies for persuasion. Success in negotiation relies heavily on effective preparation. If you follow the principles of a well-formed outcome you will achieve this. It helps you to become crystal clear about your minimum and maximum settlement price. You can also use this process to establish a long list of 'tradeables' – things you're happy to give away to achieve a win–win.

If your sensory acuity is sharp you'll pick up on subtle signals that reveal how the other person is responding to you. This allows you to flex your approach as needed while maintaining superb rapport skills throughout the meeting. As any poker player will tell you, state management is an important ingredient for success. Our bodies constantly give away how we're feeling through micro-movements such as our facial expressions. The state we're in is important because it affects how we behave. If we're uncertain it will be reflected in our body language and our behaviour. NLP offers techniques that help you to maintain a calm and alert emotional state.

The Meta Model provides even the most experienced negotiators with the tools they need to achieve an advanced level of probing skills. When you understand the principles you're able to cut through the surface and uncover any lurking deletions, distortions or generalizations to obtain a better understanding of what the other party wants.

No matter what level of experience you have, NLP has something to offer to take your skills to the next level.

NLP in leadership

You don't have to be a CEO of a multi-national company or a manager of a large team to be a leader. Leadership applies to us all. To be personally successful we need to have a clear vision – a well-formed outcome – of where we're heading and a strategy to get us there. While some leaders are responsible for vast numbers of employees, others need to communicate that vision to a small group or just themselves. The clearer we are about our end goal the more likely it is that people will receive and implement our message. If a leader communicates in a dry, dull way or lacks conviction their team is less likely to follow them; if they believe in what they hear because it's expressed with passion they will. Self-talk is highly influential too. Telling yourself you'll make it to the end of the London marathon or climb to the top of Kilimanjaro helps to maintain your motivation. Energy, enthusiasm and self-belief are not enough on their own though. Your deeds need to match your words – you need to be seen to 'walk the talk'. Congruence is critical for effective leadership.

NLP perspectives
Judith DeLozier – Effective leadership abilities are one of the keys to our future success and survival

'Leaders are people and organizations who go first, this means that there is something that moves us to want to go first. The question is what moves in us that we are so passionate about that we are willing to risk our self importance?

(Contd)

During times of uncertainty, changing markets and social change, leadership plays a more and more important role in managing families, communities, organizations and ourselves. This is not to mention our planet. There are many models of leadership and many tomes related to different kinds of leadership. NLP, however, offers the tools and processes to define and explore specific models, principles and skills that allow us to become a more successful leader. NLP allows us to define effective leadership from different perceptual positions as well as define the differences between a leader, leadership and leading. Being in a formal role of leadership does not necessarily mean that the person in the role has the capabilities, skill or the degree of influence to guide a group or organization through the maze of change. Leaders are people who are committed to creating something better and commit their heartbeats in service to something larger than themselves.

Leadership then becomes a landscape that is accessible to everyone; the natural abilities a person has can be enhanced and polished for even more effective and healthy influence. Healthy systems are calm, flexible, adaptable and understand the difference between energized rest and frenzied collapse, whether it be an individual or group. All of these characteristics can be modelled through NLP principles.'

Judith Delozier is a member of Grinder and Bandler's original group of students; she contributed extensively to the development of NLP models and processes. She is the co-author with John Grinder of *Turtles All The Way Down* and *The Encyclopedia of Systemic Neuro-linguistic programming and NLP New Coding* which she wrote with Robert Dilts.

Values are also crucial to leadership. They act like a compass on our journey to achieving the outcome we have set our sights on. Good leaders know what makes their people tick and by communicating and getting buy-in to the company's values they create unity and alignment. Like a cox with a crew of rowers the leader takes responsibility for the team's safety and they not only direct and control activity, but also coach and motivate their team.

NLP and training

While not all trainers know about and use NLP, in our experience it adds richness and depth to the learning experience. You need to be able to build rapport with a group, calibrate their emotional state and use your sensory acuity to tell you whether what you're doing is working or not. The best trainers are constantly adapting what they do to make sure their course participants' needs are satisfied.

Not every trainer is expert at NLP but many have some experience of it or interest in it. It is one of a number of tools, along with accelerated learning, transaction analysis (TA), and emotional intelligence that trainers use. It's popular among soft skills' trainers because it provides a useful model of human communication. Effective training is all about communicating effectively. If a trainer doesn't understand how to communicate clearly and effectively in a way that works for the participants the group is unlikely to learn much.

Trainers who do use NLP typically draw upon a wide range of techniques, concepts and principles. In some training courses the learners are introduced to aspects of NLP such as the Four Pillars: well-formed outcomes, sensory acuity, behavioural flexibility and rapport. Sales, negotiation, customer service and managing conflict are obvious areas where these skills are valuable.

NLP perspective
Amanda Vickers – The key to learning is caring about being the best you can be

'There are many tools in the average trainer's kitbag. The best trainers though are better than merely run of the mill. They aspire to something more. They don't simply keep their skills and knowledge up-to-date. They have a thirst for learning and care deeply about the people they work with. Because they care they seek out new and improved ways to facilitate learning. NLP provides trainers with a rich and deep understanding of what makes people tick. More than that – the process of learning about it means they enhance their skills as a trainer. They develop their ability to calibrate and connect with a group quickly and easily, create a state that is conducive to learning and facilitate the process of bringing about lasting change by working with beliefs and values.

As someone who has been a trainer and worked in this field for twenty years I can't imagine running a training session without using NLP. While I do not exclusively draw upon it in my work, it is such an integrated part of what I do that I barely notice it and often take it for granted. When I "dig into" a course participant's outcomes it's natural to ask them "What specifically do you want?" or "How will you know when you've achieved it?" These are classic NLP questions. Sensory acuity and behavioural flexibility are indispensable skills for every trainer. Without them you can all too easily go "off-track" and disengage a group. Being aware of the participants' maps of the world, emotional states, primary representational systems, beliefs and values allows me to pace their experience, create an environment that is conducive for helping people learn and to build trust with a group rapidly.'

Amanda Vickers is Director of Speak First Ltd, one of the UK's fastest growing international training and coaching consultancies, and co-author of *Teach Yourself Presenting*.

www.speak-first.com

Some courses lend themselves to using techniques such as the New Behaviour Generator which helps people to install a new strategy or way of behaving in a particular situation such as speaking confidently to strangers at a networking event. The Circle of Excellence is great where you want people to be able to access resources that will be useful to them in a specific situation such as speaking articulately and persuasively to colleagues who you want to buy into your ideas.

NLP in education

Given its capacity to accelerate learning and assist people in achieving their potential, it's surprising that NLP has not been more enthusiastically and more widely embraced by the world of education. Many of its tools and techniques are perfect for developing individuals of all ages to use their minds as effectively as possible. But despite NLP having been around for nearly four decades, its impact in the classroom has been modest to say the least.

Steadily, slowly and surely, though, things seem to be changing. Awareness among educationalists of the benefits NLP can deliver is growing – but we're still a long way from it being considered a core element of the teacher-training curriculum.

The publication of several books has helped spread the word. One of the most recent is *NLP for Teachers: How to Be a Highly Effective Teacher* by Richard Churches and Roger Terry. Published as a 'powerful resource for all those who wish to extend their portfolio of strategies to support effective learning and teaching', it sets out a strong case for incorporating NLP into the classroom. Another book worth tracking down – a classic in this area – is Don A. Blackeby's *Rediscover the Joy of Learning*, which is aimed specifically at the classroom practitioner.

In an article for *Positive Health* magazine, Don asserts what he believes NLP can do for education and what needs to happen: 'In my opinion, we in education spend too much time and effort in theorizing about education and get away from the actual learning process. We pile words upon words, bigger words upon bigger words and bury what has to happen in the subjective experience of students in order for successful learning to occur. These theories sound good, and are needed, but don't translate into action at the level where help is needed – at the subjective experience level. The good news is that NLP operates at the subjective experience level. That is what we practitioners of NLP do! Therefore, the application of NLP in education is a magnificent opportunity for practitioners of NLP.'

Many of us will have suffered at least one teacher – possibly even several – who struggled to connect with students and communicate ideas effectively. By developing rapport skills, understanding the different VAK learning modalities and managing their state better, educationalists will be able to get their message across more successfully. NLP has also been of help with students who have learning challenges such as dyslexia and Attention Deficit Hyperactivity Disorder (ADHD).

Perhaps one day it won't only be educationalists who are taught NLP – it will be students as well. Imagine a world in which everyone left school with at least a basic, working knowledge of NLP. Well, it may not be tomorrow, but it may come eventually. Some NLP training companies have started developing courses specifically for children. If it catches on, we may see an NLP revolution.

NLP and spirituality

Some people are surprised to hear the word 'spirituality' used in relation to NLP, since it's widely perceived as eminently practical and grounded in 'getting what you want'. If you've read this book in order, and have been following its arguments, you might find it curious that a form of applied psychology which says the only way you can experience the world is through your five senses could even begin to consider something beyond. Yet some people do find that NLP gives them a spiritual dimension to their lives – a sense of being part of a larger system.

The word spirituality is even used in the widely-used 'neurological levels' model developed by Robert Dilts. It sits at the top of a sequence that looks like this (others argue they are all at the same level, a heterarchy not a hierarchy):

▶ *Spirituality*
▶ *Identity*
▶ *Beliefs and Values*
▶ *Capabilities*
▶ *Behaviours*
▶ *Environment*

What is certainly true is that NLP will give you a fantastic set of tools for exploring your personal reality – and that may well take you somewhere spiritual.

Insight

There are so many situations where you can apply NLP and reap the benefits it brings. In our view the best way to keep the skills you acquire sharp is to practise and make NLP an integrated part of your life.

NLP perspective
Robert McDonald – To a hammer
everything is a nail

'NLP is a cognitive science used by practitioners to examine subjective experiences, copy them, and create goal-oriented procedures, designed to help people achieve measurable results.

From perhaps the largest perspective, the Perennial Philosophy, NLP fits snugly within the Great Chain of Being, which has identified five levels of reality: matter, life, mind, soul and divine. NLP clearly belongs to the psychological domain and effectively relates to the first three levels. The relationship of NLP to the two Spiritual levels, however, reveals a limitation inherent in NLP: Like a hammer to which the whole world is a nail, NLP reduces Spirituality to mental representations, ultimately based on the body's sensory systems.

This unavoidable reduction is the glory and the gloom of NLP. Glory because, being single-mindedly utilitarian and not encumbered by questions of the Good, the True and the Beautiful, this reduction has made possible the creation of tools that rapidly resolve many forms of human suffering, all the while improving self-confidence and astounding professionals and the lay public alike. That is, by reducing nominalizations to sensory-based representations, NLP transforms ideas, opinions and conclusions into useful observations and step-by-step procedures, the foundation of measurable achievement.

Gloom because this same reduction either ignores or leads people away from the Divine, the numinous, the ultimate Good, "the many-splendoured thing". By explaining all human experiences, including the Spiritual – infinite existence, infinite consciousness, infinite bliss – in terms of modalities, submodalities, perceptual positions, and physiology, NLP reveals its fundamental limitation: Being a cognitive science, the highest level of reality it can acknowledge is its own.

One remedy is the Destination® Method, which uses the extraordinary power of NLP but continually opens to heart-felt compassion, based on a Spiritual model that includes and fosters authenticity, humility, mercy, forgiveness, grace, wisdom and love.'

Dr Robert McDonald, Master Trainer and Developer, Founder of The Destination® Method, The Telos Healing Center. Co-Author of *Tools of the Spirit* (with Robert Dilts) and *NLP: The New Technology of Achievement*.

www.TelosCenter.com

TEN KEY POINTS TO REMEMBER

1   *Many people turn to NLP for personal development and it is not uncommon for people to make significant changes in their life as a result.*

2   *NLP provides lots of techniques for helping presenters manage their state. Modelling great presenters is a good way to substantially improve the quality of delivery.*

3   *NLP can be a powerful tool for maintaining your mental and physical heath. Some successful sports people use NLP to challenge limiting beliefs about what it's possible for them to achieve.*

4   *Relationships hold the key to a good life at home, with friends and at work. NLP provides numerous techniques for improving the way we communicate, understand and connect with one another.*

5   *NLP has its origins in therapy and the trail of techniques that's been created is widely used by practitioners in this field.*

6   *Communication is a central contributory factor in business success, which means that NLP provides a multitude of techniques for improving business performance.*

7   *Sales people who embrace NLP are better equipped to win business and create lasting relationships founded on trust.*

8   *The qualities of effective leaders can be modelled using NLP. Effective leaders create well-formed outcomes and use values to guide their team's behaviour in working towards achieving it.*

9 *Many trainers and coaches draw on NLP techniques, concepts and principles in their work. This is also true in the world of education where NLP is used to accelerate learning and help children achieve their potential.*

10 *NLP gives you a fantastic set of tools for exploring your personal reality, which may take you somewhere spiritual.*

Taking it further

If you have only a passing interest in NLP, or you picked up this book on impulse, you may have learnt all you want by now. Our aim has been to explain the central principles in a practical way. But many people find that once they've had a glimpse of the possibilities offered by NLP they want to learn more – perhaps by studying a particular area in more depth or by engaging with advanced material.

Using the internet

There are various ways of developing your understanding. One of the cheapest, quickest and easiest is to check out the wealth of information available on the internet. Type 'NLP' into any search engine and you'll be rewarded with thousands of different links to websites around the world. While many have been put up by training and publishing companies in the hope of persuading visitors to attend their workshops or buy their books, others exist simply in a spirit of sharing information. And even the commercial sites tend to have useful material which you can read and sometimes download free of charge.

However, trawling through dozens of websites can be a time-consuming business, so we've picked a few to get you started. Most have 'links' pages which take you to other NLP sites worth seeing. Of course, websites come and websites go, and their content changes. That's the nature of the internet. These sites are all current at the time of publication, but some may have changed or disappeared over time.

NLP University – www.nlpu.com – A fantastic resource with dozens of free articles by NLP developer Robert Dilts which you can read on screen or print out. It's also home to the online Encyclopedia of NLP, where you can get detailed explanations of NLP terms and concepts.

NLP Schedule – www.nlpschedule.com – A useful site with articles, book reviews, links and a searchable database of NLP practitioners.

Honest Abe's NLP Emporium – www.Bradburyac.mistral.co.uk – Run by Andy Bradbury, this is a friendly site featuring loads of book reviews, extensive links listings, several interesting articles, and a collection of NLP FAQs (frequently asked questions).

NLP World – http://nlp-world.com – A professionally designed site with lots of information and links to other sites within the NLP community.

NLP Platform – http://nlp-platform.com – Has articles organized into categories, and useful links to various countries around the world.

NLPtCA – http://www.nlptca.com – This is the Neuro Linguisic Psychotherapy and Counselling Association which is aimed at psychotherapists and counsellors using NLP. It offers support and guidance for those in practice, training or considering a career as an NLP Psychotherapist or Counsellor.

There are also plenty of groups where you can ask questions and read discussions relating to NLP. A good place to start is with Yahoo. Go to www.yahoo.co.uk or www.yahoo.com and look for 'Connect' then click on 'Groups'. If you don't already have a Yahoo ID you'll need to get one. Go to new users and choose an ID. All the obvious IDs will have already been chosen – Yahoo has millions of users worldwide – so you may need to go for something like johndoe555. Having started with the following groups you can then carry out a search using 'NLP' as a keyword to find others.

http://groups.yahoo.com/group/NLP-Readings

http://groups.yahoo.com/group/NLPOnline

http://groups.yahoo.com/group/nlptalk-reserve

There is also an excellent newsgroup called alt.psychology.nlp –
and the newsgroup alt.hypnosis sometimes includes discussion
about NLP. You can access these groups a number of ways, but
most quickly and easily by going to www.google.co.uk, selecting
the 'groups' option and typing in 'NLP'.

Visit Michael Beale's **NLP Training Blog** – www.nlp-blog.co.uk –
if you want to participate in or read about some interesting NLP
debates and listen to podcasts on various topics.

Further reading

In recent years there has been an explosion of NLP books, ranging
from introductions and general guides to titles exploring specific
areas or leading edge thinking in greater depth.

Amazon, of course, is an excellent resource, and you'll find most
of the popular titles available there. But for a more comprehensive
inventory, check out www.nlpbooks.com – where you'll be able to
find pretty much any NLP book currently in print, along with titles
on hypnosis, accelerated learning, gestalt etc. Although based in the
UK, the company ships all around the world.

Which titles should you read? As ever, it depends what your
outcome is. Do you want depth or breadth? Classic principles or
cutting-edge thinking? The extensive books review page on the
Honest Abe's NLP Emporium site is a good place to start. They're
just one person's view, but do give a flavour of what most of the
well-known titles are about and how they stack up.

Certainly worth reading are some of the early NLP books by Richard Bandler and John Grinder, such as *The Structure of Magic Vol 1* (Science & Behaviour Books Inc, ISBN 0-8314-0044-7) and *Frogs into Princes* (Eden Grove Editions, ISBN 1-870845-03-X).

If it's personal development using NLP techniques and patterns that interests you, check out *NLP – The New Technology of Achievement* by Steve Andreas and Charles Faulkner (Nicholas Brealey, ISBN 1-85788-122-2) and *Unlimited Power* by Anthony Robbins (Simon & Schuster, ISBN 0-671-69976-8).

The ultimate NLP book, however, is the printed version of the *Encyclopedia of NLP*, which runs to 1,625 pages in two handsomely bound volumes of American A4 (210 × 280 mm). It's an astonishingly comprehensive work, with somewhere in the region of one million words overall, plus hundreds of diagrams and photographs. You can get details of the current price from www.nlpuniversitypress.com – and view sample pages before you decide whether to buy or not.

NLP magazines

Considering the popularity of NLP, there are relatively few publications covering the field. Some trainers produce a newsletter, and most associations have their own journal, but there are not many independent titles.

ANLP produces *Rapport* magazine for members which is full of useful articles that are of interest to NLPers (www.anlp.org).

Anchor Point is a printed magazine published in the USA, but you can take out a subscription anywhere in the world. Full details are on the website – www.nlpanchorpoint.com – along with a large number of articles from previous issues which you can download as PDFs.

ReSource magazine provides a range of stimulating and inspiring articles with a strong strand of NLP. To subscribe or find out more go to www.resourcemagazine.co.uk

If online magazines are more your bag try *NLP Weekly* which is an online magazine/blog that aims to provide updated NLP and hypnosis information including techniques and patterns provided from a variety of sources.

NLP training

However, at the end of the day there's only so much you can learn about NLP from a book, magazine or the internet. Many of the skills, such as rapport, are interpersonal, and some of the techniques and patterns are difficult to do on your own.

For that reason you might like to consider undertaking some training in NLP. There are many companies offering courses of varying duration. A good starting point is to attend a workshop lasting a day or maybe two. This will cover many of the essentials, and give you a taste of NLP in practice. If that works for you, and you still want to know more, the next stage could be to sign up for a 'Practitioner' course. This is a much greater commitment, both in terms of time and money.

Traditionally, such courses were based around 125 contact hours over a 20-day period – typically ten weekends over a ten-month period or one long weekend each month (often Friday to Monday) over a five-month period. However, an increasing number of training companies now offer 'intensive' practitioner programmes as an alternative. These are usually seven days long – 60–70 contact hours – with a requirement for those attending to listen to a set of NLP tapes before commencing the course.

Critics of this approach say the reduced amount of time actually spent in face-to-face training, and the lack of opportunity for material to be assimilated and put into practice between modules, means those taking intensive programmes end up learning and knowing less. Advocates, on the other hand, assert that being immersed in NLP for a full week, having been pre-exposed to the concepts by listening to the tapes, is a richer experience.

Proving this one way or another is difficult, if not impossible, and you will have to make your own mind up. If you have the time and the budget we'd definitely recommend a 20-day programme. However, we recognize that some people have commitments which make it difficult for them to get away at weekends, or simply prefer to take a week off work and complete their Practitioner training all in one go. And the cost of travel and, in some cases, accommodation for 20 days can for some be prohibitive.

Either way, Practitioner training is something that's really worth doing. For many, it's a life-changing experience, both personally and professionally.

There are many courses on offer from different companies, and it's important to choose the right one. INLPTA, the International NLP Trainers Association (www.inlpta.co.uk), sets standards for its registered trainers – and there are many other excellent companies in addition. While there is a generally agreed 'curriculum', some trainers have a particular orientation or emphasis, such as therapy, business or personal growth, and you will get the best from it if it matches your interests and outcomes.

It's also important to make sure that you connect with the person actually doing the training. Some companies run 'taster' sessions or give presentations at NLP conferences which give you a chance to check this out. Over the course of a couple of hours you'll get a sense of whether their style will suit you or not.

If the training organization you're considering doesn't offer this option, read the brochure carefully and then ring with any questions you might have. Things to think about are what experience the trainer has and the size of the group – some have just a handful of participants, others more than 100.

Having completed their Practitioner training, many people go on to do Master Practitioner training, which involves more advanced concepts and patterns, and is also run both as 20-day and intensive programmes.

NLP organizations

The **Association for Neuro-Linguistic Programming** (ANLP) is an independent organization with a reputation for promoting standards, professionalism and good practice in NLP. All members are governed by their code of ethics. The website, where you can get more details, is www.anlp.org.

The **Global Organization of Neuro-Linguistic Programming** (GONLP) and the **British Board of NLP** (BBNLP) is a community of trainers, practitioners, master practitioners and authors of NLP from around the globe. They offer more then 50 benefits to members to support their businesses and personal development. For more information go to www.bbnlp.com.

The **Professional Guild of NLP** provides information on a range of topics and provides a facility for searching for NLP training courses and for people who practice NLP professionally. Practitioners and training providers can become members and therefore position themselves in the public domain. Details can be found at www.professionalguildofnlp.com.

The **NLP Register** is an organization that formed out of a desire to avoid dilution of standards and to maintain the quality of training practice. They clearly set out the standards members adhere to in order to help those new to NLP to have clear information about what training providers cover on their courses. Visit www.thenlpregister.com for details.

NLP conferences

Jo Hogg has successfully hosted NLP conferences in the UK for several years. They attract many well-known names from the world of NLP and lots of delegates. If you want to keep yourself up to date with the latest thinking and mingle with other NLPers go to www.nlpconference.co.uk and make sure the latest dates are in your diary. The links page on this site will direct you to lots of useful sites and is a good place to go to find a local NLP practice group.

Contact the authors

Finally, if you have any questions about NLP, or any comments you'd like to make, you are most welcome to contact the authors by email at enquiries@speak-first.com. We will do our best to give you a personal reply and help you with any queries you may have.

Glossary

4-tuple method for representing internal experience at a moment in time using the four representational systems – Visual, Auditory Kinaesthetic and Olfactory/Gustatory (VAKO)

accessing cues unconscious behaviours, including breathing, posture and eye movements that indicate which representational system a person is using to process information

ambiguity a language pattern of the Milton Model – statements or commands that have several meanings

anchoring the pairing of a cue or trigger, internal or external, with a specific response. This can happen accidentally or be set intentionally

'as if' frame to pretend or act 'as if' something were true or an outcome had already been achieved

associated experiencing fully using one's own senses – seeing through own eyes, hearing with own ears, etc.

auditory one of the representational systems; to do with hearing and speaking

behaviour in NLP terms, behaviour is what you do or say – one of the neurological levels

behavioural flexibility ability to vary one's approach in order to achieve a desired result

belief generalizations about what we consider to be true. One of the neurological levels

calibration the process of using sensory acuity to tune into changes in another person's state by reading signals such as voice tone, skin colour, micro muscle movement, and gestures

capability relates to skills, abilities and strategies – how you do something

causal connections a language pattern of the Milton Model – statements that imply a link between two events

cause and effect a linguistic distinction in the Meta Model that indicates there is a causal relationship within a statement

chunking changing perception by focusing on bigger, more general units (chunking up) or smaller, more specific units (chunking down)

comparative deletion Meta Model distinction in which a comparison is implied in a statement without saying what it's being compared to

complex equivalence Meta Model distinction in which two or more statements or actions are taken to mean the same thing

congruence when all aspects of a person, especially beliefs and values, are aligned

consciousness what we are aware of in the present moment

content reframing giving a statement another meaning. Sometimes called meaning reframing

context reframing reframing approach that involves identifying where a specific behaviour would be appropriate

contrastive analysis the process of comparing different events, states and internal representations to determine the difference that makes the difference between them

conversational postulate Milton Model pattern in which a question is interpreted as a command

criteria the standards on which an evaluation is based

crossover matching matching a person's body language with a different form of posture or movement

deep structure the underlying complete representation of a communication from which the surface structure thought or utterance arises

deletion the process of selectively paying attention to some aspects of experience and excluding or deleting others

dissociation experiencing something from the viewpoint of a detached observer, not 'in' an experience, but 'outside' it

distortion inaccuracy of representation, one of the Meta Model processes

downtime turning attention inwards, resulting in a light trance state

driver submodality crucial submodality distinction, which influences the rest

ecology taking account of all the elements in a system

elicitation gathering information, usually by asking questions but also by watching

embedded command Milton Model pattern that entails making a command out of a statement by emphasizing particular words

epistemology the study of knowledge, how we know what we know. NLP operates as an epistemology

explicit modeling involves moving to a dissociated position to describe the specific structure of the model's subjective experience

eye accessing cues unconscious eye movements that indicate the use of visual, auditory and kinaesthetic thinking

first position experiencing the world from one's own perspective. One of the perceptual positions

fourth position experiencing the whole system at one time – the three perceptual positions interacting with one another

frame the boundaries or constraints of an event or an experience

future pacing technique for making sure new responses are anchored by imagining future situations

generalization process by which specific experiences come to represent a broader category of experiences

gustatory one of the representational systems – the sense of taste

identity your sense of who you are or who you are not. Self-image. One of the neurological levels

implicit modeling modelling process or stage, which involves being with the exemplar (model) and absorbing what they do and how they behave

imprinting imprinting takes place when a significant experience results in beliefs being formed in a short period of time. In NLP the imprint or pattern becomes fixed or wired into the nervous system

. . . .

incongruence state of disharmony and inner conflict

. . . .

installation process of establishing a new mental strategy or behaviour so that it operates automatically

. . . .

intention the deeper purpose or desire behind a behaviour

. . . .

kinaesthetic one of the representational systems – relating to feelings, internal sensations and emotions

. . . .

lack of referential index Meta Model distinction that indicates that the noun, object, person or event isn't specified in a statement

. . . .

leading altering one's behaviour so that others follow; requires rapport

. . . .

lead system the representational system someone uses to search for information

. . . .

lost performative Meta Model distinction in which opinion is expressed as fact

. . . .

mapping across the process of transferring elements of one state or situation to another

. . . .

map of reality model of the world unique to each person

. . . .

matching copying what someone else is doing to strengthen rapport. (See also **mirroring**.) Sorting for similarities

. . . .

meaning reframing giving a statement another meaning. Sometimes called **content reframing**

. . . .

meta above or beyond, as in Meta Model and Meta Mirror. Stepping back or to one side (or floating above)

Meta Model a model for identifying language patterns that obscure meaning in a communication through deletion, distortion and generalization. Provides a set of challenges for recovering information

meta outcome the outcome of an outcome. The desired effects of an outcome or goal

metaphor indirectly communicating something through a story or by implying a comparison. Thinking about one situation in terms of something else

Meta Program perceptual filters that help us organize our thinking and decide where to focus our attention

Milton Model a set of language patterns based on the work of Milton Erickson used for inducing trance and communicating with the unconscious mind

mind reading Meta Model distinction – knowing what someone else is thinking

mirroring accurately matching aspects of someone else's behaviour, usually to strengthen rapport

mismatching behavioural mismatching is the opposite to matching. Breaking rapport by adopting different patterns of behaviour. In Meta Programs, 'sorting' for differences

modal operators (of possibility and necessity) Meta Model categories that define the limits of what a person considers possible, indicated by words such as 'should', 'shouldn't', 'ought', 'must', 'can't', 'can'

modelling observing and mapping across the successful strategies, beliefs, behaviours and processes underpinning someone's exceptional performance

Neuro-Linguistic Programming (NLP) the study of the structure of subjective experience. 'Neuro' the brain, 'Linguistic' language and 'Programming' the patterns created by the interaction between the brain and language. Founded by Richard Bandler and John Grinder

new code a description of NLP developed by John Grinder and Judith DeLozier in their book *Turtles All The Way Down*. Based upon the concepts of states, perceptual positions, multiple descriptions, perceptual filters and conscious/ unconscious relationships

nominalization Meta Model distinction in which a verb has been changed into an abstract noun

olfactory one of the representational systems – the sense of smell

outcome a specific, sensory-based and desired goal that has met the well-formedness conditions

overlap using one representational system to gain access to another. For instance, creating a mental image of something and then hearing the sounds

pacing gaining and maintaining rapport with someone by matching their map of the world through language, behaviour, beliefs and values

parts a metaphor for aspects of our psyche. Seen as unconscious parts or sub-personalities that appear to take on a life of their own

perceptual positions experiencing life and viewing situations from our own perspective (first position), that of another person (second position) and that of a detached position (third position). Also referred to as triple description

predicates sensory-based process words that show which of the representational systems is being used

preferred system the representational system a person uses most often for internal processing and organizing experiences

presupposition Meta Model distinction in which something is implicitly required to make sense of a statement

presuppositions the concepts and models at the heart of NLP, explained in Chapter 2

quotes Milton Model language pattern where the message it's intended to communicate is placed within quotation marks

rapport building trust, harmony and responsiveness in a relationship

reframing transforming the meaning of something by changing the context or frame of reference

representation sensory-based internal coding, i.e. pictures, sounds and feelings

representational systems internal coding system based around the five senses: visual, auditory, kinaesthetic, olfactory and gustatory

resource anything that can be accessed and utilized to assist in achieving a desired state or outcome

secondary gains additional benefits – not the main purpose – that derive from apparently negative behaviours and actions, e.g. getting time away from your desk when smoking at work

second position experiencing the world viewpoint of another person. One of the perceptual positions

selectional restriction violation Milton Model language pattern where qualities are attributed to something that couldn't have them, e.g. the tomato plant can be comfortable

sensory acuity the ability to make refined sensory distinctions

sensory-specific evidence information that is based on what can be seen, heard, felt, tasted and smelt

simple deletion Meta Model distinction in which an important element has been left out of a statement

sleight of mouth verbal reframes devised by Robert Dilts that influence beliefs and can be used to widen perspective

spiritual being part of a larger system – about higher purpose and what we have to offer our family, community, society and the world at large. One of the neurological levels

state how we feel at any moment in time, which is determined to a large degree by what's happening in our physiology and neurology

strategies sequences in the way people use their senses in carrying out cognitive tasks such as thinking, recalling, learning, making decisions and so on

submodalities fine distinctions within the representational systems. The building blocks of how experience is coded

surface structure thoughts and utterances – the results of the process of deletion, distortion and generalization

synaesthesia automatic from one representational system with another, often visual or auditory to kinaesthetic

systemic NLP Robert Dilts and Todd Epstein developed the systemic approach to NLP in the late 1980s, emphasizing cybernetics, systemic thinking and ecology

tag questions a language pattern of the Milton Model. A question is placed at the end of a statement with the intention of displacing the attention of the listener

third position experiencing an interaction from the detached viewpoint of an external perspective. One of the perceptual positions

timeline a way of describing how we mentally store and utilize pictures, sounds, feelings, tastes and smells of events in our past, present and future

trance a naturally occurring altered state in which the focus of attention is inward

transderivational search (TDS) searching back through stored memories to find reference experiences relating to a current behaviour or response

transformational grammar a theory of language developed by linguist Noam Chomsky

triple description comes from NLP New Code and the idea of three perceptual positions

unconscious everything that is not in our awareness in the present moment

universal quantifiers Meta Model distinction – a term for words that imply absolutes such as never, always, every and only

....

unspecified verb a linguistic distinction in the Meta Model, which indicates verbs that have the adverb deleted so the specifics of the action are deleted

....

uptime state where attention is focused outwards

....

values what is most important to someone. A primary source of motivation in people's lives. One of the neurological levels

....

visual one of the representational systems – to do with the sense of sight

....

visualization the process of forming images, sounds and feelings in the mind

....

well-formedness conditions rules for the creation of outcomes that make them achievable, compelling and verifiable. Stated in positive terms, sensory-based evidence, context considered, within the person's control, access to resources and ecologically sound

....

Index